# CONFOUND

## THE CRITICS

Answers for Attacks on Biblical Truths

# BODIE HODGE

First printing: August 2014
Second printing: November 2014

Master Books®, P.O. Box 726, Green Forest, AR 72638

Master Books® is a division of the New Leaf Publishing Group, Inc.

ISBN: 978-0-89051-838-0
Library of Congress Number: 2014943928

Cover by Diana Bogardus

Please consider requesting that a copy of this volume be purchased by your local library system.

**Printed in the United States of America**

Please visit our website for other great titles:
www.masterbooks.net

For information regarding author interviews,
please contact the publicity department at (870) 438-5288

Master
Books®
A Division of New Leaf Publishing Group
www.masterbooks.net

Special thanks: Dr. Georgia Purdom, Dr. Terry Mortenson, Dr. Tommy Mitchell, Dr. Jason Lisle, Frost Smith, Stacia McKeever, John Upchurch, Andrew McKenzie, Jeremy Ham, Tim Chaffey, Paul Taylor, David Wright, Troy Lacey, Tim Lovett, Jeremy Ham, Eric Lutz, and Ken Ham.

# Contents

## Section 3: How to respond to people on topics about biblical authority, theology, and compromised positions

# ①NTRODUCTION

## *How can this book help me?*

For years, hosts of people have asked Answers in Genesis to help them reply to newspapers, opinions, internet websites such as blogs or debate boards, books, DVDs, and other media by non-Christians who are attacking creation or other aspects of the Bible, the character of God, or Christianity in general. Many of these attacks are rather hostile in their approach, and Christians really struggle with answering many of the claims.

Many Christians have written books that help people answer these questions, and I've been a part of some of these books (e.g., *The New Answers Book* series, Ken Ham, gen. ed.; *How Do We Know the Bible Is True?* series, Ken Ham and Bodie Hodge, gen. eds.; *Demolishing Supposed Bible Contradictions* series, Ken Ham, Bodie Hodge, and Tim Chaffey, gen. eds.). Some Christians have written books that discuss the theory behind how to answer (e.g., *Always Ready*, Dr. Greg Bahnsen; *The Ultimate Proof of Creation*, Dr. Jason Lisle), but this book is unique in that it helps put the theory and answers into practice. By the way, these books that I just mentioned, I highly recommend.

For example, let's use a game to provide a good analogy. Let's say you want to play pool. You can study the science of momentum about how balls move and interact with each other. You can even study the various games (8-ball or 9-ball) and learn all about them, and this is good, but until you put what you've learned into practice, that knowledge does you little good. You need to be able to hit the pool ball into the pocket when the time comes.

That is the thrust of this book. It is to help show you *how* to use the answers and *how* to use the theory when the time comes. I do this by giving you practical examples of situations that I've been in and how I responded when the time came. So hopefully, these examples will help you apply answers when the time comes for you. Consider some verses to get you going:

> We destroy arguments and every lofty opinion raised against the knowledge of God, and take every thought captive to obey Christ (2 Corinthians 10:5; ESV).

> But in your hearts honor Christ the Lord as holy, always being prepared to make a defense to anyone who asks you for a reason for the hope that is in you; yet do it with gentleness and respect,

having a good conscience, so that, when you are slandered, those
who revile your good behavior in Christ may be put to shame (1
Peter 3:15–16; ESV).

See to it that no one takes you captive by philosophy and
empty deceit, according to human tradition, according to the ele-
mental spirits of the world, and not according to Christ (Colossians 2:8; ESV).

## Stats

At the ministry of Answers in Genesis, we receive a large volume of correspondence that needs a response. In the years that I strictly worked correspondence, we received about 10,000 to 16,000 emails, phone calls, and
written letters. One year, I did some statistics on the emails and found that
about 6.5 percent were hostile non-Christians (mostly atheists and agnostics
or other forms of humanism). And sadly, about 3 percent were from hostile
Christians (mostly those who believed in an old earth and/or evolution and
mixed it with the Bible)!

If this percentage is largely accurate (and it seems consistent with other
years as well), that means we've had to deal with about 950 to 1,520 negative
correspondences per year! Reading such diatribes can get you down, but you
need to look at it as an opportunity to witness to people and help correct
them where they have misunderstood biblical Christianity. Don't take such
attacks personally, but remember:

"If the world hates you, you know that it hated Me [Jesus]
before it hated you" (John 15:18).

## Getting started in a response: a few helpful hints

As I dealt with quite a bit of hostile correspondence, I realized that I needed
to look at this as a positive. I had an opportunity to reach out to an unbeliever, or perhaps a compromised Christian.[1] I needed to be discerning for
several reasons. Up front, it is our responsibility to get the person to realize
the importance of Christ for their lives and repent (2 Peter 3:9), or *if they*

---

1. A compromised Christian is a Christian, but he has allowed another worldview or religion to infiltrate his Christianity (think of when the Israelites mixed true worship with Baal
worship). The most common way this happens today is by giving up the straightforward reading
of Genesis 1–11 and replacing it with aspects of the religion of humanism. Some compromised
Christians buy into geological evolution (millions of years), astronomical evolution (big bang or
other old universe worldviews), chemical evolution (chemical origin of life), or biological evolution (man evolved from single-celled organisms).

*are a Christian* to realize the importance of God's Word in their lives *as the authority in all areas* (2 Timothy 3:16).

### Discernment in general

First, you need to be able to determine the stance of the writer of a negative letter. Is the writer a Christian, atheist, compromised Christian, Mormon, Hindu, Islamic, angry, sad, mocking, etc.? This will help you determine how to reply. And you need to keep in mind that these people are *not* the enemy, but that the false philosophy has taken them captive (Colossians 2:8).

### Discernment about their view of the Bible

Also, you need to be discerning about how they might *view* the Bible. If they appear to believe the Bible, then use Scripture (and a lot of it!) and set up the debate as *that faulty belief system* vs. *God's Word*. By setting it up as "a viewpoint vs. Bible," they should be helped to realize that it is really about a "false philosophy vs. God." It takes the battle away from "you vs. them" and puts it where it should be: God, demolishing the false view (Hebrews 4:12). Many of these people do not realize that they have bought into a secularly biased worldview, or if they do realize it, they fail to realize why it is wrong or inconsistent, especially with God's Word.

If they don't seem to believe the Bible or even mock it, you should still use it but make sure to address why it can be trusted, using things like "presuppositional apologetics" or other aspects of the ultimate proof (don't let this scare you, as these are addressed in some of the books I've previously mentioned).[2] Essentially, you need to "pull the rug out" from underneath the unbeliever's worldview by showing how they are borrowing from a biblical worldview to even make their case and, hence, revealing that the Bible is true whether they have realized it or not.

### Discerning the real issue

Next, we need to answer the *underlying* issue. We need to read between the lines and realize **why** they are asking the questions/sending the hostile letter. Often, answering the questions won't address **why** they don't trust the Bible and ultimately Jesus Christ (e.g., I've repeatedly answered people's questions, only to have them turn and ask more, showing that the questions they asked *originally* were not causing them to stumble but something greater, perhaps

---

2. To understand this presuppositional, ultimate proof approach, it may be good to read from *Always Ready* by Dr. Greg Bahnsen or *The Ultimate Proof of Creation* by Dr. Jason Lisle, though this is not entirely needed for this book.

more foundational). You need to address this issue if possible. Sometimes they will lash out with a number of questions, but these are usually not the main reason they are struggling. We need to try to figure out and address the root of the issues they are having.

Often people misspell things or use poor grammar, but be gracious on such points. It is better to talk about the real issues behind the letter, than to point out little things like that, but always try to use good grammar, spelling, and punctuation when you respond. As you will surely notice, many of the initial correspondences included in this book contain a great many grammatical errors and misspellings (and these have remained unedited). But even in that category, I'm not without error myself. So please be forgiving to those with whom you are corresponding.

### Be patient

It is always good to be sincere and kind, regardless of how much hate and vitriol you may encounter. Again, don't take it personally. I found that when people are angry about an issue, it means they are thinking about it more than others and finding conflict within their own worldview — so they want to lash out and not address it; which is all the more reason for you to point out why their *worldview* is inconsistent, arbitrary, and so on.

From my experience with those who are angry, sometimes it is good to wait at least two weeks to a month to reply. This not only gives them time to "cool off" so that they will be more open to listening, but often they have forgotten about their letter by then, too. Then, when they receive a kind and respectful response, they will often apologize for their rude tone and you can carry on a good conversation.

### How many times should you respond?

How many times should you respond to someone who refuses to listen or learn? The Bible tells us:

> But avoid foolish controversies, genealogies, dissensions, and quarrels about the law, for they are unprofitable and worthless. As for a person who stirs up division, after warning him once and then twice, have nothing more to do with him, knowing that such a person is warped and sinful; he is self-condemned (Titus 3:9–11; ESV).

The answer is twice. If you think they are sincere, then continue corresponding, but that will be up to you. But there is a point where it is "casting pearls to swine" (Matthew 7:6) and you need to "brush the dust from your shoes" (Acts 13:51) and move to on to those who are willing and awaiting answers.

## Style: single letter or point-by-point

Before you start your written response, you need to decide if you are going to write one big response (single letter), or break their correspondence into parts and answer each part accordingly (point-by-point). My preference is usually point-by-point when they have multiple claims. This helps you avoid missing something that may be important. Also, there is no confusion over what you are responding to, since it is the section immediately above. When we get into the responses, this should be fairly clear, so if you have never done a point-by-point response, don't fret.

## Challenge-riposte: when to use it?

Another thing that needs to be addressed is using a method called "challenge-riposte." This is a debate method that is very aggressive and is appropriate to use *in the right circumstance*. Many who use it today, though, don't use it properly. Let me explain.

The challenge-riposte method is very direct and was used by some biblical persons in rebuking, including Christ. Elijah, for example, used it when taunting the prophets of Baal in 1 Kings 18:27. John the Baptist even called the Pharisees and Sadducees a "brood of vipers" in Matthew 3:7.

Christ "had a go" at the religious leaders (Pharisees) in Matthew 12:1–8. Twice Jesus said, "Haven't you read?" This "stepped up" rebuke by Christ was directed at the people who were learned and even taught the Scriptures, and Jesus basically insulted them when He asked if they had even read the Scriptures on this subject. Christ went so far as to say "Woe to you, hypocrites!" in Matthew 23:15. There are other places in Scripture where rebukes were given, so there is precedence for this method. However, take note of the timing of when this method was used in Scripture. Jesus did not use it the first time He was challenged by the Pharisees. For example, in Luke 5:17–26 Jesus was challenged by the Pharisees for forgiving sins and Jesus kindly responded. He was questioned by the Pharisees regarding eating with tax collectors and sinners in Matthew 9:11, Mark 2:16, and Luke 5:30, and He kindly responded.

It was after the Pharisees continued to disregard Jesus' teaching and continued to oppose Him that Jesus stepped up His response to a challenge-riposte style. This lesson should also be mimicked by Christians. We are to be respectful and gentle in our responses initially as per 1 Peter 3:15. However, if we are met with continued attacks from the same person, then we can step it up a bit, as Christ did, when challenged publicly. My preference is not to engage in challenge-riposte unless forced into it. To see an instance of this go to appendix 2, "How to Respond to a 'Repeat Offender.' "

### Presuppositional approach

Answers in Genesis is a presuppositional, biblical authority ministry. God and His Word are presupposed to be the truth, and the methodology of presuppositional apologetics is truly devastating to false worldviews that are set up to oppose Christ. There is nothing greater than God or His Word. Often, in efforts to share that the Bible is the truth, Christians inadvertently use evidential apologetics[3] (or its sister form of classical apologetics), which ultimately results in man's ideas being the authority over God by starting with something *other* than God.[4]

> Evidential: The evidence proves the Bible (or more appropriately, "Our understanding of the evidence gives a good probability that the Bible is true").

> Presuppositional: Evidence is a good confirmation of the Bible.

Closer look: All evidence needs to be interpreted, and there are two ways of doing so — God's way or man's way. In all debates, it is not about the evidence but the worldview by which that evidence is looked at. So it is a religious debate. Let's evaluate these worldviews in light of God's Word. In the first sentence, is God the authority? No. *Man's interpretations* of the evidence are seen as the authority and raised up to be greater than God, since man's interpretations of the evidence are what is trying to dictate whether God's Word is true (Matthew 10:24).

The second sentence uses the Bible as the starting point, and evidence is merely seen in light of God's Word. So God is the authority. This doesn't

---

3. Evidential apologetics does not mean, "using evidence"; in other words, there is a big difference between being evidence heavy and evidential. Evidential apologetics is a methodology of defending the faith by leaving the Bible out of the discussion and trying to develop probabilistic arguments to say the Bible is *likely* true; whereas evidence heavy means you use a lot of evidence. In other words, the Bible is divorced from the discussion of evidence. In presuppositional apologetics, the Bible is never divorced from the evidence but is the absolute authority and basis by which we look at all evidence. For a concise understanding of evidential apologetics see: Evidential Apologetic: Faith Founded on Fact, Bible.org website, February 26, 2006, http://bible.org/seriespage/evidentialist-apologetics-faith-founded-fact.

4. Ken Ham and Bodie Hodge, gen. eds., *How Do We Know the Bible Is True?* Volume 2 (Green Forest, AR: Master Books, 2012), p. 61–80.

mean evidence is neglected; it is still used as confirmation. In a presuppositional viewpoint, evidence and logic are used, but they are predicated on God's Word.

This short example is only a touch of presuppositional apologetics. In presuppositional apologetics, it is good to spot things in a particular way. Look for the following:

- arbitrariness

- inconsistencies within the opposing worldview

- What must be true for their claims to make sense (preconditions of intelligibility)? Does this worldview have a basis for knowledge, logic, etc.? Are they borrowing from Christian presuppositions to make sense of the world, etc.?

- How does the professed worldview lead to absurdity?

These are good ways to quickly refute the false worldview people often present.

Often evidentialist arguments, whether Christian or non-Christian, *inadvertantly* go back to assuming God's Word is truth. They "can't not," as God is the ultimate authority regardless of what anyone thinks or says. This is because to understand anything means assuming the Bible is true (whether people want to believe it or not). Such things as:

1. Truth, logic, and other nonmaterial entities exist, like information and knowledge.

2. The laws of the universe are uniform, as God has stated (unless in rare instances God works a miracle that may defy such things, which is not arbitrary).[5]

3. Morality has an absolute basis in God's Word.

These things are predicated on God existing and His words being true.

### Love the sinner, not the sin

When you are responding to someone, always keep in mind that they are made in the image of God and are your relative. They are not the enemy! It is the false philosophies that they have been taught (that they now believe in) that are the enemy. I like to use the four "Bs" as a guideline in responding:

---

5. Not all miracles are in defiance of the laws of nature. Many occur as a matter of timing and perhaps others are well within the laws of nature, where we simply do not know *all* the laws operating in the world God created.

1. Be picky.

2. Be biblical.

3. Be kind (and gracious).

4. Be humble.

Be picky because the Bible is picky when it comes to false arguments. In other words, we want to be the best we can be and not let things slide unless we are being gracious on a point (e.g., grammar). Don't be picky for picky's sake though. First Peter 3:15 says to always be prepared to give an answer, it doesn't say always give an answer. Deem when it is inappropriate to respond to a comment. For example, if the person uses foul language, it may be best to not deviate from the original topic to debate the Christian morality of bad words, but focus on the main issues in the debate points.

Ever heard that you are your own worst critic? Be just as critical toward false arguments. As a Christian, you represent Christ and so your best should be the best you can be. Christ never waffled. So do what you can to word things correctly and check your facts and biblical statements.

Always be biblical, even if others oppose the Bible. Don't let them dictate that the Word of God should not be used, when God makes it clear that it should be used (2 Timothy 3:16). Try to be as kind as possible and at the same time gracious, as the Lord showed us grace (Galatians 5:22; 1 Peter 1:13), and let this lead to humbleness. Remember that when it comes down to it, we are all sinners and all compared *to Christ,* who is perfect. We have all fallen short and we need to remain humble when witnessing to others (James 4:10).

### Checklist of other points

Here is a checklist for responding:

1. First, check and make sure they include their information in good faith (legitimate name, address, and email address). We do this at Answers in Genesis so that we do not waste our time answering long emails from Charles Darwin with the address of the North Pole. If you work in ministry (church, organization, and so on), this may be a good policy to have in place; for the rest, this may not be a big deal. The point is to make sure the address they give you for a response (email, phone, or letter) is legitimate. If not, then don't bother spending the time. I once answered a long letter, only to realize that the letter came from "Satan" with an address of "Hell." (The post office, I realized, was not interested in delivering mail

there — perhaps that is one of the punishments of being in hell. Okay, you are allowed to smile at that one.)

2. Pray for them.

3. Do the discerning — what do they believe, how do they view the Bible and God, what is their real issue?

4. Check each "fact" that they claim. If they didn't send documentation for it, ask for it.

5. Check each journal, article, or web link on anything they claim and read about it in detail. If they don't send it, ask them for it. This helps avoid "answering a fool according to his folly." In other words, don't buy into a false claim and then try to answer.[6]

6. When checking their facts and articles, check and see where they break logic by reviewing the logic list in appendix A or books on logic (*Discerning Truth*, Dr. Jason Lisle, or *The Fallacy Detective*, Nathaniel and Hans Bluedorn). It is always good to point out the specific fallacy *with kindness*, as it helps them learn how to think (especially considering that precious few people have been taught logic nowadays since an evolutionary worldview causes people to violate many laws of logic).

7. Also, open the reply by thanking them for contacting you and telling them that your response is said with sincerity and respect (1 Peter 3:15). And be humble, as we have all fallen short too and in many instances have been in their shoes as well. We need to show the same grace to the unbeliever as Christ showed to us.

8. *Usually* respond via "point-by-point" analysis, addressing each point, questioning their conclusions if they are not biblical, and inserting Scripture. It is often good to include the verse so they can read it as opposed to simply mentioning the reference. Sadly, few actually look up the verse. I realize that writing out the Scriptures can't always be done, though. Do not do any of this in a judging way but be bold and use sincerity to rebuke them by using the discerning factions in #3.

9. Check and link to the facts that you present. Use articles and books as supplements, not as the basis. Make the argument and give

---

6. Dr. Jason Lisle, "Fool-Proof Apologetics," *Answers* magazine, vol. 4, no. 2, p. 66–69, http://www.answersingenesis.org/articles/am/v4/n2/fool-proof.

them the biblical reasons, then use articles as *backup* for further information. Double check what you write and even get a second or third set of eyes on it to be sure it is biblically and scientifically correct.

10. Encourage them and present the gospel if needed — especially if they are not a believer.

11. Always finish with something like "I pray this helps, God bless," or "Kind regards."

# Chapter 1

# TEACHING BY EXAMPLE

To start off, I want to do something different. I want to show you how I break down a hostile letter and look at it biblically. Hopefully, this will give you some pointers on how to respond to similar inquiries in the future, whether in person, email, or on forums, before we jump into the bulk of the responses.

One of the first things I do is pray for wisdom and discernment in responding. My prayer is that each response I make will honor and glorify God. Then I read the letter and try to discern what the person believes.

When I read R.B.'s email (see below), I saw that he is very hostile toward the Bible, appearing to be a non-Christian. He is likely an atheist (or unaware of being one variant of atheist called a "humanist," who, perhaps inadvertently, sees humans as the ultimate authority — for instance, on a subject like morality as opposed to God being the authority). He has obviously encountered Christians who were not well versed in apologetics — or he is basing his claims on common caricatures of creationists from skeptics.

This gives us a head start on how to handle the response: use the Word of God but also show *why* we use it. We may also have to use some philosophy to show that the view the inquirer is using is not well grounded. Remember that each hostile email is an opportunity to share the truth. Here is R.B.'s letter, exactly as it arrived:

> i would just like to comment that the only proof of creationism is the bible. the bible was written by men. men can lie. man is capable of the most horribly attrocities on the planet. you ask us not to believe in the word of God, but the word of men who claim that they are speaking for God. most people pick ad choose what they want to believe in the bible. if you believe one part of the bible, you have to believe every single word. you can't take parts word-for-word, and change the rest of it through your own interpretation. all i hear is that science is all wrong because it disputes the bible, but the bible itself is the only evidence of any creationist claims. dinosaur bones were burried by the devil to test our faith. you can just discredit any scientific evidence by saying "it doesn't say that in the bible." it doesn't say anything

**about chemistry in the bible. does that mean that all chemists are
wrong because their explanation is not in the bible?**

**R.B.**

Thanks for the inquiry. I am responding below with both sincerity and
respect. [Note: I like to start many letters like this to show the author that
I am not trying to be harsh by any means. It is difficult to read the tone of
a letter or email, so be up front and say (and mean!) that it is written with
kindness. Even though someone may send a hostile email, we should not
treat him or her as an enemy. The false philosophy and false principalities
are the enemy (Ephesians 6:12). We need to keep in mind that all Christians
were once enemies of God who were saved by grace through faith in Jesus
Christ (Romans 5:10; Ephesians 2:8). God first loved us, setting the example
for us to pass along love and respect for others created in His image (1 John
4:9; John 15:17). In fact, we are commanded to use gentleness and respect (1
Peter 3:15)]; this response will also be done in a point-by-point style.

**i would just like to comment that the only proof of creationism
is the bible. the bible was written by men.**

Of course, the Bible was written by men, but his claim here is that God was
NOT involved. He has no way of substantiating the validity of his claim (no
God involved in the production of the Bible) except by blind faith, which
is arbitrary. For someone to truly make this statement, he would have to be
transcendent and omnipresent. He would have to be able to "see" into the
spiritual realm and verify that God did not influence the writers of the Bible
many years ago. Such attributes that this person is inadvertently claiming are
attributes of God. So, in essence, R.B. is claiming to be God, or just repeating what he has heard from others, who claim to know more than God.

This is a worldview issue right from the start. One can believe R.B., or
any human, is "god" (i.e., humans seen as the ultimate authority), or one
can place his faith in the true Creator God and His eyewitness account in
His Word, seeing Him as authoritative. One can respond by pointing out
that he is claiming to be God with this statement.

**men can lie.**

This is true, but not because R.B. is saying it. It is true because God says
it (Romans 3:4). And R.B. apparently believes that lying is morally wrong.
In a response, one can point out that for R.B. to say this he is borrowing
morality from the Bible by at least admitting to the concept of moral truth.

But interestingly, one could ask R.B., "Were you lying when you claimed the Bible was written merely by men?" What this shows is that, logically, by the writer's own standards, he could be lying. Of course, this should be done with gentleness and respect (1 Peter 3:15).

**man is capable of the most horribly attrocities on the planet.**

Again, this is true, but not because R.B. said it. In fact, I am glad that he recognizes this, because it gives us two ways to respond.

    1. Originally, God made the world perfect, and there were no atrocities. But because of man's sin, the world is now subject to such things. It serves as a reminder that we need a Savior from sin and this sin-cursed world.[1]

    2. Many people often try to blame God for such atrocities, yet the reader rightly recognizes that man is involved. Man's sin, again, is why such things exist.

Both of these answers lead into the gospel message.[2]

Another thing that is useful is to show that R.B. is borrowing Christian morality to argue against it. Consider the accompanying illustration. He is borrowing from the Bible's morality to say such things are wrong.

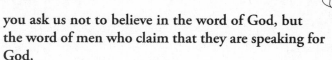

**you ask us not to believe in the word of God, but the word of men who claim that they are speaking for God.**

Note the fallacy here. He is assuming that his statement above (that leads to a human claiming to be God because he has elevated his own thoughts to be greater than God's Word) is true; hence, he is building on it. We need to point out the fallacy and then show what this philosophy leads to (the "don't answer, answer" strategy from Proverbs 26:4–5). One could say:

    I don't accept your proposition that God had nothing to do with His Word, but let's assume for a moment that you are correct.

---

1. For more on this, please see "Why Does God's Creation Include Death and Suffering?" http://www.answersingenesis.org/articles/nab/why-does-creation-include-suffering.

2. For more on this please see: "The Gospel of Jesus Christ," http://www.answersingenesis.org/about/good-news.

How do you propose to save yourself from sin and death if salvation has not come through Jesus Christ?

Also, why would you be upset with horrible atrocities and lies? By saying lies and horrible atrocities are wrong, you are borrowing from a biblical worldview. In a worldview that does not acknowledge the God of the Bible, why are such things wrong? Such things would be governed by chemical reactions in the brain. Why would anyone be upset about titanium reacting with boron?

**most people pick ad choose what they want to believe in the bible.**

Sadly, this is true, and it reveals how much humanism has influenced Christians. In essence, what happens is that people (even Christians) use their own ideas to pick and choose what they want to believe from the Bible.

So, Christians, take note of what the real authority is in this situation: a person's own ideas, not God's Word. The real authority to those who "pick and choose" is a human, not God, i.e., humanism. Sadly, many Christians in today's culture are mixing Christianity with humanism (recall Exodus 20:3). As Christians, we should always use God's Word as the authority, not our own sinful, fallible reasoning.

In response to R.B., one could point out that R.B. is doing the same thing. He is opting to believe that lying and horrible atrocities are wrong. He is picking and choosing these things from the Bible to believe, whether he realizes it or not, yet rejecting the rest — including its authority statements.

**if you believe one part of the bible, you have to believe every single word.**

If R.B. really believed this, then why doesn't he believe the whole Bible, since he already borrowed from its morality and concept of truth?

**you can't take parts word-for-word, and change the rest of it through your own interpritation.**

Take note of R.B.'s assumption here. He assumes that the entire Bible is written in the same literary style. A remedial look at the Bile reveals poetry, metaphors, literal history, prayers, genealogical data, etc. He gives a false assumption and tries to build on it, so his entire argument breaks down.

The issue is letting God interpret His own Word (Scripture interprets Scripture). This is why understanding the context and the complementary nature of Scripture is so important. It has nothing to do with human interpretation. Many, like R.B., may be assuming "no God," and therefore that God cannot interpret, so people must. But this is not the case.

Proverbs 8:8–9 and 2 Corinthians 4:2 reveal that the Scriptures are to be taken plainly or straightforwardly. I like to put this in simple terms: metaphors are metaphors; poetry is poetry; literal history is literal history; and so on. So there should be no reason for outlandish interpretations, unless one does it in one's own mind (e.g., mixing it with humanism).

**all i hear is that science is all wrong because it disputes the bible,**

I wanted to cut this phrase off here and explain two things. First, science is not all wrong. It is a methodology that actually confirms the Bible. And second, R.B. is confusing the term "science" with secular interpretations of science and evolution.

**but the bible itself is the only evidence of any creationist claims.**

In reality, the Bible is the foundation for creationists' claims. But all facts can be used by creationists as evidence. For example, dinosaurs are often taught as evidence for evolution and millions of years, but they are used by creationists to teach that God created them on day 6 and that the bulk of the dinosaurs died in the Flood of Noah's day, leaving their fossils behind (that is, those that were not on the ark).[3]

**dinosaur bones were burried by the devil to test our faith.**

If this is intended as a caricature of our position (or a general creationist position), it's just a plain straw man argument. As just stated, dinosaurs existed and their bones were buried in the Flood. Interesting that for someone who is arguing against the Bible, R.B. seems to adhere to biblical teaching that the devil exists!

**you can just discredit any scientific evidence by saying "it doesn't say that in the bible."**

Again, take note that R.B. is equating interpretations with "scientific evidence." We do not dispute dinosaur bones, we dispute the dates given for them, and we have reasonable doubt for those dates.[4] Scientific models and interpretations offer great support for the Bible. However, at Answers in Genesis we like to point out that scientific models can change with new

---

3. Ken Ham, gen. ed., *The New Answers Book 1* (Green Forest, AR: Master Books, 2006), p. 149–177, http://www.answersingenesis.org/articles/nab/what-happened-to-the-dinosaurs.

4. Ibid., p. 77–86, 113–124.

information, but the Bible is still the inerrant framework within which to interpret scientific facts.

**it doesn't say anything about chemistry in the bible.**

When there is an absolute (i.e., "doesn't say anything") in a statement, it is good to re-read it and see if that absolute is true. As a side note, in an atheistic worldview, in which absolutes do not exist, it is interesting that absolutes are used quite often!

Regardless, the Bible does touch on chemistry, but the Bible isn't a chemistry textbook. Consider passages about iron, bronze, and copper. To purify such items and mix alloys requires some chemistry. In fact, materials processing requires considerable amounts of chemistry. Naturally, there are some subjects not mentioned in Scripture, but that is not a problem. For example, the Bible doesn't say that using a club (or gun, or rope, etc.) to kill someone is wrong; it says murder is wrong. The framework is in place.

**does that mean that all chemists are wrong because their explanation is not in the bible?**

Note another absolute (all) that tries to set up that creationists think all chemists are wrong. Of course, there are creationists who are chemists, and because of God's attributes that we know from the Bible (logical, non-contradictory), we know that chemistry is possible. So it has little to do with this, even though R.B. claims that it does.

Now that we have answered the inquirer, it is good to sum up with the gospel — whether in a few lines or even more in-depth. It is always good to close with some encouraging words about what to do next and even an invitation to learn more about Jesus Christ and the Bible. Remember the Great Commission at the end of Matthew. We want to see people saved. Perhaps you could say something like this:

> I can see that you have a strong moral conscience (lying is wrong, atrocities by man are horrible, etc.), and this is good, since it comes from the Bible. R.B., I hope that this response has challenged you to consider the truth of the Bible, which seems to be your biggest stumbling block. I want to encourage you to study this further and consider the claims of Christ.

Then perhaps include a link to an article or chapter that explains the gospel to make it a little easier for him and close with the words "With kindness in Christ."

# How to respond to people On topics About Ethics, Philosophy, and Morality

## Chapter 2

# BEING BRAINWASHED

Letter, unedited:

> All I want to say is that you people should open your mind from ancient archaic beliefs and see the real world. God can exist hear today, and the things I have read seem so misinformed that I could almost feel as if I were being brain washed. I think everyone should be entitled to hold faith in what they choose as long as it is moral, but I do not think that misinforming people of true hard facts that have been proven is moral! Furthermore, as a student of religion and archeology I think it is time to bridge the gap between science and religion and come to an understanding that they do infact work together most of the time.
>
> A., U.S.

Response:

It is nice to hear from you. Please see my comments below and note that they are said with respect, though they are meant to challenge you.

> All I want to say is that you people should open your mind from ancient archaic beliefs and see the real world.

If this was all you wanted to say then why continue? Our beliefs are just as relevant today as they were thousands of years ago.

> God can exist hear today,

Which God? Are you referring to the God of the Bible? The God of the Bible created time, so God is not limited to existing yesterday, today, or tomorrow. I agree that God exists (the God of the Bible). The question should be, do you trust what God *says* in His Word (e.g., Exodus 20:11; Mark 10:6)?

> and the things I have read seem so misinformed that I could almost feel as if I were being brain washed.

Did you consider the possibility that you are already brainwashed to believe something else?

**I think everyone should be entitled to hold faith in what they choose**

They why tell us *"you people should open your mind from ancient archaic beliefs"*? This is a contradiction within the worldview being espoused.

**as long as it is moral,**

What do you mean by moral? Do you mean the morals in the Bible where God, who is the ultimate authority on morality, sets them? I thought you rejected that by your comment *"ancient archaic beliefs"*?

**but I do not think that misinforming people of true hard facts that have been proven is moral!**

We love facts! Did you know we all have the same facts, same science, and same evidences? It is the *interpretation* of those facts that are different. Furthermore, what makes you think truth exists? That comes from the Bible where God is the truth (John 14:6). This same Bible refutes the position you are trying to profess.

**Furthermore, as a student of religion and archeology I think it is time to bridge the gap between science and religion and come to an understanding that they do infact work together most of the time.**

I do believe they work together. I think you have confused operational and historical science. Let me explain in more detail. *Operational science* is the highly reliable repeatable science that has a tremendous reputation. This is the type of science that put men on the moon, builds computers and automobiles, genetic mapping, etc. Most of these fields of science are well respected. As Christians, we fully believe in operational science. In fact, most of these fields of science were developed by Christians.[1]

The other science is called *historical science*. It isn't repeatable because it deals with events in the past. Evolution, radiometric dating, etc., deal with reconstructing the past. So quite a few assumptions are required to fill in the gaps. These assumptions are called "interpretations," and they are not repeatable science.

Many times, these assumptions change and are shown to be wrong and the whole concept of what was believed changes. This happens frequently in

1. Please see "Which Scientists of the Past Believed in a Creator?" http://www.answersingenesis.org/Home/Area/bios/default.asp#pastsci.

historical science. This science is not very reliable and changes quite often. Sometimes, I wonder why it is even called "science," with such a bad reputation and non-repeatability. It makes people lose hope in good operational science just because it uses the name "science."

But in the same respect, some people get confused and think the reputation of operational science can be applied to historical science. This is a fallacy of transfer. Please take a look at the following:

Operational/experimental science                Historical science

These illustrations help us visualize the differences. In historical science, there is quite a bit of imagination. In historical science what is said to be "correct and true" today will probably be wrong tomorrow. In operational science, what is "correct and true" today will likely be "correct and true" tomorrow.

When using the Bible as the basis for interpreting the evidence, how can anyone go wrong? God is perfect and His Word is also perfect. The entire creation is cursed (Genesis 3 and Romans 8) so why trust something that is cursed over God and His Word, which aren't cursed? The issue is about trusting God's Word. I pray this helps, and God bless.

## Chapter 3

# CAN GOD CREATE A ROCK SO BIG HE CAN'T LIFT IT?

Letter, unedited:

> An atheist friend of mine once asked me a baffling question—one to which I could not respond any other way.
>
> "According to the Bible God is Omnipotent, he is All Powerful. . . . Could God create a rock so heavy that he could not lift it?" I answered No, and then he laughed and said, Well if he can't create a rock so heavy that he can't lift it, then isn't he logically NOT Omnipotent? This question has left me in deep prayer and concern, even though I know that God is beyond our understanding. What can I say that challenges this atheist's claim?
>
> M.R., U.S.

Response:

Thank you for contacting Answers in Genesis with an oft-used challenge question: Can God create a rock so big He can't lift it?

For this to be a valid question, God would need to be bound by the laws of gravity. Obviously, God is not bound by His creation (i.e., gravity), as it is part of the universe He created. That would be like asking on what page of Shakespeare's *Hamlet* can we find Shakespeare? It is an illogical question. One could argue that Shakespeare's characteristics are in the play, but he, as the playwright, is certainly not bound by the pages of his work.

In other words, this question first assumes that gravity is greater than God. How can something God creates be greater than God? The assumption is illogical right from the start, and thus the question is illogical right from the start — this is called the contrary-to-the-premise fallacy. Since this question assumes God is bound to His creation, it cannot be referring to the Creator God of the Bible. One way to reveal this fallacy when someone asks this question is to ask: "What 'god' are you talking about?"

They will probably respond: "The God of the Bible" (as this person apparently intended).

Then you can respond: "The God of the Bible is not bound by His creation, and since this question has this 'god' bound by gravity, it cannot be referring to the God of the Bible."

Along a similar line, a coworker relayed this conversation to me that she had with her ten-year-old daughter: She asked, "Can God lie?" to which I said, "No." Then she asked, "Can't He do anything?" and I said, "Yes, but He wouldn't want to lie." Then she asked, "Well, could He if He wanted to?" to which I replied, "He wouldn't want to." But she kept asking, "But what if He wanted to?" So I answered, "According to the biblical account of His character, He wouldn't want to and He wouldn't. Whether or not He could is a question that misses the point. The answer is He wouldn't want to and so He would not, and that's the end of it."

Additional to the general biblical account of God's character indicating He would not lie is Hebrews 6:18, which says it is impossible for God to lie. Remember that God is not like us, and even when God the Son was in human form on the earth, He was tempted in all ways as we are, yet He did not sin (Hebrews 4:15). Always examine the logic behind these sorts of questions; you will find that these sorts of challenges don't stand up to logic or scrutiny.

But consider the converse, if there was no God of the Bible . . . would logic exist and, furthermore, would existence exist? The sheer fact that people try to use logic to argue "there is no God" undercuts the very worldview they profess to follow. Keep proclaiming the truth. With kindness, God bless.

*Chapter 4*

# ⭢PRESUPPOSITIONS: THE EVIDENCE DOESN'T SPEAK FOR ITSELF

Letter, unedited:

> **Evolution does not PRESUPPOSE no God. It merely attempts to discern the mechanisms of God's universe. What you are saying is that you find it believable that God created a universe filled with evidence to teach us about how the world works. But that evidence shouldn't be believed. Instead, we should believe a book written by primitive people with one foot still in a cave dwelling, rather than everything our God-given human abilities can see in God's universe around us every day.**
>
> **First of all, evolution is simply a collection of observations. If you prefer, you can see the hand of God in action within evolution. I do. I don't see your problem.**
>
> **Steve, U.S.**

Response:

It is nice to hear from you and I'm glad that you are willing to make conversation about presuppositions and evolutionary thoughts. My comments below are said with sincerity and kindness.

**Evolution does not PRESUPPOSE no God.**

First of all, evolution doesn't "think," "presuppose," or otherwise have human qualities — that is called the fallacy of reification. It is a worldview based on human thought. It would be better to say "*evolutionists* do not. . . ."

Strangely, Darwin, the father of the modern evolutionary models, disagrees with you in his book *The Descent of Man*. He makes it clear that man invented the concept of a God/spiritual realm. He even said: "The same high mental faculties which first led man to believe in unseen spiritual agencies, then in fetishism, polytheism, and ultimately in monotheism, would infallibly lead him, as long as his reasoning powers remained poorly developed, to various strange superstitions and customs."[1]

Also saying: "The idea of a universal and beneficent Creator does not seem to arise in the mind of man, until he has been elevated by long-continued culture."[2]

Claiming that man invented God makes this a godless philosophy from the start and clarifies what Darwin's position was. It was essentially a rehash of Epicureanism [which was a Greek mythology that was evolutionary by nature with no God(s)] or the more recent version of Lamarckian evolution.

**It merely attempts to discern the mechanisms of God's universe.**

Actually, that is what experimental science does (as opposed to historical science). Most fields of experimental science were developed by Bible-believing Christians, like us, to understand the laws of science God created.[3]

**What you are saying is that you find it believable that God created a universe filled with evidence to teach us about how the world works. But that evidence shouldn't be believed.**

Not so. We believe the evidence. We all have the same evidence but it doesn't speak for itself.[4] All evidence must be interpreted based on a belief system. As a Christian, I use the Bible to explain the evidence.

It would be illogical to think that God, who is perfect and who eyewitnessed His creation, wouldn't know how to explain it and that imperfect men who weren't there would know more than God.

So when it comes to evidence, one's faith needs to be in a perfect God or imperfect men to interpret it. I simply don't have the "faith" in fallible men that some do.

**Instead, we should believe a book written by primitive people**

Primitive? I don't accept your presupposition that man was originally primitive. The Bible is the proper presupposition, and it makes Adam out to be

---

1. Charles Darwin, *The Descent of Man*, chapter 3, www.literature.org/authors/darwin-charles/the-descent-of-man/chapter-03.html.

2. Ibid., chapter 21, www.literature.org/authors/darwin-charles/the-descent-of-man/chapter-21.html.

3. "Which Scientists of the Past Believed in a Creator?" *Answers in Genesis* website, http://www.answersingenesis.org/Home/Area/bios/default.asp#pastsci.

4. Ken Ham, "Creation: Where's the 'proof'?" December 1, 1999, *Answers in Genesis* website, http://www.answersingenesis.org/articles/cm/v22/n1/creation-proof.

very intelligent. Adam had perfect DNA ("very good" in Genesis 1:31), and God programmed him with perfect knowledge (not infinite knowledge) so as to communicate with him right from the start. For more on Adam's characteristics please see "What Was Adam Like?"[5]

Even looking into the past, there is evidence to confirm the biblical account that man has always been intelligent, not primitive, having ancient batteries, incredible ship-building technology, and let's not forget the pyramids![6]

**with one foot still in a cave dwelling,**

Again, I don't accept your presupposition that man was primitive, but as you probably know there are still people today living in caves and that doesn't make them primitive — some have cable TV!

**rather than everything our God-given human abilities can see in God's universe around us every day.**

I agree with the *observations*. In fact, Romans 1:20 makes it clear that God's attributes can be seen in what is made so we are without excuse:

> For since the creation of the world His invisible attributes, His eternal power and divine nature, have been clearly seen, being understood through what has been made, so that they are without excuse (NASB).

In essence, it is enough to condemn, but not enough to save. We all still need Jesus Christ.

**First of all, evolution is simply a collection of observations.**

Then why haven't we observed these?

1. No one has been able to make life from nonlife (matter giving rise to life which is foundational to pond-scum-to-people evolution).

2. No one has been able to change a single-celled life form like an amoeba into a cow or goat, etc.

---

5. This article can be found at: http://www.answersingenesis.org/articles/cm/v13/n4/adam and is by Ken Ham.

6. See David Criswell, "Ancient Civilizations and Modern Man," March 1, 1995, http://www.answersingenesis.org/articles/cm/v17/n2/ancient-civilizations; Larry Pierce, "The Large Ships of Antiquity," Answers in Genesis website, http://www.answersingenesis.org/articles/cm/v22/n3/ships; David Down, "The Pyramids of Ancient Egypt," September 1, 2004, http://www.answersingenesis.org/articles/cm/v26/n4/pyramids-of-ancient-egypt.

3. No one has been able to observe and repeat the big bang (which is foundational to pond-scum-to-people evolution).

4. We haven't observed the billions of information-gaining mutations required to build the DNA strand to give rise to new kinds of life forms.

5. Matter has never been observed to give rise to new information.

Evolution is clearly a worldview and, more specifically, it is a subset of the religion of secular humanism, in the same way creation is a subset of Christianity.

**If you prefer, you can see the hand of God in action within evolution. I do.**

You are confusing *natural selection* with evolution. Natural selection is good, observable science. In fact, natural selection was developed by Ed Blyth, a creationist, about 25 years before Darwin, and is an excellent confirmation of God's created kinds in Genesis.

Natural selection clearly shows dogs making dogs, cats making cats, weasels making weasels, etc. This is biblical. However, we don't observe dogs giving rise to horses or mice giving rise to cats. Natural selection is not goo-to-you evolution.[7]

**I don't see your problem.**

The issue is simple — you can either trust God's Word or trust man's ideas about the past. In whom will your faith be placed? God says:

> And without faith it is impossible to please Him, for he who comes to God must believe that He is and that He is a rewarder of those who seek Him (Hebrews 11:6; NASB).

> It is better to take refuge in the LORD than to trust in man (Psalm 118:8; NASB).

Our goal here isn't to win or lose an argument, but to get people thinking, help people get saved, and then disciple them as Jesus commanded in Matthew 28. I'm sure you've heard the "good news" of Jesus Christ before, but I'm not sure if you understand what this means.

---

7. Ken Ham, gen. ed., *The New Answers Book 1*, "Is Natural Selection the Same Thing as Evolution?" by Dr. Georgia Purdom (Green Forest, AR: Master Books, 2006), http://www.answersingenesis.org/articles/nab/is-natural-selection-evolution.

The "good news" of being saved goes back to the "bad news" in Genesis. God originally created a perfect world (Genesis 1:31); there was no death and suffering (Genesis 1:29–30). Then man sinned against a perfect and holy God (Genesis 3). God cursed the animals and the ground because of man and sentenced them to die (Genesis 3). It is due to man's actions that sin and death entered the world. Now we are all sinners as a result and in need of a Savior (Romans 5:12).

When man sinned, God sacrificed animals (Genesis 3:21 — coats of skins) to cover their sin because God commanded that sin is punishable by death (Genesis 2:17). This covering could only cover, not forgive and take away sins (Hebrews 9:22).

But God loved us enough to take that punishment upon Himself. He stepped into His creation as a perfect man, Jesus Christ, to live and suffer and die a painful death — to be the final sacrifice to cover our sins for good and offer forgiveness (John 3:16).

For those who receive Jesus Christ, there will be salvation and a new heaven and new earth (Isaiah 65:17; Revelation 21:1). They will one day see a perfect world again with no pain and sorrow (Revelation 21:4) — the curse will be removed (Revelation 22:3). When you remove the reason for the gospel and replace it with goo-to-you evolution, it undermines the reason for Christ.

I want to encourage you to consider this. Kind regards in Christ.

## Chapter 5

# What is the Basis for Morality?

Letter with reference added to quote so readers know where to find that response; otherwise unedited:

> Whilst reading through some of your feedback archive, I was somewhat takenaback at the response given to a scientist concerning evolution.
>
> You said:
>
> "Why not steal, why not lie, why not murder your fellow students, why not put falsehoods in museums[—]especially if it benefits you in some way? The current generation put this together and that is why they arent afraid to put on pro-evolution shirts with Natural Selection written on them and kill their fellow students."[1]
>
> Are you suggesting that the only thing preventing you from commiting such acts is a fear of God? If you happened to have been raised outside religion, do you honestly believe you would be compelled to rape, murder and steal? It is a very revealing comment to make if true.
>
> M.F., Southampton, UK

Response:

Thank you for contacting Answers in Genesis. First, I'm not sure that anyone can escape being raised without any religion whatsoever — whether secular humanism, naturalism, evolutionism, Christianity, Islam, etc. I had the privilege of being raised in a family that respected the Bible and its teachings, whereas many others were raised with evolutionary religion or even had it forced on them.

But let's answer your two questions. 1. **"Are you suggesting that the only thing preventing you from committing such acts is a fear of God?"** Let's face it, without God, there is no reason not to be a rapist, murderer,

---

1. Bodie Hodge, "Feedback: 'A False Version of Our History,' " August 6, 2006, http://www. answersingenesis.org/articles/2006/08/18/feedback-false-version-history.

etc. They are being consistent in their religion. All should have a fear of God and that would be to hate evil (Proverbs 8:13), but that is not the sole reason Christians abstain from common animals acts like rape, murder, cannibalism, and so on. The other reason is out of love for God and His Word (John 14:26).

2. **"If you happened to have been raised outside religion, do you honestly believe you would be compelled to rape, murder and steal?"** This "what if" question is essentially useless and as such, it is impossible to know. But let me answer like this: if one has been raised to believe they are just animals and there is no right and wrong, like many evolutionists commonly teach even though this is a religion, then *why not* do like animals?

Logically, though, if people are taught from a young age that nothing matters, that there are no morals, and that they can do whatever pleases them, and that "survival of the fittest" is "the way the world works," then what type of society should we expect? After all, leading evolutionary spokesperson Richard Dawkins makes it clear that there is no basis for morality in evolution:

> Jaron Lanier: "There's a large group of people who simply are uncomfortable with accepting evolution because it leads to what they perceive as a moral vacuum, in which their best impulses have no basis in nature."
>
> Richard Dawkins: "All I can say is, That's just tough. We have to face up to the truth."[2]

Let's look at a few examples of evolutionary beliefs causing terrible crimes.

> 1. Jeffrey Dahmer: "If a person doesn't think there is a God to be accountable to, then — then what's the point of trying to modify your behaviour to keep it within acceptable ranges? That's how I thought anyway. I always believed the theory of evolution as truth, that we all just came from the slime. When we, when we died, you know, that was it, there is nothing. . . ."[3]

> 2. Adolf Hitler (Hitler's atrocities certainly fulfilled Darwin's call to eliminate certain races): "At some future period, not very distant as measured by centuries, the civilized races of man will almost certainly exterminate and replace the savage races throughout the world. At the same time the anthropomorphous apes . . .

2. "Evolution: The Dissent of Darwin," *Psychology Today* (January/February 1997): p. 62.
3. Jeffrey Dahmer, in an interview with Stone Phillips, *Dateline NBC*, Nov. 29, 1994.

will no doubt be exterminated. The break between man and his nearest allies will then be wider, for it will intervene between man in a more civilized state, as we may hope, even than the Caucasian, and some ape as low as a baboon, instead of as now between the negro or Australian [aborigine] and the gorilla."[4]

Sir Arthur Keith, a British anthropologist, was an atheistic evolutionist and an anti-Nazi, but he still drew this chilling conclusion:

> The German Führer, as I have consistently maintained, is an evolutionist; he has consciously sought to make the practice of Germany conform to the theory of evolution.[5]

But let's allow Hitler to speak for himself. Consider this quote in his unpublished second book:

> The types of creatures on the earth are countless, and on an individual level their self-preservation instinct as well as the longing for procreation is always unlimited; however, the space in which this entire life process plays itself out is limited. It is the surface area of a precisely measured sphere on which billions and billions of individual beings struggle for life and succession. In the limitation of this living space lies the compulsion for the struggle for survival, and the struggle for survival, in turn contains the precondition for evolution.[6]

Hitler continues:

> The history of the world in the ages when humans did not yet exist was initially a representation of geological occurrences. The clash of natural forces with each other, the formation of a habitable surface on this planet, the separation of water and land, the formation of the mountains, plains, and the seas. That is [was] the history of the world during this time. Later, with the emergence of organic life, human interest focuses on the appearance and disappearance of its thousandfold forms. Man himself finally becomes visible very late, and from that point on he begins to understand the term "world history" as referring to the history of his own development — in other words, the representation

---

4. Charles Darwin, *The Descent of Man*, 1874 (2nd ed.), p. 178.
5. Arthur Keith, *Evolution and Ethics*, 1947, p. 230.
6. Adolf Hitler, *Hitler's Second Book*, edited by Gerhard L. Weinberg, translated by Krista Smith (New York: Enigma Books, 2003) , p. 8.

of his own evolution. This development is characterized by the never-ending battle of humans against animals and also against humans themselves.[7]

Stalin:

> One of [Stalin's] friends later said in a book . . . that when Stalin began to read Darwin he became an atheist. . . . [T]hree years after Stalin's death, Communist Party leader Nikita Khrushchev charged Stalin with perpetrating "mass arrests and deportations of many thousands of people, execution without trial and without normal investigation." Khrushchev also stated that during Stalin's reign 70 per cent of the members and candidates of the party central committee in 1934 were subsequently arrested and shot. Most of these, claimed Khrushchev, were simply "innocent communists." Darwinian "survival of the fittest" ideas thus powerfully shaped Stalin's approach to society. Oppression, self glorification, atheism and murder resulted from Stalin's rejection of his Creator after reading and believing the evolutionary ideas of Darwin.[8]

These are but a few who based their own moralities on themselves. We all know that teaching influences people's lives. As sad as it is, what do we see today? We see kids killing kids in schools, rape, merciless theft and vandalism, the murder of unborn children, and an overall disregard for the law. And research confirms that this decline in morals is linked to a rejection of biblical absolutes as people embrace evolutionary ideas, as the Bible *is* the source of morality. Simply look at the results of evolution this past century to see its devastating effect on human life.[9]

As Christians, the basis of all morality is dictated by God and His Word. When rejecting God, we make ourselves the final authority in matters of morality, and there is no basis for consistent morality applied to everyone. (This is not to say that people who do not believe the Bible are all criminals; most are not, but they have no basis for their morality — no real justification for why people should be moral.)

But following the moral guidelines the Bible gives is not done solely out of fear — though, certainly, there is recognition of God's judgment. Rather,

---

7. Hitler, *Hitler's Second Book*, p. 9.

8. "What Happened When Stalin Read Darwin?" *Creation* 10(4):23, 1988.

9. Bodie Hodge, "The Results of Evolution: Is It the Bloodiest Religion Ever?" Answers in Genesis website, July 13, 2009, http://www.answersingenesis.org/articles/2009/07/13/results-evolution-bloodiest-religion-ever.

people can act morally when they understand why morals exist, have a relationship with the foundation behind them, and realize that morality exists to protect us, not to restrict us.

We do not avoid murder just because we fear God's judgment, but also because the Bible shows us why all human lives are valuable, and why murder is truly wrong (and not just "undesirable"). And, of course, this all stems from understanding the creation account in Genesis, and that God made us in His image.

Additionally, a personal relationship with Christ frees us from bondage to the sin nature we all inherited through Adam and indwells us with the Holy Spirit. We possess this sinful nature until we are freed from our bodies — which is why we, as Christians, still sin. Sadly, this is gleefully pointed out when a prominent Christian leader succumbs to the lust of the flesh. But it is God's desire for His people to be set apart (sanctified) and conformed to His perfect Son (Romans 8), and it is God who works in us "both to will and to do of his good pleasure" (Philippians 2:13, KJV).

In kindness.

## Chapter 6

# THE BIBLE AND SLAVERY

Letter, unedited:

> This is a response to Paul Taylor's article "A Leader for Biblical Equality".
>
> Just because human beings are from "one blood" doesn't mean that the bible is anti-slavery. The bible supports and regulates slave ownership and doesn't say that owning a slave is wrong. White Christians have often used the bible to convince themselves that owning slaves is OK and the slaves should obey their "earthly masters". White Christians also owned white slaves during and after the fall of the Roman Empire. So to say that White Christians need to believe that their slaves are inferior to them in order to justify slave ownership is also false. A slave is slave in the mind of White Christians that have owned them and the bible supports slave ownership.
>
> Find me one verse in the bible that condemns owning a slave. I dare you. I've already found several that support it. Your "god" should be destroyed. Here are Bible verses in support of slave ownership new and old testament (Leviticus 25:44-46 NLT), (Exodus 21:2-6 NLT), Jesus Christ thinks slaves should be beaten too (Luke 12:47-48 NLT), (1 Timothy 6:1-2 NLT), (Ephesians 6:5 NLT), (Exodus 21:20-21 NAB).
>
> A.

Response: [Since this letter was directed to a ministry friend and former coworker in our UK office, we have replied together.]

We are pleased that you decided to contact us. We have no idea what angle you approach this issue from. Because of your concentration on what "White Christians" have said, we assume that you are probably neither of light complexion nor Christian.[1]

---

1. It should be noted that the authors and Answers in Genesis oppose both racism and slavery. According to the Bible, there is only one race — the human race where all people are descended from Adam and Eve.

I, Paul Taylor, am both — by background, I am "White"[2] Anglo-Saxon Protestant, having been brought up in the Church of England in the North of England, in a "white," working-class family. My Christianity is not due to my Anglican upbringing — my faith stems from the fact that I was born again at the age of 15.

I, Bodie Hodge, am what I affectionately call a "Mutt" Christian who is of lighter complexion. I am a mixture of German, Irish, English, Dutch, Portuguese, and Native American. In fact, I probably have a few others that I'm not aware of! I received Christ as Lord at the age of nine.

It is possible that our views could be influenced by our background, though we have had these comments checked by a "Black" Christian colleague and a Christian of Asian descent to assure that we are being biblically minded (Proverbs 11:14). You have used the terminology "White." We are therefore using the term "White" to refer to what we would normally call peoples of European descent (especially Anglo-Saxon origin) and "Black" to refer to peoples we would normally say are primarily of African descent. We do not wish to cause offense by terminology.

You state that "White Christians have often used the Bible to convince themselves that owning slaves is OK and the slaves should obey their 'earthly masters.' " You are correct. Regrettably and shamefully, "White" people claiming to be Christians have frequently taken verses of Scripture out of context to justify the most despicable acts. I could argue that most of these people were not really Christians; they were not really born again but were adhering to a form of Christianity for traditional or national reasons. Nevertheless, I think we have to concede that there are genuine "White" Christians who have believed the vilest calumnies about the nature of "Black" people and have sought support for their disgraceful views from the pages of the Bible.

Some "White" Christians have assumed that the so-called curse of Ham (Genesis 9:25) was to cause Ham's descendants to be black and to be cursed. While it is likely that African peoples are descended from Ham (Cush, Phut, and Mizraim), it is not likely that they are descended from Canaan — the curse was actually declared on Canaan, not Ham.

However, there is no evidence from Genesis that the curse has anything to do with skin color. Others have suggested that the "mark of Cain" in Genesis 4 was that he was turned dark-skinned. Again, there is no evidence

2. We are using the term "White" to refer to peoples of European origin and "Black" to refer to peoples primarily of African origin. We are actually not too thrilled about these terms either since all people are really the same color, just different shades, but for the sake of understanding, we will use them in this chapter in a reluctant sense.

of this in Scripture, and in any case, Cain's descendants were possibly wiped out in the Flood.

Incidentally, the use of such passages to attempt to justify some sort of evil associated with dark skin is based on an assumption that the other characters in the accounts were light-skinned, like "White" Anglo-Saxons today. That assumption can also not be found in Scripture, and is very unlikely to be true. Very light skin and very dark skin are actually the *extremes* of skin color, caused by the minimum and maximum of melanin production, and are more likely, therefore, to be the genetically selected results of populations moving away from each other, after the Tower of Babel incident recorded in Genesis 11.

The first thing we need to say is that neither slavery in New Testament times nor slavery under the Mosaic covenant had anything to do with the sort of slavery where "Black" people were bought and sold as property by "White" people in the well-known slave trade over the last few centuries. No "White" Christian should think that they can use any slightly positive comment about slavery in these sections to justify the historic slave trade, which is still a major stain on the histories of both the U.S. and UK.

The U.S. and the UK were not the only countries in history to delve into harsh slavery and so be stained.

1. Ham's son Mizraim founded Egypt (still called *Mizraim* in Hebrew). Egypt was the first recorded nation in the Bible to have harsh slavery, and it was imposed on Joseph, the son of Israel, in 1728 B.C., according to Archbishop Ussher. Later, the Egyptians were slave masters to the rest of the Israelites, and Moses, by the hand of God, freed them.

2. The Israelites were again enslaved by Assyrian and Babylonian captors about 1,000 years later.

3. Other ancient nations were also involved in slavery; the Code of Hammurabi discussed it soon after Babel.

4. "Black" Moors enslaved "Whites" during their conquering of Spain and Portugal on the Iberian Peninsula in the eighth century A.D. for over 400 years. The Moors even took slaves as far north as Scandinavia. The Moorish and Middle Eastern slave market was quite extensive.

5. Norse raiders of Scandinavia enslaved other European peoples and took them back as property beginning in the eighth century A.D.

Even in modern times, slavery is still alive in the Sudan and Darfur.

We find many other examples of harsh slavery from cultures throughout the world. At any rate, these few examples indicate that harsh slavery was/is a reality, and in all cases, is an unacceptable act by biblical standards.

The extreme kindness to be shown to slaves/servants commanded in the Bible among the Israelites was often prefaced by a reminder that they, too, were slaves at the hand of the Egyptians. In other words, they were to treat slaves/servants in a way that they wanted to be treated.

But was slavery that is discussed in the Bible the same as the harsh slavery? For example, slaves and masters are referred to in Paul's epistles. In Ephesians 6:5, a better translation is to use the word "bondservant." The Bible is in no way condoning the practice of bondservants, who were certainly not being paid the first-century equivalent of the minimum wage. Nevertheless, they were being paid something, and were therefore in a state more akin to a lifetime employment contract rather than "racial" slavery. Moreover, Paul gives clear instructions that Christian "masters" are to treat such people with respect and as equals. Their employment position did not affect their standing in the Church.

Passages in Leviticus show us the importance of treating "aliens" and foreigners well, and how, if they believe, they become part of the people of God (for example, Rahab and Ruth, to name but two). Also, the existence of slavery in Leviticus 25 underlines the importance of redemption, and enables the New Testament writers to point out that we are slaves to sin, but are redeemed by the blood of Jesus. Such slavery is a living allegory, and does not justify the "racial" and "racist" form of slavery practiced from about the 16th to 19th centuries.

As we already know, slavery was common in the Middle East as far back as ancient Egypt. If God had simply ignored it, then there would have been no rules for their treatment and they could have treated them harshly with no rights. But since they did have rights and rules for their protection, it showed that God cared for them as well. However, this is often misconstrued for an endorsement of slavery, which it is not. God listed slave traders among the worst of sinners in 1 Timothy 1:10 (kidnappers/men stealers/ slave traders). This is no new teaching as Moses was not fond of forced slavery either:

> He who kidnaps a man and sells him, or if he is found in his hand, shall surely be put to death (Exodus 21:16).

In light of such rules, slaves/servants in Israelite culture came about by their own actions, whether from among the Israelites or neighboring cultures.

In fact, take note of the punishment of Egypt, when the Lord freed the Israelites (Exodus chapters 3–15). God predicted this punishment well in advance:

> Then He said to Abram: "Know certainly that your descendants will be strangers in a land that is not theirs, and will serve them, and they will afflict them four hundred years. And also the nation whom they serve I will judge; afterward they shall come out with great possessions" (Genesis 15:13–14).

Had God not protected slaves/bondservants by such commands, then many people surrounding them, who did have harsh slavery, would have loved to move in where there were no governing principles as to the treatment of slaves. It would have given a "green light" to slave owners from neighboring areas to come and settle there. But with the rules in place, it discouraged slavery in their realm.

Now let us directly discuss the passages that you bring up for clarification:

> "Blessed is that servant whom his master will find so doing when he comes. Truly, I say to you that he will make him ruler over all that he has. But if that servant says in his heart, 'My master is delaying his coming,' and begins to beat the male and female servants, and to eat and drink and be drunk, the master of that servant will come on a day when he is not looking for him, and at an hour when he is not aware, and will cut him in two and appoint him his portion with the unbelievers. And that servant who knew his master's will, and did not prepare himself or do according to his will, shall be beaten with many stripes. But he who did not know, yet committed things deserving of stripes, shall be beaten with few. For everyone to whom much is given, from him much will be required; and to whom much has been committed, of him they will ask the more" (Luke 12:43–48).

As for Jesus' supposed support for beating slaves, this is in the context of a parable. Parables are stories Jesus told to help us understand spiritual truths. For example, in one parable, Jesus likens God to a judge. The judge is unjust, but eventually gives justice to the widow when she persists. The point of that story was not to tell us that God is like an unjust judge — on the contrary, He is completely just. The point of the parable is to tell us to be persistent in prayer. Similarly, Luke 12:47–48 does not justify beating slaves. It is not a parable telling us how masters are to behave. It is a parable telling us that we must be ready for when Jesus Himself returns. One will be rewarded with eternal life through Christ, or with eternal punishment (Matthew 25:46).

> Let as many bondservants as are under the yoke count their own masters worthy of all honor, so that the name of God and His doctrine may not be blasphemed. And those who have believing masters, let them not despise them because they are brethren, but rather serve them because those who are benefited are believers and beloved. Teach and exhort these things (1 Timothy 6:1–2).

Writing to Timothy, Paul doesn't give an endorsement to slavery or servants. He merely gives commands to those who are *already* either masters or bond-servants. Again, bondservants or slaves were paid a wage and, being brothers in Christ, Paul makes it clear that they are equals:

> There is neither Jew nor Greek, there is neither slave nor free, there is neither male nor female; for you are all one in Christ Jesus (Galatians 3:28).

> Bondservants, be obedient to those who are your masters according to the flesh, with fear and trembling, in sincerity of heart, as to Christ; not with eye service, as men-pleasers, but as bondservants of Christ, doing the will of God from the heart, with goodwill doing service, as to the Lord, and not to men, knowing that whatever good anyone does, he will receive the same from the Lord, whether he is a slave or free. And you, masters, do the same things to them, giving up threatening, knowing that your own Master also is in heaven, and there is no partiality with Him (Ephesians 6:5–9).

Again, Paul in Ephesians is not giving an endorsement to slavery/bondser-vants and masters but gives them both the same commands. Again, bond-servants were to be paid fair wages:

> Masters, give your bondservants what is just and fair, knowing that you also have a Master in heaven (Colossians 4:1).

> "If you buy a Hebrew servant, he shall serve six years; and in the seventh he shall go out free and pay nothing. 'If he comes in by himself, he shall go out by himself; if he comes in married, then his wife shall go out with him. If his master has given him a

wife, and she has borne him sons or daughters, the wife and her children shall be her master's, and he shall go out by himself. But if the servant plainly says, 'I love my master, my wife, and my children; I will not go out free,' then his master shall bring him to the judges. He shall also bring him to the door, or to the doorpost, and his master shall pierce his ear with an awl; and he shall serve him forever" (Exodus 21:2–6).

This is the first type of bankruptcy law I've encountered. With this, a government doesn't step in, but a person who has lost himself to debt can sell the only thing he has left, his ability to perform labor. This is a loan. In six years the loan is paid off, and he is set free. Bondservants who did this made a wage, had their debt covered, had a home to stay in, on-the-job training, and did it for only six years. This almost sounds better than college, which doesn't cover debt and you have to pay for it!

This is not a forced agreement either. The bondservants enter into service of their own accord. In the same respect, foreigners can also sell themselves into servitude. Although the rules are slightly different, it would still be by their own accord in light of Exodus 21:16.

"If men contend with each other, and one strikes the other with a stone or with his fist, and he does not die but is confined to his bed, if he rises again and walks about outside with his staff, then he who struck him shall be acquitted. He shall only pay for the loss of his time, and shall provide for him to be thoroughly healed. And if a man beats his male or female servant with a rod, so that he dies under his hand, he shall surely be punished. Notwithstanding, if he remains alive a day or two, he shall not be punished; for he is his property" (Exodus 21:18–21).

This passage closely follows Moses' decree against slave traders in Exodus 21:16. We include verses 18 and 19 to show the parallel to servants among the Israelites. The rules still apply for their protection if they already have servants or if someone sells themself into service.

I am the LORD your God, who brought you out of the land of Egypt, to give you the land of Canaan and to be your God. And if one of your brethren who dwells by you becomes poor, and sells himself to you, you shall not compel him to serve as a slave. As a hired servant and a sojourner he shall be with you, and shall serve you until the Year of Jubilee. And then he shall depart from you

— he and his children with him — and shall return to his own family. He shall return to the possession of his fathers. For they are My servants, whom I brought out of the land of Egypt; they shall not be sold as slaves. You shall not rule over him with rigor, but you shall fear your God. And as for your male and female slaves whom you may have — from the nations that are around you, from them you may buy male and female slaves. Moreover you may buy the children of the strangers who dwell among you, and their families who are with you, which they beget in your land; and they shall become your property. And you may take them as an inheritance for your children after you, to inherit them as a possession; they shall be your permanent slaves. But regarding your brethren, the children of Israel, you shall not rule over one another with rigor (Leviticus 25:38–46).

God prefaces this passage specifically with a reminder that the Lord saved them from their bondage of slavery in Egypt. Again, if one becomes poor, he can sell himself into slavery/servitude and be released as was already discussed.

Verse 44 discusses slaves that they may *already* have from nations around them. They can be bought and sold. It doesn't say to seek them out or have forced slavery. Hence, it is not giving an endorsement of seeking new slaves or encouraging the slave trade. At this point, the Israelites had just come out of slavery and were about to enter the Holy Land. They shouldn't have had many servants. Also, this doesn't restrict other people in cultures around them from selling themselves as bondservants. But as discussed already, there are passages for the proper and godly treatment of servants/slaves.

The slavery of "Black" people by "White" people in the 16th to 19th centuries was harshly unjust, like many cultures before. This harsh slavery is not discussed in Moses' writings, because such slavery was unknown in Hebrew culture. This is not surprising. Paul tells us in Romans 1:30 that people are capable of inventing new ways of doing evil.

"White" on "Black" slavery was opposed by Christians such as William Wilberforce, not by examining passages on slavery, because the slaveries were of different types. "Racial" slavery was opposed because it was seen to be contrary to the value that God places on every human being, and the fact that God "has made from one blood every nation of men to dwell on all the face of the earth" (Acts 17:26). The use of the term "one blood" is so significant. If "races" were really of different "bloods," then we could not all be saved by the shedding of the blood of one Savior. It is because the entire human race is descended from one man — Adam — that we know we can trust in one Savior, Jesus Christ.

You say our "god" needs to be destroyed. If by this you refer to a sort of petty "god" invented by "White" Christians to justify "racist" attitudes, then you are right. The true God of the Bible is not like that. As we have tried to show, yet again, God's Word, the Bible, teaches that there is only one race of people — Adam's race — and there is one Savior, Jesus Christ.

A few pointers to remember:

1. Slaves under Mosaic Law were different from the harshly treated slaves of other societies; they were more like servants or bondservants.

2. The Bible doesn't give an endorsement of slave traders but the opposite (1 Timothy 1:10). A slave/bondservant was acquired when a person *voluntarily* entered into the arrangement when he needed to pay off his debts.

3. The Bible recognizes that slavery is a reality in this sin-cursed world and doesn't ignore it, but instead gives regulations for good treatment by both masters and servants and reveals they are equal under Christ.

4. Israelites could sell themselves as slaves/bondservants to have their debts covered, make a wage, have housing, and be set free after six years. Foreigners could sell themselves as a slave/bondservant as well.

5. Many forget that it was biblical Christians who led the fight to abolish harsh slavery in modern times.

The issue of racism is just one of many reasons why we oppose evolution. Darwinian evolution can easily be used to suggest that some "races" are more evolved than others. Biblical Christianity cannot be used that way — unless it is twisted by people who have deliberately misunderstood what the Bible actually teaches. Recall Darwin's prediction of nonwhite "races":

> At some future period, not very distant as measured by centuries, the civilized races of man will almost certainly exterminate and replace the savage races throughout the world. At the same time the anthropomorphous apes . . . will no doubt be exterminated. The

break between man and his nearest allies will then be wider, for it will intervene between man in a more civilized state, as we may hope, even than the Caucasian, and some ape as low as a baboon, instead of as now between the negro or Australian [aborigine] and the gorilla."[3]

I pray this helps clarify, and we want to encourage you to consider the good news of Jesus Christ. Please take some time to read this short article on the subject (see appendix 4). With sincerity in Christ,

Paul Taylor, formerly with Answers in Genesis–UK
Bodie Hodge, Answers in Genesis–US

---

3. Charles Darwin, *The Descent of Man* (New York, A.L. Burt, 1874, 2nd ed.), p. 178.

*Chapter 7*

# WHAT ABOUT THE "HARSH" GOD OF THE OLD TESTAMENT?

Letter, unedited:

> **For a while a question has been on my mind; how come in the Old Testament God seems so mean and brutal? I hear of unbelievers using this against christians and it also makes me doubt my faith a bit. I want to try to find an answer. Please, help.**
>
> **D., U.S.**

Response:

This view of God is commonly referred to in the secular media. We often hear that the God of the Old Testament seems very harsh/brutal and "evil." But as Christians, we need to evaluate such claims against the Bible and see if they are with or without merit.

Such claims are an attack on God's character, but are the claims true or are they missing something? Knowing that God is good (Mark 10:18), when I hear this, the first verse that pops into my head is:

> Woe to those who call evil good, and good evil; who substitute darkness for light and light for darkness; who substitute bitter for sweet and sweet for bitter! (Isaiah 5:20; NASB)

The intent of many of those who make such claims is to make a good God look evil to justify their position of rejecting Him, His Word, or even His existence. Of course, this doesn't make much sense . . . to reveal the fallacy consider if someone said, "Hitler was evil harsh and mean, so therefore he didn't exist!"

But if *God* didn't exist and the Bible weren't His Word, there would be no basis to say that good and evil exist in the first place, and therefore, brutality would be neither good nor bad. Few that I have spoken with realize this when they attack God's character in an effort to make a case that He doesn't exist.

At any rate, let's analyze this and see if God really is harsh/brutal and evil. Among the common events in the Bible where I've heard people say

God is harsh, they usually begin in Genesis: the Flood or Sodom and Gomorrah. There are others, too, but for this short response, I will just discuss these.

## The Flood

God is often attacked for killing "all the innocent people and even children" in the Flood. But judging Scripture by Scripture, we read that no one is truly innocent (Romans 3:23) and all will die eventually anyway — a repercussion of our own actions (1 Corinthians 15:22; Romans 6:23). Second, let's see what brought such a judgment on the people before the Flood:

> Then the LORD saw that the wickedness of man was great in the earth, and that every intent of the thoughts of his heart was only evil continually (Genesis 6:5).

What a strong statement! Every intention and thought was evil all the time. Imagine the murders, rapes, thefts, child sacrifices, cannibalism, and so on. This was happening continually. Yet this was about 120 years (maximum) before the Flood (Genesis 6:3). So God was still patient, allowing time for repentance and change (1 Peter 3:20). God even called Noah to be a preacher of righteousness (2 Peter 2:5), yet people still refused to listen and continued to murder, rape, do child sacrifice, and so on.

God even went so far as to offer a way of salvation! He provided an ark through Noah and his family and yet others didn't come. Only Noah's family was saved (2 Peter 2:5). The means of salvation, preaching of righteousness, and God's patience were there, yet everyone else refused them and received their judgment.

As an aside, the claim of children dying in the Flood has always been of interest to me. If people really were evil and their thoughts evil all the time, then abortion, child murder, and child sacrifice were likely commonplace. And disobedience to God would mean disobeying God's command to be fruitful and multiply (Genesis 1:28). Resisting this command would result in drastically fewer children, so I wonder if many children were even around at the time of the Flood. Noah himself had no children until he was 500 years old (lending to my postulation that children were few and far between in those days — I wouldn't be surprised if Noah took a long time to find a godly wife who wanted children as well).

Even so, children are sinners and can also have every evil intentions and thoughts (Romans 3:23). Today, for example, we see children killing children in school, rape among children, and so on. But consider this . . . who was it that kept their children from entering the ark? It was their parents/guardians continuing in their own violence.

## Sodom and Gomorrah

Please read Genesis 18:20–33. In this section, the Lord revealed to Abraham that Sodom and Gomorrah had sinned exceedingly. Their wickedness was not *entirely* revealed (Ezekiel 16:49) but we do know their acts of sodomy (later in the chapter) had overtaken them in their actions, enough to rape.

Abraham asked if God would sweep away the righteous with the wicked. He asked the Lord if there were 50 righteous, would the Lord spare the city; He said yes. He asked the Lord if there were 40 righteous, would the Lord spare it; He said yes. He asked the Lord if there were 30 righteous, would the Lord spare it; He said yes. He asked the Lord if there were 20 righteous, would the Lord spare it; He said yes. He asked the Lord if there were 10 righteous, would the Lord spare it; He said yes.

This reveals how wicked and sinful the people were. They were without excuse and judgment was finally coming. This also reveals something interesting about the Flood. If God would spare Sodom and Gomorrah for only 10 righteous people, then would God have spared the earth if 10 people were righteous before the Flood? It appears that He did. Methuselah and Lamech, Noah's father and grandfather *may* have been those 2 that made 10 (along with Noah, his wife, his 3 sons and their wives). Of course, there may have been others who were righteous, too, up until the Flood. But at the time of the Flood, we can surmise there were only 8 (Methuselah and Lamech had died just before the Flood).

Lot and his family numbered less than 10 in Sodom and Gomorrah (Lot, his wife, his two daughters, his two sons-in-law, and two angels only made 8, the same as the Flood). Yet God provided a means of salvation for them. The angels came and helped them get to safety.

Were there children in Sodom and Gomorrah? The Bible doesn't reveal any, and homosexual behavior was rampant, so there may not have been any children. Since God made it clear that not even 10 people were righteous in the city, then even the children (if any) were being extremely sinful.

I hope this helps explain that God acts justly, punishing those whose crimes reach a point that it is time to act. Interestingly enough, people who say God is cruel want justice when they are wronged; for example, if someone steals from them or attacks them. So they really have a double standard.

God is the same God of the Old Testament and New Testament. In both cases, people have/had the opportunity to get back to a right relationship with Him. In both cases, God judges sin (2 Peter 3:5–7). Mercy and patience were to be found through God's vessels Noah, with his preaching for years, and Abraham, with his pleading for Sodom and Gomorrah (even Lot urged the people not to be so wicked) — just as mercy and patience are still available today (2 Peter 3:9). And He has provided a means of salvation in Jesus Christ (1 Peter 3:18), as the ark was with the Flood and the angels were in urging Lot and his family to flee Sodom and Gomorrah. In fact, there were many more that I could have commented on. Here is a chart of a few, including the ones we discussed:

| Event/people | Were they sinning? | Did God provide justice? | Did God provide a means of salvation? |
| --- | --- | --- | --- |
| The Fall: Adam and the woman | Yes | Yes | Yes |
| The Flood | Yes | Yes | Yes |
| Sodom and Gomorrah | Yes | Yes | Yes |
| The Egyptians | Yes | Yes | Yes |
| Canaanites | Yes | Yes | Yes |
| The Benjamites | Yes | Yes | Yes |
| Non-Christians | Yes | Yes | Yes |

No one can blame God for not providing a merciful alternative or call Him evil for providing justice against sin. Please pray that people will open their eyes and realize that they should hate sin (Romans 12:9) and love God (Deuteronomy 6:5), who acts justly against sin (2 Thessalonians 1:5–10). Yet He offers abundant mercy to those who love Him (Exodus 20:6; Deuteronomy 7:9; Ephesians 2:4). I pray this helps, and for those reading this who are not familiar with the good news of Jesus Christ, please take some time to read this short article on the subject (appendix 4).

Kindness in Christ.

# ᴀ Righteous Lie? Parts 1 ᴀɴᴅ 2

Letter, reference so everyone knows where to find that alleged Bible contradiction and response, otherwise unedited:

> **You, know I almost hate to do this because I know how much email you guys handle . . . But I want to respond to Bodie Hodge's "contradictions" article on Rahab's "lie".[1] Bodie is almost always right on the mark and is probably my favorite feedback man, but in this case I have to take exception to his saying that it is always wrong to lie . . . The ninth commandment says we should never bear false witness against our neighbor (or anyone). But if the Nazis are looking for Jews, and you know where they are, it would not be wrong to lie, in order to protect them, nor would this be bearing false witness "against" someone . . . I think in the same way the Israeli midwives lied to the Egyptians about the birthing of male babies in Moses's day . . . I know its a rare exception, but there may be other circumstances when it might be appropriate to "lie", although obviously, 99% percent of the time it would be wrong . . . Keep up the good work, all of you, your ministry is the most awesome in the world, just blows me away**
>
> **M.H.**

Response: [FYI: M.H. and I had a great conversation on this topic and have the utmost respect for one another. He was even praying for my wife when she was giving birth, immediately after this last response. But this shows how Christians can engage in debate in an iron sharpening iron fashion as Christian brothers.]

Thank you for contacting Answers in Genesis and thanks for the comments. I know this can be a touchy subject, but please bear with me as I try to explain. Keep in mind that I, too, am not perfect but will try to answer as scripturally as possible. (Also, sorry for the length — but this feedback will

---

1. Bodie Hodge, "Contradictions: A Righteous Lie?" Answers in Genesis website, November 3, 2008, http://www.answersingenesis.org/articles/2008/11/03/contradictions-a-righteous-lie.

allow me the breadth that I did not have with the contradiction article on Rahab on the website.)

## A righteous lie? Part 1

Bearing false witness is a lie, and in Hebrew the word for *false* in Exodus 20:16 is *sheqer*, which literally means "lie." It is derived from the Hebrew word *shaqar*, which means "deal falsely, be false, trick, and cheat." There are many verses in the Bible that reaffirm the Ninth Commandment, and a couple are given here:

> You shall not steal, nor deal falsely, nor lie to one another (Leviticus 19:11).

> I have not written to you because you do not know the truth, but because you know it, and that no lie is of the truth (1 John 2:21).

The devil is the father of lies (John 8:44), and one lie to God the Holy Spirit was worthy of instant death for Ananias (Acts 5:3–5). Paul points out that even if he were to lie for the glory of God, he would be deemed a sinner for such an act:

> For if the truth of God has increased through my lie to His glory, why am I also still judged as a sinner? (Romans 3:7).

In light of such passages, does a "righteous lie" really exist? The most common example sent to me was envisioning the Holocaust and being placed in the position of lying to potentially protect someone's life. Like most, if placed in such a difficult situation, it would be very difficult. In fact, I could never be sure what I would do, especially if it were a loved one.

But consider for a moment that we are all already sentenced to die because we are sinners (Romans 5:12). It is going to happen, regardless. If a lie helps keep someone alive for a matter of moments compared to eternity, was the lie, which is high treason against the Creator, worth it?

It would be like sitting in a cell on death row and when the guards come to take your roommate to the electric chair, you lie to the guards and say you don't know where the person went — while your roommate is hiding under his covers on the bed. Does it really help? Since we are all sinners (Romans 3:23), death is coming for us, and there is an appointed time (Ecclesiastes 3:2).

> The truthful lip shall be established forever, but a lying tongue is but for a moment (Proverbs 12:19).

Is it worth sinning against God to try to buy a moment of time next to eternity? Intentionally lying is foolish and would only harm the extent of your own life (Ecclesiastes 7:17). Let's look further at Scripture for an example of a situation where a lie could have saved a life.

## Stephen

Stephen in Acts 6–7 preached Christ, and men came against him. This culminated with a question by the high priest in Acts 7:1 who said: "Are these things so?"

At this point, Stephen could have done a "righteous lie" to save his life so that he could have many more years to preach the gospel. However, Stephen laid a long and appropriate foundation for Christ — then preached Christ. And they killed him.

But this event triggered a persecution that sent the gospel to the Gentiles (Acts 11:19) and peaked with Paul (who consented to Stephen's death) coming to Christ and taking the message to the Gentiles and writing several books of the New Testament. The Lord had a greater purpose for Stephen — even though it cost him his life. Keep in mind, however, that this, and other examples, are about the person in question — not another.

## Do we know what God had in mind?

I often wonder if a Nazi soldier had asked if someone was there hiding and they told the truth before God, could the Lord have in mind a greater purpose? Could God have used that person to free a great many people who ultimately died in the Holocaust? Or have done something to stop the war earlier? Or cause a great number of Jews and Nazis to come to know Christ? It is possible, but we simply cannot know. And one should not dwell too long on "what ifs" anyway.

No doubt, there is great value in the truth (John 8:32). As fallible, sinful human beings, our imperfect thoughts may not be able to comprehend what God has in mind, and we need to strive to trust God when He speaks on this subject, regardless of how hard it may be. We need to place our faith fully in Christ and trust in God in all things — and not lean on our own understanding (Proverbs 3:5).

I'm not saying this to be "preachy," because I really don't know what I would do in such a situation. However, I would pray that the Lord would grant me the wisdom to know what to say and how to say it — but more preferably, how to avoid being in that situation in the first place.

## If forced into this situation . . . what then?

Let's consider again the Nazi-Holocaust situation. There seems to be a conflict in the situation to lie before God to try to save someone else's life. The result is often called the "greater good" or "lesser of two evils."

I've been told in the past that the lesser of these two evils would be to lie to save a life — hence the common phrase "a righteous lie." This is often justified by appealing to the command to love our neighbor (Romans 13:9).

But how does God view this, remembering that God is a discerner of our motives? To God, a lie for selfish motive was worthy of death for Ananias. But, in fact, just one sin is worthy of death (Genesis 2:17). (This should be a reminder that we should continually praise God for His grace that is bestowed upon us.) But let's look at Scripture again. The two greatest commandments are as follows:

> Then one of the scribes came, and having heard them reasoning together, perceiving that He had answered them well, asked Him, "Which is the first [meaning greatest/foremost] commandment of all?"
>
> Jesus answered him, "The first of all the commandments is: 'Hear, O Israel, the LORD our God, the LORD is one. And you shall love the LORD your God with all your heart, with all your soul, with all your mind, and with all your strength.' This is the first commandment. And the second, like it, is this: 'You shall love your neighbor as yourself.' There is no other commandment greater than these" (Mark 12:28–31).

Jesus tells us that all the commandments can be summed up into these two statements. But of these two, the first is to love the Lord your God with all your heart, with all your soul, with all your mind, and with all your strength. So, this would trump the second. Our actions toward God should trump our actions toward men. Peter also affirmed this:

> But Peter and the other apostles answered and said: "We ought to obey God rather than men" (Acts 5:29).

If we love God, we should obey Him (John 14:15). To love God first means to obey Him first — before looking at our neighbor. So, is the greater good trusting God when He says not to lie or trusting in our fallible, sinful minds about the uncertain future?

Consider this carefully. In the situation of a Nazi beating on the door, we have assumed a lie would save a life, but really we don't know. So one would be opting to lie and disobey God without the certainty of saving a life — keeping in mind that all are ultimately condemned to die physically. Besides, whether one lied or not may not have stopped the Nazi solders from searching the house anyway.

As Christians, we need to keep in mind that Jesus Christ reigns. All authority has been given to Him (Matthew 28:18), and He sits on the throne of God at the right hand of the Father (Acts 2:33; Hebrews 8:1). Nothing can happen without His say. Even Satan could not touch Peter without Christ's approval (Luke 22:31). Regardless, if one were to lie or not, Jesus Christ is in control of timing every person's life and able to discern our motives. It is not for us to worry over what might happen, but rather to place our faith and obedience in Christ and to let Him do the reigning. For we do not know the future, whereas God has been telling the end from the beginning (Isaiah 46:10).

## A righteous lie? Part 2

Letter, unedited:

> Wow, you put a lot of work in to that answer Bodie, and from a biblical basis too. I agree with you 100% about lying to protect yourself, that could be interpreted as mere cowardice, and I think most of your biblical examples dealt with that. However there is a scripture in Exodus ch.1 vs. 15–22, in which the Jewish midwives are told to kill all the male babies they delivered but refused to do so. When asked why they hadn't destroyed the babies, they told the Egyptians the Hebrew women simply gave birth faster than the Egyptian women, and had the babies before the midwives got there. Vs.17 however says that the Jewish midwives saved the male children alive, so here they are lying not only to save the male babies but probably to escape punishment from the Egyptians. Vs. 20 says that God dealt well with the midwives for doing this. I think this is one of the rare examples or cases where lying would truly not be offensive to our Creator. At any rate, I think this scripture shows that not all lies are equal, at least to my mind. In that most lies are done for self advancement, self protection, greed, etc., but some are done at least with the intention of protecting others, their reputations or physical

selves. I can't fault your stance though, your conscience and the Word must be your guide. Keep up the good work.

M.H.

Response:

I looked up the passage about the midwives, and I, personally, don't believe they lied. Scripture doesn't really say they did. Please see the context:

> Then the king of Egypt spoke to the Hebrew midwives, of whom the name of one was Shiphrah and the name of the other Puah; and he said, "When you do the duties of a midwife for the Hebrew women, and see them on the birthstools, if it is a son, then you shall kill him; but if it is a daughter, then she shall live." But the midwives feared God, and did not do as the king of Egypt commanded them, but saved the male children alive. So the king of Egypt called for the midwives and said to them, "Why have you done this thing, and saved the male children alive?"
>
> And the midwives said to Pharaoh, "Because the Hebrew women are not like the Egyptian women; for they are lively and give birth before the midwives come to them."
>
> Therefore God dealt well with the midwives, and the people multiplied and grew very mighty. And so it was, because the midwives feared God, that He provided households for them.
>
> So Pharaoh commanded all his people, saying, "Every son who is born you shall cast into the river, and every daughter you shall save alive" (Exodus 1:15–22).

Naturally, their fear of God led them to refuse the order to murder. It makes more sense to me that they could have informed the Hebrew wives what the pharaoh had commanded, and, thus, many of the Israelite women were giving birth before the midwives would arrive so they would not be in a position of killing the child. Perhaps the midwives took their time to arrive as well. That would allow the children to survive and the midwives to speak the truth to Pharaoh.

What would make pregnant mothers more vigorous or lively and able to have children born quickly? Make them aware that if they do not give birth quickly their child's life may be in danger. There are any number of ways the mothers and midwives could have avoided a lie.

With humbleness in Christ.

## Chapter 9

# HILARIOUSLY ILLOGICAL!

Letter, expletive edited out:

> The information on your website is so illogical and wrong that it's hilarious. Yet I feel worried that there are so many people who obviously believe this @!*&%$. I'm an Australian and I feel utterly embarrassed to think that Ken Ham is an Australian. And also someone that supposedly has an applied science degree from the university of queensland? Just because you believe in something doesn't make it true. It's one thing to read the bible's stories and garner moral lessons from them, but to take its word literally? The bible is a historical book, which has been edited and changed over history. This site's utter hate of science is ridiculous. Scientific thought is logical and critical thinking. The thoughts and ideas on this site are illogical and disgusting. Just because you can't explain something or science is yet to explain it, doesn't mean that the unexplainable is attributed to an unseen entity. This site even tries to refute things that science clearly explains. It's just sad!
>
> A.D., Australia

Response:

Thanks for sending us an email. I am replying below to your comments and questions. Please note that my comments are said with sincerity. (I understand that tone is sometimes difficult to display in writing, so I wanted to be upfront about it.)

**The information on your website is so illogical and wrong**

Such as? This is called an unsubstantiated allegation, which you agreed not to send when you agreed to the website's feedback rules.[1] So I'm surprised such a claim was made without any backing. We want the information on

---

1. Answer in Genesis has feedback rules to aid in a proper response: http://www.answersingenesis.org/feedback/sendmail.aspx?TopicID=inquiries.

the website to be both logical and correct, so if there was anything to be challenged, please point it out so we can revisit it to make sure it is accurate and modify it if necessary.

Based on the humanistic worldview promoted in your email (i.e., the Bible is not true), why do you think logic exists? For logic to exist, the Bible must be true. The sheer fact that you believe logic exists betrays the very worldview to which you pay lip service. In other words, your worldview is self-refuting.[2]

### that it's hilarious.

This is an epithet fallacy. But consider the humor of someone claiming something is wrong and chuckling about it, and yet they cannot name why it is wrong.

### Yet I feel worried

Why would an evolutionist worry (see Luke 12:22)? If everything follows either purely random processes or purely predetermined material results of chemical reactions, then why worry? In such a worldview, this is illogical.

Again, the fact that people worry reveals that they want some sort of moral code, which is meaningless in an evolutionary worldview, by the way. But I'm glad you have the sense of worrying because it means that *you want morality*. I want to encourage you to realize that morality comes from God.

### that there are so many people who obviously believe this @!*&%$.

This is another epithet fallacy.

### I'm an Australian and I feel utterly embarrassed to think that Ken Ham is an Australian.

Why? The feeling of embarrassment in an evolutionary worldview is simply chemical reactions in the brain and is no different from chemical reactions for love and compassion.[3]

But again, why the sense of morality in an evolutionary worldview? What is going on here is that in your heart of hearts, you know God exists (Romans 1:20–21), and God is the basis for morality since He is the

2. Dr. Jason Lisle, "Atheism: An Irrational Worldview," Answers in Genesis website, October 10, 2007, http://www.answersingenesis.org/articles/aid/v2/n1/atheism-irrational.

3. For the reader, Ken Ham, who is originally from Australia, is the president and CEO of Answers in Genesis.

ultimate *Law Giver*. You are trying to suppress that knowledge (Romans 1:18), but you must still borrow from the biblical worldview in order to uphold some form of morality.[4]

**And also someone that supposedly has an applied science degree from the university of queensland?**

Not supposedly; Mr. Ham earned it years ago. This should come as no surprise since Christians earn advanced degrees every year at universities all over the world and are not anti-science. But consider that science is possible simply because the Bible is true, so this should come as no surprise either. In fact, most of the great founders of scientific disciplines believed the Bible, such as Newton, Boyle, Galileo, etc.

**Just because you believe in something doesn't make it true.**

Ditto. What makes things true is predicated on the possibility of truth existing. In a materialistic, atheistic universe, why would truth, which is immaterial, exist? This is a major problem for materialists like atheists. Of course, truth is not a problem for Christians since God is both the truth (John 14:6) and the source of truth.

Without His Word, truth is meaningless. Of course, there is so much more we could dive into from this point, but that's another discussion.

**It's one thing to read the bible's stories and garner moral lessons from them,**

But morality is meaningless if God does not exist. In a purely evolutionary worldview, chemicals react. Why would anyone care about morality unless there is an ultimate standard to reveal what morality is? God is that standard, and in His Word He has told us what is right and what is wrong.

**but to take its word literally?**

What do you mean by literally? *Literally* has traditionally meant to take something the way it is written (not the false modern concept that everything must be taken in a strict literal sense — i.e., that the metaphorical use of "pillars of the earth" means the earth is sitting on top of pillars in space). If it is a metaphor, then it should be understood as a metaphor. If the writing

---

4. Dr. Jason Lisle, "Evolution and the Challenge of Morality," Answers in Genesis website, April 14, 2008, http://www.answersingenesis.org/articles/2008/04/14/evolution-challenge-of-morality.

style is literal history, then it is literal history and should be interpreted as such. If it is a song, then follow the principles for understanding a song. This concept is entirely biblical.

But consider something else here. What if I were to argue that evolutionists should not interpret evolutionary papers literally when they use metaphors? They should interpret them in a strict literal sense. Would the evolutionists accept this? Not at all. So why attack Christians for trusting what God's Word says in its context and literary style?

### The bible is a historical book,

Yes, but it is more than that (psalms and songs, genealogies, prayers, prophecies, etc.). But I'm glad you agree that it is a historical book *in some sense anyway*. This premise challenges the evolutionary ideas of origins at their very core. So how can one trust an evolutionary history of billions of years, knowing the Bible is indeed history?

### which has been edited and changed over history.

This is basically a *contrary to the fact conditional error* fallacy. Any student of this subject would say the opposite after only a little research. The Bible's words have been attested to through thousands of ancient manuscripts that repeatedly affirm the texts have been faithfully transmitted to us.

### This site's utter hate of science is ridiculous.

This is false and is another epithet fallacy, as well as equivocation. As an aside, it should have been obvious on our website how much we do love and enjoy science. However, I think the equivocation fallacy is pertinent here. Equating science with an evolutionary worldview is a fallacy.

The issue is not science versus religion, as many seem to think. It is worldview versus worldview. More specifically, it is humanism (with its views of evolution and millions of years) versus biblical Christianity (with its views of creation and thousands of years).[5]

We both have the same science, and when it comes to repeatable, experimental science (known as operational science), both evolutionists and creationists would agree almost every time! Where we disagree is our interpretations of the past (i.e., origins).

---

5. See *The New Answers Book 2*, Ken Ham, gen. ed., "How Old Is the Earth?" by Bodie Hodge (Green Forest, AR: Master Books, 2008), http://www.answersingenesis.org/articles/2007/05/30/how-old-is-earth.

The reason we disagree here is due to our differing *authorities*. Is God the ultimate authority on the subject or is man? This is the debate — humanism versus biblical Christianity.

> It is better to trust in the LORD than to put confidence in man (Psalm 118:8).

It will be a sad day when people who rejected God stand before Him in judgment (Hebrews 9:27) and tell Him that they trusted the false ideas of man over what God lovingly revealed to mankind. How should a just God respond?

**Scientific thought is logical and critical thinking.**

We agree, but again, this view is only possible because the Bible is true. (Keep in mind that the point is not that people *need to believe* the Bible is true, but simply that the Bible is true.)

**The thoughts and ideas on this site are illogical and disgusting.**

Again, this is an unsubstantiated allegation and question-begging epithet.

**Just because you can't explain something or science is yet to explain it, doesn't mean that the unexplainable is attributed to an unseen entity.**

This is a reification fallacy. "Science" doesn't explain things; it is a methodology. People use it as a tool to help explain things, but *science* doesn't make the statements; people do. This reveals how much faith is given to the religion of humanism. People have such faith *in other people* to come up with strange stories to explain things. This puts the ultimate authority in mankind. When the ancient Greeks didn't know the answers, they came up with some fancy stories that fit within their worldview. And sadly, generations of people believed those stories, and now we look back and call those stories "mythology."

The same thing is going on today. In an evolutionary worldview, when people don't know an answer, they come up with stories that fit within their worldview (e.g., Oort cloud, abiogenesis, missing links, etc.). I look forward to a time when people look back and recognize the evolutionary stories as mythology. But the point is that evolution, like Greek mythology, is a product of the religion of humanism.

The issue is that when God speaks on a subject, He cannot be wrong, but fallible, sinful, imperfect human beings can *and will* be wrong when they try to explain things, especially about the past, apart from God and His Word.

**This site even tries to refute things that science clearly explains.**

Again, this is a reification fallacy. "Science" does not explain things; *people* do. I've heard some people say science *speaks, tells,* or *explains* things to them, but what they really mean is that *scientists* speak, tell, or explain their views of the data.

Also, this is another unsubstantiated allegation.

**It's just sad!**

This is an appeal to emotion fallacy, which is especially illogical in an evolutionary worldview because everything would ultimately be meaningless (like sadness) in a strictly chemical universe. This actually undercuts the anti-Bible argument that has been presented in this email.

I want to encourage you to consider abandoning the humanistic worldview with its materialistic evolutionary bent. A materialistic evolutionary worldview is illogical on many fronts (such as having no basis for logic, which is immaterial, and no basis for truth or knowledge).

With that in mind, I would like you to consider a biblical worldview, which does have a basis for logic, truth, knowledge, and more — including morality, which seems to be important to you (to your credit). Please take some time to read this message entitled "What Does It Mean to Be 'Saved'?" [http://www.answersingenesis.org/articles/2009/04/21/what-does-it-mean-to-be-saved]. This extended article explains salvation, one of the major themes in the Bible in an easy-to-read fashion starting at the beginning.

With kindness in Christ.

*Chapter 10*

# OPPOSITION TO THE CREATION MUSEUM

Letter, unedited:

> The very idea that $25 Million will be spent on a Creationist Museum is absurd in and of itself, but even more so considering the number of actual living human beings in dire need of help. What about the poor and the homeless in America and abroad? Millions suffering and dying everyday by starvation, war, disease, lack of water, lack of shelter, and so on. Why not use this money to help out those less fortunate than us? Isn't THAT what Jesus taught? Isnt't THAT what compassionate Christians should energize themselves as individuals and as a group to help combat? The hypocrisy is stunning and there is no good argument to support the notion that building a museum prosthelytizing a theory based entirely on faith is more important and more desperately needed than to actually help your fellow man. Jesus weeps for you and cringes in disgust by these inexplicably selfish actions. You are the heathens.

C.M., U.S.

Response: [David Wright, a friend and coworker at Answers in Genesis, has coauthored this letter with me.]

Preface: As the Creation Museum neared the opening date, we received more and more opposition from non-Christians, and we expected that:

> These things I have spoken to you, that in Me you may have peace. In the world you will have tribulation; but be of good cheer, I have overcome the world (John 16:33).

Much of this opposition is disingenuous in saying certain parts of the Bible are true or important (that Christians are to help the poor and needy), while ignoring the rest of Scripture (where we are to disciple and teach and proclaim the gospel). This email is but one criticism that we commonly took the time to answer.

**The very idea that $25 Million will be spent on a Creationist Museum is absurd in and of itself,**

It is actually $27 million due to expansions, but regardless, what is so absurd? For the level of professional workmanship and design that has gone into this state-of-the-art, cutting-edge museum that glorifies God and His Word, $27 million is relatively inexpensive, especially when compared to the Field Museum's recent $17 million exhibit. So why are you not writing to them about the absurdity/wastefulness of their exhibit?

Our funds have come through faithful donations by fellow Christians. We receive no government tax money, unlike other institutions or museums that push their humanistic religious beliefs, money that could have been spent feeding the homeless and hungry.

**but even more so considering the number of actual living human beings in dire need of help.**

And you think their salvation from this sin-cursed world through Jesus Christ is not a worthy need? This is what the Creation Museum is all about. We are not here to merely teach that God's Word is true about creation, but to see people saved. It appears that priorities need to be sorted out:

> For what will it profit a man if he gains the whole world, and loses his own soul? (Mark 8:36)

**What about the poor and the homeless in America and abroad?**

We agree that these are troubling issues and they need to be dealt with, and indeed there are hundreds — if not thousands — of ministries that do just that, taking care of the poor and homeless. The Church (that is, Christians as a whole) shares the burdens as a whole, and we are one special-ized aspect of the Church. The Bible points out an incredible analogy with regards to this in 1 Corinthians 12:12–28. Please take a moment to read this passage.

If all gave money to feed the poor, then who would give them shelter? Who would teach them, who would give medical care, and so on? These ministries are vital and many at Answers in Genesis donate to these minis-tries. Have you?

Also, something you probably did not consider is that those who give to the Creation Museum do so sacrificially — both money and time. What people donate to us is often given after they have already given to their local churches, communities, and other charities.

**Millions suffering and dying everyday by starvation, war, disease, lack of water, lack of shelter, and so on.**

This should be a stark reminder for everyone that we live in a sin-cursed world. It is because of sin that there is starvation, war, disease, lack of water, lack of shelter, and so on. And many of our supporters devote their time and money to helping those in need. As a matter of fact, when Hurricane Katrina hit the Gulf Coast, Answers in Genesis asked its supporters to give to relief efforts, and also set up our own relief effort. Because of Answers in Genesis' generous supporters, we were able to provide thousands of supplies to those in Ocean Springs, Mississippi, many of whom lost almost everything in the hurricanes. Much of this information can be found on our website (answersingenesis.org).

Also, we have a prison ministry that has reached about 200 prisons so far (with hundreds to go). We receive hundreds of letters a year from prisoners who are indigent. We can't send them money, but we can send them materials that will help them while in prison to walk with Christ and let them know that there is hope, and that they are accountable to God for their actions.

How many secular museums do you know of that give materials to prisoners or to those who are poor and homeless?

**Why not use this money to help out those less fortunate than us? Isn't THAT what Jesus taught?**

That certainly is something that Jesus taught. Jesus also taught us to disciple people in all nations and teach them to obey everything that He has commanded (Matthew 28:19–20), which is a primary aspect of the Creation Museum. On what basis do you judge that some of Jesus' commands are not to be obeyed and others should be?

But first let's think about why there are so many of those less fortunate. Secular museums spend millions of dollars indoctrinating people to think that there is no God, and accordingly that we are not accountable for our actions (since they claim we are just animals). Because the Bible's foundation has been taken away, generation after generation has strayed further from the truth of God's Word. And if someone doesn't believe God's Word about creation, salvation, etc., then why would they have any reason to believe it when it says to take care of those who are less fortunate?

Incidentally, it is inconsistent with the teachings of molecules-to-man evolution to help those in need. After all, evolution progresses as the weak die off and the "fittest" survive with less competition. But imagine a museum that calls people back to the Word of God and lets them know that the Bible is trustworthy and authoritative. We want the museum to teach that the Bible's history is true — and because its account of history is true, so is its message of salvation. We want thousands of people to come to know the Lord and receive Christ as Lord. Then imagine all these people truly believing God's Word and then truly believing Jesus' teachings about taking care of the poor instead of viewing them as being "no different than a fruit fly."

**Isn't THAT what compassionate Christians should energize themselves as individuals and as a group to help combat?**

That is what millions of Christians are doing, including those who support, volunteer for, and work at Answers in Genesis and the Creation Museum. But why would an evolutionist help, or even care?

**The hypocrisy is stunning**

How so? As individuals at Answers in Genesis, we give to missions who help the poor and homeless. As an example, I (Bodie) have helped build a home and a church in Mexico, and have given money to feed the poor in those regions. And now, that church is reaching out to its community. Others in the ministry sponsor children in poor countries, donate to tsunami relief, etc.

**and there is no good argument to support the notion that building a museum prosthelytizing a theory based entirely on faith**

So you must be in opposition to the many secular museums that hold high "faith" in the evolutionary religion. Then by all means, please show me the emails that you send them. I'm interested, especially considering the massive money they have spent on exhibits alone!

**is more important and more desperately needed than to actually help your fellow man.**

Again — many parts to the body; we can't all be the eye or all be the ear.

**Jesus weeps for you and cringes in disgust**

Where does the Bible say this? And also, on what basis do you speak for Christ? Again, when you do this, you are raising your own thoughts above God and His Word. Besides, since we are doing what the Lord has commanded in the Great Commission, then this statement is without merit.

**by these inexplicably selfish actions.**

How are our actions selfish, especially when we sacrifice so much to do the Lord's bidding with the museum? We have already seen people saved in the museum — and it isn't even opened yet! What makes you think Christ would cringe, when people are coming to know Him through the museum?

**You are the heathens.**

So are you now trying to speak for God and say who is saved? We will pray for you to realize that the Bible is true in all areas. It is for this reason that the Church and Answers in Genesis work together to help people in their needs, whether feeding the poor, giving shelter, ministering to needs, or other things.

The Creation Museum is just one small aspect of Christ's Church that is reaching people around the globe. Seeing people come to know the Lord at the museum already is a tremendous blessing. Unlike the many secular, evolution-based museums — some of which survive in part with tax money — the Creation Museum teaches that the Bible is true, and it is being built with donations from people who love God and His Word and who want to see God receive the glory in a museum.[1]

I really want to encourage you to reevaluate your priorities and consider giving your life to Christ. For Christ did not come down to merely feed the poor and water them, but to giving them living water (John 4:10–28) and make it so they would never go hungry again (John 6:35).

In Christ,

David Wright and Bodie Hodge

---

1. For those reading this, please prayerfully consider giving a donation to help with the upkeep of the Creation Museum. Donations can be made online or by calling 1-800-778-3390. There are also memberships available.

*Chapter 11*

# WHY BUILD AN ARK INSTEAD OF GIVE MONEY TO THE POOR?

When we decided to build a full-sized replica of Noah's ark, this was one of the common objections we heard:

**Why spend so much on an Ark when starving children could be fed in third-world countries?**

Response:

Skeptics and some Christians often question Answers in Genesis and the Creation Museum about our beliefs. We are used to this kind of questioning, and we expect it because we stand for biblical truth in a world that continues to turn its back on the Word of God. With the announcement of the Ark Encounter, we received numerous letters questioning Answers in Genesis's next major project. These are some of the common objections:

- Why spend so much on an ark when starving children could be fed in third-world countries?

- Why not give the money to a Christian school?

- Why not spend the money on looking for the ark?

- Why not give the money to other ministries?

Certainly, some of these are sincere questions and should be addressed. Why not give to the poor? Well, we encourage people to share with those in need, and many Answers in Genesis employees and supporters do. In fact, I love it when Christians stand up and start a ministry to care for the needy because they are passionate about it. One of our ministry's founders worked for a relief ministry in the 1980s during the devastating Ethiopian famine. But if Christians give only to the poor, would that negate the need for other giving?

Some Christians give to Christian schools and universities to help keep their doors open, and we encourage such support of Bible-upholding institutions. Some wish to search for Noah's ark or give to other ministries, and again, we also encourage that.

But when people say the money donated for the full-size Noah's ark should be spent instead on feeding the poor or giving to another cause, they are essentially arguing that no money should be given to building the Ark Encounter. Yet consider the words of the Great Commission given by Jesus Christ.

> And Jesus came and spoke to them, saying, "All authority has been given to Me in heaven and on earth. Go therefore and make disciples of all the nations, baptizing them in the name of the Father and of the Son and of the Holy Spirit, teaching them to observe all things that I have commanded you; and lo, I am with you always, even to the end of the age." Amen (Matthew 28:18–20).

Taking care of the poor is an important ministry (2 Corinthians 8), but Christ also made it clear that we are to make disciples of all nations.[1] One thing that has been lacking in many churches is a strong emphasis on discipleship, and this is especially true in the area of apologetics (i.e., how to defend the faith, including the most-attacked part of the Bible, Genesis). For nearly 200 years, attacks on Genesis chapters 1–11 have been rampant, and parts of the Church are just now waking up to this attack. Sadly, this is only after countless people have walked away from the Church because they saw the Bible as untrustworthy.

First, the ark project is about discipleship. It will stand as a monument to the truth of the Bible in Genesis 6–9 and will call the Church back to the authority of the Bible from its very first book. As believers learn the importance and trustworthiness of these early chapters, they will have the proper foundation for understanding the biblical worldview. So the Ark will stand to help us and other Christians fulfill the Lord's command in Matthew 28 to make disciples.

But the Ark is also about evangelism. We want to challenge the secular world and help people realize the authority of the Bible and the truth of the gospel of Jesus Christ.

### Who are the neediest people of all?

Frankly, we can't think of a more effective way to share the gospel with many millions of people today than by using an Ark. The Ark of Noah is a picture of salvation, which allows us to share with future visitors that Christ is our modern-day Ark of salvation. People who might not ever attend a church service will be powerfully presented with the gospel message at the ark, where they will learn about Christ.

A feasibility study predicted that 1.6 million people will visit in the first year alone, with hundreds of thousands who will not be Christians. Because so many people will be visiting the Ark each year, this will be a wonderful, unique evangelistic opportunity. In fact, we can think of no more vital project in the world today that will reach out to the very neediest people — those who are heading to a Christ-less eternity.

The Ark Encounter will also bring several thousand jobs to the region (perhaps 900 people alone at the Ark Encounter). With unemployment still at 10 percent in the state, a job generator like the Ark will be welcome news to many families. In addition, the state and local governments will receive hundreds of millions of dollars in tax revenue over the Ark's first ten years, which will help fund health care, libraries, and other services. The Ark Encounter will be an absolute boon to Kentucky and its families.

We point out, too, that the Ark Encounter will be a wholesome, family-friendly attraction, and it will be a great asset to visiting children and adults and to the community as a whole.

As more people become disciples of Christ and are immersed in the Scriptures (understanding and gaining wisdom from them), they, too, become supporters of Christian schools, the poor, and other ministries.

In their support of the Ark Encounter, should Christians decrease giving to their local church, Christian schools, or ministries that support the impoverished? We hope not. Our hope and prayer is that people will donate above and beyond their normal giving as they reason in their hearts to give (2 Corinthians 9:7).

The Ark Encounter will be a testimony to the world that the Bible is true and, therefore, the message of the gospel is also true. And as a side note, Christians have an opportunity to be good witnesses to the world by giving cheerfully. In all this, may the world see our love for God, and may His people give God the glory.

## Chapter 12

# Took a Hundred Years to Refute

This letter is an excerpt from *The Bluegrass Blade* on February 11, 1900:

> **Fifteen hundred years ago, Constantine, who murdered his own wife and children, started the Christian religion.**
>
> **From that day to this that religion has been the greatest curse that ever afflicted the earth.**
>
> **This religion teaches that 6,000 years ago God made the first man out of dust — not even mud — and the first woman out of a bone; that God cursed the whole human race because a snake made the woman eat an apple; that God had a son by another man's wife, and that he had this son murdered in order to keep himself from sending all the human race to hell.**
>
> **This son taught that any man who did not believe that piece of ignorance and priestly lying would go to hell and burn eternally in fire and brimstone.**
>
> **The Bible, in which these things are taught, favors drunkenness, murder, slavery, lying, stealing and lechery.**
>
> **Charles Chilton Moore**

Response:

Atheists today are giving praise to atheist Charles Moore as someone who was like an anti-God "blogger" from over a hundred years ago. But are his arguments any better than those that atheists employ today? Or are his comments just the same stuff we see over and over again in modern blogs, emails, and letters? Well, in truth, it is nothing new, just another person attacking God and His Word with false claims. Such things began in the days of our grandparents, Adam and Eve, and are still at the forefront.

> **Fifteen hundred years ago, Constantine, who murdered his own wife and children,**

Yes, he sinned, and so did Moore. But we are all sinners and all in need of Christ.

**started the Christian religion.**

False. God/Christ started the Christian religion from the beginning, and the names *Christian* and *Christianity* originated from the word *Christ*, meaning "Messiah" or "Anointed One" (John 1:41, 4:25), who was often mentioned in the Old Testament as the one to come. Christ's earthly ministry was about 250 years before Constantine. In fact, the first use of the term *Christians* was at Antioch (Acts 11:26), and even extra-biblical writers used the term before the emperor was born.

**From that day to this that religion has been the greatest curse**

If Christianity is a lie, why is anything good or bad? A curse in that view is no different from a blessing because nothing would ultimately matter, since without Christianity, there is no ultimate authority to give us moral standards.

**that ever afflicted the earth.**

False. Sin was the worst thing that ever happened to the earth.

**This religion teaches that 6,000 years ago God made the first man out of dust — not even mud — and the first woman out of a bone;**

This shows that God cared and specially created man. In other words, we are not worthless pieces of pond scum, as is commonly taught in schools today.

**that God cursed the whole human race**

In essence, it is as if God no longer upholds the world in a perfect state. Never does the Bible say mankind was cursed, though.

**because a snake made the woman eat an apple;**

This serpent didn't make her eat anything. She was deceived by the serpent, and then *she desired* the fruit, and *she* took the fruit and *she ate*. And *she* got punished for it.

Besides, the Bible never specifically mentioned that it was an apple. It was the fruit of the Tree of the Knowledge of Good and Evil.

**that God had a son by another man's wife,**

False. Mary was not married to Joseph at the time (Matthew 1:18). And secondly, she was an Israelite, which meant she was the Bride of God first (see Genesis 17:17 and many other passages about this covenant between God and Israel, especially Ezekiel 16:32, which calls the Israelites — via the national capital — an adulterous wife).

Such an argument, perhaps inadvertently, accepts what the Bible teaches about marriage (being one man and one woman) and that marriage should be honored by all:

> Marriage is honorable among all, and the bed undefiled; but fornicators and adulterers God will judge (Hebrews 13:4).

So Moore is being hypocritical when he argues against what the Bible teaches, all the while relying on biblical principles.

**and that he had this son murdered**

Remedial theology from the Bible reveals that God's Son is God (John 1, Colossians 1, and Hebrews 1). God sacrificed Himself to pay the infinite punishment (that naturally stems from an infinite God). Those in Christ (God) will be spared; the rest still have that infinite punishment awaiting them in hell for all eternity.

**in order to keep himself from sending all the human race to hell.**

Rather kind and loving gesture, isn't it? Would you have died to save someone who despised you? However, God doesn't merely send people to hell. He grants those who despise Him what they want: eternity apart from Him.

**This son taught that any man who did not believe that piece of ignorance and priestly lying would go to hell and burn eternally in fire and brimstone.**

False. A holy and just God must judge unrighteousness with the only fitting consequence: infinite punishment from an infinite God. In fact, all of us are condemned already because we are all sinners. However, Christ has already paid the debt. As far as we know, Mr. Moore never received Christ, but you (the readers) can still receive Christ.

> For God so loved the world that He gave His only begotten Son, that whoever believes in Him should not perish but have everlasting life. For God did not send His Son into the world to condemn the world, but that the world through Him might be

saved. He who believes in Him is not condemned; but he who does not believe is condemned already, because he has not believed in the name of the only begotten Son of God (John 3:16–18).

**The Bible, in which these things are taught, favors drunkenness, murder, slavery, lying, stealing and lechery.**

False. While the Bible honestly depicts the sinfulness of humanity in the context of specific cultures, God's Word strongly condemns these failings and offers a much better way.

> Now the works of the flesh are evident, which are: adultery, fornication, uncleanness, lewdness, idolatry, sorcery, hatred, contentions, jealousies, outbursts of wrath, selfish ambitions, dissensions, heresies, envy, murders, drunkenness, revelries, and the like; of which I tell you beforehand, just as I also told you in time past, that those who practice such things will not inherit the kingdom of God. But the fruit of the Spirit is love, joy, peace, longsuffering, kindness, goodness, faithfulness, gentleness, self-control. Against such there is no law. And those who are Christ's have crucified the flesh with its passions and desires (Galatians 5:19–24).

> "Honor your father and your mother, that your days may be long upon the land which the LORD your God is giving you. You shall not murder. You shall not commit adultery. You shall not steal. You shall not bear false witness against your neighbor. You shall not covet your neighbor's house; you shall not covet your neighbor's wife, nor his male servant, nor his female servant, nor his ox, nor his donkey, nor anything that is your neighbor's" (Exodus 20:12–17).

And there are many more similar verses. This is just a start. Besides, if the Bible were not true, why would these actions be wrong?

Even false claims from over a hundred years ago can easily be responded to. I was saddened that there were so many false claims in Mr. Moore's comments. Had he taken a few minutes to look up the passages he erred on, perhaps he could have done a better job.

Sadly, Mr. Moore has long since gone to face the Creator of the universe and receive his judgment from God. What will God say to you when it is your turn to stand before Him?

## Chapter 13

# DOES THE BIBLE TEACH FEMALE INFERIORITY?

Letter, unedited:

> I just wonder, as a feminist, how you can make Darwin out to
> be a bad guy for saying women are inferior, when your bible has
> been changed through out the years to make women to be the
> biggest sinner ever known to mankind? oh i am an athiest by the
> way . . (please don't be mean to me) i'd also love to know how you
> dated the dinosaurs lives as the science people have dated them
> A LOT farther back than you have. . . . do tell me as i am most
> curious. thanks for your time . . . sorry if i've offended you . . .
> but i'm sure as i will never judge you or be mean to you, i know
> you will do me the same curteousy.
>
> K.F., U.S.

Response: [My lady colleague and friend, Dr. Georgia Purdom, has joined
me in this response. We are coworkers at Answers in Genesis.]

> **I just wonder, as a feminist, how you can make Darwin out to be
> a bad guy for saying women are inferior,**

To begin, let us ask you on what basis you, a self-confessed atheist, use the
term "bad"? In an atheistic worldview, standards of morality are without
basis. The Bible defines what is good and what is bad, and for an atheist to
refer to something as "bad" means that she is borrowing from the Bible's
standard of right and wrong. Since the Bible is true, this presents a problem
for both atheism and Darwinism. Other atheists point out that in atheism,
there is no basis for right and wrong.

   We are assuming you are referring to the article in *Answers* magazine
entitled "Darwin Taught Male Superiority Regarding Darwin's Views on the
Inferiority of Women."[1] Darwin made it very clear in his writings that he
believed women were inferior to men. He said:

---

1. Dr. Jerry Bergman, "Darwin taught Male Superiority," *Answers* magazine, January 1,
2007, http://www.answersingenesis.org/articles/am/v2/n1/darwin-taught-male-superiority.

. . . a higher eminence, in whatever he takes up, than can women — whether requiring deep thought, reason, or imagination, or merely the use of the senses and hands. If two lists were made of the most eminent men and women in poetry, painting, sculpture, music (inclusive of both composition and performance), history, science, and philosophy, with half-a-dozen names under each subject, the two lists would not bear comparison. We may also infer, from the law of the deviation from averages, so well illustrated by Mr. Galton, in his work on "Hereditary Genius" that . . . the average of mental power in man must be above that of women.[2]

Darwin "bolstered" his claims with assertions that women were "childlike" and "less spiritual." We (one of us is a female) believe most females, feminist or not, would find Darwin's views on women completely unacceptable.

In addition, Darwin's views of women are in direct odds with the Bible in regards to the status of women. According to Galatians 3:28, "There is neither Jew nor Greek, there is neither slave nor free, there is neither male nor female; for you are all one in Christ Jesus." Therefore, Darwin's views on women are also in complete opposition to the Word of God; thus, biblically, we can condemn his views.

### when your bible has been changed through out the years

This claim is baseless. What evidence is there to claim that the Bible has been changed throughout the years? God can easily preserve His Word flawlessly throughout time. Textual criticism, Dead Sea Scrolls, and so on are a great confirmation that the words of the Bible have been preserved. This is no ordinary book; this is the Bible, the written Word of God, who knows and has revealed the past, so people can understand the world around us!

### to make women to be the biggest sinner ever known to mankind?

What verses are you specifically referring to in regard to women being portrayed as "the biggest sinner ever known to mankind"? Is it the fact that Eve ate of the Tree of Knowledge of Good and Evil *before* Adam, thus making her out to be the "biggest sinner"? God clearly attributes sin and the subsequent Curse on creation to Adam. Romans 5:12 says, "Therefore, just as

---

2. Charles Darwin, *The Descent of Man and Selection in Relation to Sex* (New York: D. Appleton and Company, 1896), p. 564.

through one man sin entered the world, and death through sin, and thus death spread to all men, because all sinned." And 1 Corinthians 15:22 adds, "For as in Adam all die, even so in Christ all shall be made alive." Sin entered through Adam — not Eve.

This really makes Adam out to be the "biggest sinner." But note 1 Corinthians 15:22: we *all* sinned. We can't simply blame Adam entirely, since we all sin, too. Adam is on record with this one sin, and one was exceeding the sin limit since God is holy and cannot look upon sin (Habakkuk 1:13). Any sin is so bad that it caused the Curse and death to enter creation. But since God is good, He cannot allow sin to continue forever. Judgment is coming. But with Christ, one can be forgiven and return to a right relationship with God. In the words of an old friend, "It is unwise to anger the one who created everything."

### oh i am an athiest by the way . . (please don't be mean to me)

As an atheist, why does it matter to you what God, or even Darwin, thought about women? According to atheism, truth is relative, and human reason is the full and final authority (which is why there are many "truths" out there in this view — there is more than one person!). If that is the case, then Darwin was perfectly justified to believe women were less evolved and inferior. What basis is there for judging his thinking on this matter? However, using the Bible as the full and final authority, there is a basis to challenge Darwin's assertions.

Our comments are not meant to be "mean," and we hope you read this with the kindness that we intend. The Bible commands us to be gentle and to respond with respect (1 Peter 3:15). However, the Bible also commands us to demolish arguments (2 Corinthians 10:5) and stand for truth (Zechariah 8:16), which can set you free (John 8:32), so this will not be compromised. From an atheistic perspective, though, both "mean" and "nice" are really the same thing — chemical reactions in the brain — and have nothing to do with truth (which is a nonmaterial entity, so atheists have no basis for believing in this anyway).

Additionally, have you considered this (perhaps) hidden assumption in atheism? For one to claim there is no God means that one can see everywhere in the entire universe at the same time, as well as be transcendent, to verify that God really doesn't exist. Such attributes belong to God. So, when one claims to be an atheist, he is really claiming to be God, thereby undermining his own position.

**i'd also love to know how you dated the dinosaurs lives as the science people have dated them A LOT farther back than you have. . . . do tell me as i am most curious.**

First, Answers in Genesis and many other creation ministries employ "science people." Specifically, our on-site and affiliated PhD researchers are well qualified in their respective fields. Second, very rarely are dinosaurs dated. Ages for dinosaurs are assumed based on the uniformitarian time-scale that is applied to certain fossils. By this time-scale, dinosaurs are found in one of three places in geologic layers (Triassic, Cretaceous, and Jurassic). So the layer in which one finds a *T. Rex* is assumed to be one of those three. This is how index fossils are used. Then, the uniformitarian date is applied, which already assumes millions and billions of years.

The layers themselves are not a problem biblically. The problem is the date assigned. Most of the geologic fossiliferous layers were laid down by the Flood of Noah; hence, a better date can be ascertained by using the biblical chronologies. Dating methods have many assumptions, such as the following:

1. Initial amounts?

2. Was any parent amount added?

3. Was any daughter amount added?

4. Was any parent amount removed?

5. Was any daughter amount removed?

6. How has the rate changed due to the environmental effects?

These faulty assumptions have been shown to yield inaccurate ages of things of known age[3]; so why, logically, would anyone use these dating methods on rocks of unknown ages?

**thanks for your time . . . sorry if i've offended you . . .**

Thanks for emailing and no offense is taken. Many of us at Answers in Genesis were in the same shoes in our past — some of us being atheists and *all* of us being non-Christians before the Lord graciously brought us to repentance and faith in Him.

---

3. See *Radioisotopes and the Age of the Earth*, Eds. Vardiman, Snelling, and Chaffin, eds. (Dallas, TX: Institute for Creation Research, and St. Joseph, Missouri: Creation Research Society, 2005); and *The New Answers Book 2*, Ken Ham, gen. ed., "How Old Is the Earth?" by Bodie Hodge (Green Forest, AR: Master Books, 2008), http://www.answersingenesis.org/articles/2007/05/30/how-old-is-earth.

**but i'm sure as i will never judge you or be mean to you, i know you will do me the same curteousy.**

This email, technically, did judge us (determining that we have no right to point out that Darwin was a bad guy) and judged God (the Bible has been changed to make women look worse and that the "science people" have the highest authority when it comes to dating, not God). Yet strangely, in an atheistic worldview, there is no basis for judging us or God because, according to such a worldview, all truth is relative. But God, the Creator, does have the right to judge; and it is His Word that is the measure of judgment:

> He who rejects Me, and does not receive My words, has that which judges him — the word that I have spoken will judge him in the last day (John 12:48).

We hope this response will challenge you to get into the Bible and read it instead of making claims about it. Our hopes are that one day you will learn to trust God and His Word and place your faith in Jesus Christ and be saved.

> The Lord is not slack concerning His promise, as some count slackness, but is longsuffering toward us, not willing that any should perish but that all should come to repentance (2 Peter 3:9).

With kindness in Christ,
Dr. Georgia Purdom and Bodie Hodge

*Chapter 14*

# ARE WE HIDING OTHER VIEWS?

Letter, unedited:

> Your website discourages discussion of your views. For example,
> I had to search through several links to find this feedback page.
> The name of your organization is revealing. You appear to take
> the view that you probably already have all the answers, which is
> hardly the case.
>
> It seems that AIG has little interest in the exchange of views,
> especially views that don't support AIG's. Do you feel there is no
> need to discuss them? Do you think you know or speak for God?
> If so, how arrogant!
>
> I have to state that your contention that the interpretation of the
> evidence for evolution depends on one's world view is laughable.
> In fact, what I see with each and every claim is that AIG simply
> asserts that the evidence supports their case when by any rational
> measure it clearly does not. Worldview does not cancel gravity.
> For AIG it seems, dogma trumps all. I suggest that you simply
> reject science and relax. That, at least, would be a morally
> defensible, if misguided, position to take.
>
> S.G., Canada

Response:

Thank you for contacting us. Please see my comments below and note
the sincerity with which they are said.

> Your website discourages discussion of your views. For example,
> I had to search through several links to find this feedback page.

Discussion of our views takes place all around the Internet and churches
— on forums, blogs, Twitter, and other social networks. In fact, we often
encourage our visitors to share the articles they read (with the ShareThis
button at the top of each page). What we don't have the resources for,

however, is to take on forums and discussions on our own site. We address as many questions and thoughts as we can, and then we encourage our supporters to carry those discussions to other websites, as there are many more of them than there are of us. This is not an attempt to dissuade discussion; it is understanding our role and limitations.

**The name of your organization is revealing. You appear to take the view that you probably already have all the answers, which is hardly the case.**

This is misrepresentation fallacy. The name of our ministry, Answers in Genesis, is revealing, though. It is an effort to direct people to the foundation for what Christians should believe: the Bible. But to apply this name to a view that Answers in Genesis either has or thinks it has "all the answers" is grossly misleading. But God, indeed, does have all the answers, and we merely intend to ultimately point everyone to His Word (the Bible) as the *only* source of truth and answers.

**It seems that AIG has little interest in the exchange of views, especially views that don't support AIG's. Do you feel there is no need to discuss them?**

Since you apparently feel so strongly about exchange in views, we wonder if you have contacted schools and universities about an exchange in views — other than that of evolution, as it is very unlikely that they would agree to entertain any other view than evolution. (Note that Answers in Genesis does not advocate the teaching of creation in schools — especially by those not qualified, but we do wonder why the evolutionary religion of humanism gets free reign in the classroom, whereas other religions have been kicked out.) And we do, in fact, discuss views contrary to our own in a number of places. For example, we usually address a challenge to our views such as the responses in this book, and we specifically quote a number of anti-creation views in our other articles.

**Do you think you know or speak for God? If so, how arrogant!**

Yes and no. As Christians, of course, we know God (to the best of each of our abilities to get into God's Word), and have repented of our sins and received Christ as Lord and Savior. As Christians, we have been instructed to be ready to give a reason for the hope that is within us (1 Peter 3:15). We can know God because He knows us and indwells us and leads us in His truth.

We would encourage you to get to know Him as well — at least consider the claims of Christ with an open mind. We encourage you to also consider the straightforward reading of Scripture, putting aside any interpretation that you've heard or think.

Do we speak for God? No. God speaks for Himself in His Word — the Bible. If we ever present a view that is contradictory to Scripture, and then place it above the scriptural view, then that would be not only arrogant but blasphemy.

**I have to state that your contention that the interpretation of the evidence for evolution depends on one's world view is laughable.**

How so? It is sad that many really think that evolutionists do not interpret evidence in light of their evolutionary worldview. When evolutionists dig up a dinosaur bone, they don't announce it was created on the sixth day of creation!

**In fact, what I see with each and every claim is that AIG simply asserts that the evidence supports their case when by any rational measure it clearly does not.**

Such as? Besides, I've heard creationists assert the same basic thing about evolutionists: "In fact, what I see with each and every claim is that evolutionists simply assert that the evidence supports their case when by any rational measure it clearly does not." Why would we point this out? Because evidence does not support or refute. It is inanimate. It is not a rationally thinking being. Hence, this reveals the fallacy of reification — where people try to give humanlike qualities to something that doesn't have them. So we are back to interpretations of evidence, based on one's worldview.

**Worldview does not cancel gravity.**

Of course not, but only the Christian worldview can account for gravity's existence. In an evolutionary worldview, why would the laws of science be uniform if everything exploded from nothing? So, to do science, the Bible must be true.

Additionally, you're misunderstanding what a worldview is and does. Gravity is a physical constant that we can repeatedly test in the present. The present effects of gravity are not up for debate. Instead, a worldview informs our beliefs about the past, such as why there is the uniformity of gravity that we do observe. An evolutionist could give no reason why there is uniformity, but a Christian would say that the universe behaves in a uniform fashion because it reflects God's nature and this uniformity makes science possible. Worldview differences are not about observations of the present; they are about the unobservable past and origins.

**For AIG, it seems, dogma trumps all.**

False. God and His Word trumps all, as God is the ultimate authority. To challenge this is to raise oneself up to be greater than God. This is essentially the religion of humanism. But for the non-Christian, dogma trumps logic, science, and so on.

**I suggest that you simply reject science and relax.**

Considering science comes out of a Christian worldview, there is no need to reject science. Since we're being logical, rational, and calm — resting in the peace of God and His Word (Philippians 4:7) — why would we need a suggestion to relax?

**That, at least, would be a morally defensible, if misguided, position to take.**

To assume that morality exists, is to assume the Bible is true, as morality originates from God. Considering morality comes from a Christian worldview, this statement is also false and undermines the position taken in this email.

May we suggest that you consider the truth of God and His Word and begin with God being the authority — not me or anyone at Answers in Genesis. The issue is between you and God. Consider the God of the Bible, and consider His free gift of salvation and restoration to man.

With kindness in Christ.

SECTION 2:

# How to respond to people On topics About the sciences And Evolution

## Chapter 15

# So old You can See it!

Letter, unedited:

> I read your article in regards to Dinosaurs. My comment is that
> scientists DO have the means of determining the exact age of
> dinosaur bones and fossils through carbon dating. Also, we have
> hundreds of of other clues in our environment and universe that
> tell us that the earth is millions of years old. Please do not deny
> facts . . . . things we can see and touch.
>
> O.B., U.S.

Response:

Thank you for contacting Answers in Genesis. Please see my comments below and note that they are written to help you and are said with kindness.

> I read your article in regards to Dinosaurs. My comment is that
> scientists DO have the means of determining the exact age of
> dinosaur bones and fossils through carbon dating.

There are two major problems with this statement. The first is that the secular world is "scared" to carbon date dinosaur bones or, for that matter, any other bone they suspect is millions of years old. Creationists would love for the soft dinosaur tissue that was discovered by Dr. Mary Schweitzer to have been carbon dated. But as far as I know, such has never been done.

Granted, much carbon (including C-14) would be replaced with other materials for many fossils. This is why fossils that were formerly bone are primarily rock now; this also destroys the long-age assumptions in radiometric dating that parent and daughter isotopes cannot be added or removed. Regardless, doing C-14 testing may not reveal much on many fossils, but if even a trace of C-14 is found in fossils supposedly millions of years old, it is a major problem for those holding to long ages. And this brings me to the second problem.

Carbon dating only gives younger age dates — not millions of years. So claiming that dinosaurs have been age-dated by carbon dating means that you are agreeing that dinosaurs are *not* millions of years old — only thousands at most!

**Also, we have hundreds of of other clues in our environment and universe that tell us that the earth is millions of years old.**

Such as? But on the contrary, uniformitarian dating methods, by and large, give ages of the earth far less than billions of years.[1] Why are these ignored?

**Please do not deny facts . . . . things we can see and touch.**

Sadly, in today's culture we have all been taught that things like carbon dating are "facts," but they are merely interpretations of facts. If carbon dating is a fact, then coal layers cannot be millions of years old, and the secular "geological time-scale" breaks down, as carbon-14 is readily found in coal layers that are supposed to be millions of years old![2]

Many creationists (and evolutionists) may groan about an email like this because of the basic errors about C-14. But our goal here is to make you aware of the actual science (and lack thereof) behind many claims that are still continually used, despite the facts. When people realize that the correct scientific conclusions actually support the Bible's teaching, they are more inclined to consider the claims of Christ (it begins to lay a foundation). Because of this, please take some time to read the good news of Jesus Christ [see appendix 4] and how He came to save people from a sin-cursed and broken world.

1. Bodie Hodge, "How Old Is the Earth?" Answers in Genesis website, May 30, 2007, http://www.answersingenesis.org/articles/2007/05/30/how-old-is-earth.

2. J. Baumgardner, "$^{14}$C Evidence for a Recent Global Flood and a Young Earth," in Vardiman et al., *Radioisotopes and the Age of the Earth: Results of a Young-Earth Creationist Research Initiative* (Santee, CA: Institute for Creation Research; Chino Valley, AZ: Creation Research Society, 2005), p. 587–630.

## Chapter 16

# CLEAR EVIDENCE OF EVOLUTION OR...

Letter, unedited:

> Dear Sir:
>
> I have noted in your materials an assertion that "no evolution has ever been observed." This assertion is clearly mistaken.
>
> The Chola people live on the Altiplano of Bolivia & Peru. They are generally short, barrel-chested, with large feet.
>
> They are barrel-chested because at that altitude, bigger lungs make survival easier. They are short so their center of gravity is lower, also a help in thin altitudes. And their feet are larger than lowlanders' to help assure footing in their high environs. Since these folks, isolated until the 1920s from the rest of the world, are so different from us lowlanders, I'd say this is clear evidence of evolution.
>
> Whether or not I believe that the earth was created in 7 days is a moot point. The earth IS as it is. The fact that I believe that species have evolved does not make me unworthy of God's salvation. It means only that I have used God's gift-my mind-to think critically.
>
> Not all evolutionists believe there is no God.
>
> T.J., U.S.

Response:

> Thank you for your kind letter. I hope to respond in the same manner.
>
> Dear Sir:
>
> I have noted in your materials an assertion that "no evolution has ever been observed."

I'm not sure where you received this statement as it wasn't on our website when I searched. However, this depends on the definition of *evolution* anyway. If *evolution* simply means "change," then of course change has been observed.

In fact, many exhibits at the Creation Museum undergo "evolution" (i.e., change) by adding signage, repositioning exhibits, removing outdated material, and so on. We could also use the term "intelligently designed" to describe the change in the museum exhibits. We could further say that the "creation" of the exhibits involves changes. Isn't it strange how the terms *evolution, intelligent design*, and *creation* can be used together in this context?

These terms also have other meanings. *Evolution*, for example, can also refer to the "general theory of evolution," which is the idea that single-celled organisms gained new genetic information over millions and billions of years, and eventually arrived at "higher life-forms" such as man. It can also mean the entire worldview of naturalism where everything came from nothing.

> This assertion is clearly mistaken.
>
> The Chola people live on the Altiplano of Bolivia & Peru. They are generally short, barrel-chested, with large feet.
>
> They are barrel-chested because at that altitude, bigger lungs make survival easier. They are short so their center of gravity is lower, also a help in thin altitudes. And their feet are larger than lowlanders' to help assure footing in their high environs. Since these folks, isolated until the 1920s from the rest of the world, are so different from us lowlanders, I'd say this is clear evidence of evolution.

But this is not evidence of the general theory of evolution in which molecules change into man. Instead, it is merely an example of selection (and perhaps mutation) acting on a population. This "evolution" is "change" in the sense discussed above. People changing into people is not evolution in the grander sense. So be careful of bait-and-switch arguments. I'm surprised at the number of people who accept evolution and who can't tell the difference between the general theory of evolution (GTE) and selection (e.g., natural or artificial). The idea of natural selection began with a creationist, while the GTE is based on naturalistic ideas, which attempt to explain life without God.

When I was in Peru and went to Cusco, which is over two miles high, I found the air is indeed thin and many suffer altitude sickness. It didn't affect me very much at all. And after a few hours, my body had adjusted and I carried on like normal. Many people have migrated to those areas since the 1920s and they have little if any trouble with the altitude. So one also needs to be careful of assuming that "evolutionary changes" occurred to this population of Chola people. It makes more sense that they have a common human ancestor a few years before who was shorter, with a barrel chest and large feet, and these characteristics were merely passed to descendants.

This example you have given is merely an example of change among an already-human population. This is a fine-tuned expression of the variety in genetic information that already existed in the human population, not an example of generation of copious amounts of new genetic information. The GTE requires the addition of new information — not just a little bit, but a massive amount of genetic information.

Natural selection cannot generate brand-new genetic information. It simply doesn't work that way. Instead, it filters information that already exists. This is why most evolutionists have moved from the outdated concept of traditional Darwinism (natural selection plus millions of years [which is a rehash of Lamarckian evolution, which was a rehash of Greek mythology by the Epicureans]) to a position of neo-Darwinism or punctuated equilibrium, which claims mutations add new information (natural selection plus mutations plus millions of years).

Of course, mutations have only been shown to be nearly neutral by rearrangements or destroying (usually very detrimentally) the information already in the genome, so this process is moving in the *opposite* direction of what the GTE requires. But this doesn't mean that evolutionists don't place their faith in mutations anyway. Science fiction movies, books, and comics, like *X-men* and *Spiderman,* commonly portray mutations giving people special powers. However, mutations are not what they are purported to be; if you want to see what mutations really do, visit a cancer ward in a hospital. Mutations are destructive and are a sign that the world is under a curse, which is all the more reason to place one's faith in Christ and be saved.[1]

**Whether or not I believe that the earth was created in 7 days is a moot point.**

---

1. Please see my chapter in *The New Answers Book 2*, Ken Ham, Gen. Ed., called "Are Mutations Part of the 'Engine' of Evolution?" for a more in-depth discussion of mutations and information. http://www.answersingenesis.org/articles/nab2/mutations-engine-of-evolution.

Actually, God created in six days, not seven. He rested on the seventh.[2] And the timing of creation is not a moot point. Either God created in six days or He is being intentionally deceptive. If God lied about how long He took to create, then how would we know if God lied about salvation? God is truthful. He is the truth (John 14:6), and He doesn't lie (Hebrews 6:18). When God says He created in six days (Exodus 11:6, 31:17), then we must accept what He says. Will you trust God when He speaks about His creative acts? If not, then there is no reason for you to trust Him when He speaks about anything else in the Bible (John 3:12).

### The earth IS as it is.

I agree; the earth IS as it is . . . but did you realize the Bible explains why? Why do things die? (Genesis 3). Why are there massive geological layers that contain dead things in them? (Genesis 6–8). Why do day and night not cease (and scientific laws not change)? (Genesis 8:22, etc.).

Variation among the animal kinds and people is also a biblical concept. Jacob used animal variation to his advantage (Genesis 30:31–42), and Jacob and Esau looked different (Genesis 27:11), and so on. These changes primarily stem from variations in the already-existing genes, not from adding new information as the GTE requires.

### The fact that I believe that species have evolved does not make me unworthy of God's salvation.

Well, we are *all* unworthy of God's salvation — no matter what we believe about origins. We are saved by His grace through repentance of our sins and faith in the death, burial, and Resurrection of His Son on our behalf — not because we are "worthy" of His gift of eternal life.

However, your belief shows a lack of respect for what God *says* in His word, particularly in Genesis. Besides, what makes you equate speciation with the GTE? Part of the confusion stems from the fact that "species" is a man-made term. In Genesis 1, animals and plants are described as being created "after their kind." A "kind" is considered to be much closer to the "family" level, not in all instances, of course. Often, creationists say the animals and plants were to "reproduce after their kinds"; however, the Bible doesn't actually say this. This statement is a derivation from other biblical claims:

---

2. Some would argue that God *created* rest on the seventh day, though this would defeat the purpose of God resting from all of His creating as Genesis 2:2–3 indicates.

| Said of: | Passage: | Reproduction within kind? |
|---|---|---|
| Vegetation | Genesis 1:12: "And the earth brought forth grass, the herb that yields seed according to its kind, and the tree that yields fruit, whose seed is in itself according to its kind. And God saw that it was good." | Yes — seeds "after their kind" are the means of reproduction. |
| Sea creatures | Genesis 1:21–22: "So God created great sea creatures and every living thing that moves, with which the waters abounded, according to their kind, and every winged bird according to its kind. And God saw that it was good. And God blessed them, saying, 'Be fruitful and multiply, and fill the waters in the seas, and let birds multiply on the earth.' " | Yes — sea creatures and birds were made after their kinds and told to reproduce. |
| Land animals (on the ark) | Genesis 6:19–20: "And of every living thing of all flesh you shall bring two of every sort into the ark, to keep them alive with you; they shall be male and female. Of the birds after their kind, of animals after their kind, and of every creeping thing of the earth after its kind, two of every kind will come to you to keep them alive." | Yes — a kind is referred to as having a male and female, leading to the obvious conclusion that they will reproduce after their kind. |

It is *within these kinds* that much variation, even speciation, can take place. This would have happened after the Flood when things began to re-multiply and spread over the earth.

**It means only that I have used God's gift-my mind-to think critically.**

The basis to think critically comes from a literal Genesis as well. Man is made in the image of a logical God (Genesis 1:26–27); hence, man has a basis for reasoning. But also from Genesis, there is a basis for why man's reasoning is faulty — man's sin and the subsequent Curse that God placed on His original "very good" creation (Genesis 3). When Genesis 1–11 are denied as accounts of actual history or mythologized, which is what one who believes in the GTE must do, then there is no basis for reasoning. There is also no basis for needing a Savior!

Without Adam's sin (an actual, historical event), which brought death and the Curse into the world, there is no reason for Christ, the Last Adam, to have come (1 Corinthians 15:45). The punishment for sin was death (Genesis 2:17); this is why Jesus had to die physically. The sin against an infinite Creator demands an infinite punishment. The blood of bulls and goats (sacrificed throughout the Old Testament) cannot fully atone for this punishment; they merely provided a temporary covering for sin (Hebrews 10:4). Jesus Christ, who is the infinite God, could take on this punishment, and did so because He loved us. But Christ also showed that death could not restrain Him. He resurrected and showed the world that He has power over death, unlike all other religious leaders who are still in the grave.

When one takes away a literal Adam and Eve, there is suddenly no reason for Christ to come and no reason for a Savior to die. According to the law of non-contradiction, one cannot have "A" and "not A" in the same relationship at the same time. Mixing the GTE with the Bible has this problem. Having Adam (A) and not having Adam (not A) in the same relationship at the same time is logically impossible.

**Not all evolutionists believe there is no God.**

I agree. But as I said before, evolutionists have no basis for a belief in God when they discount Genesis. Ken Ham wrote an excellent article on this subject entitled "The God of an Old Earth," in which he said:

> Christians who believe in an old earth (billions of years) need to come to grips with the real nature of the god of an old earth — it is **not** the loving God of the Bible. . . . The god of an old earth is one that uses death as part of creating — death therefore can't be the penalty for sin — or "the last enemy" (1 Corinthians 15:26).[3]

This article often upsets people who believe in an old earth because it points out that the cruel, unloving god of an old earth is not the one described in Scripture. People falsely accuse us of implying that they are not saved, since they are following some attributes of this false, worldly god. However, we want to make it clear that one can be a Christian and believe in an old

---

3. http://www.answersingenesis.org/articles/cm/v21/n4/oldearth.

earth and/or molecules-to-man evolution. They are just being inconsistent by mixing two different religions together (secular humanism and Christianity). Really, they are using secular humanism's origins story and cancelling the Bible's origins account.

If they are brothers and sisters in Christ, however, they are being inconsistent by ascribing attributes of this cruel god of an old earth to the biblical God. Sadly, the Bible often gets dismissed because of these false attributes, as we've seen with the next generation of Christians. They see church leaders of their parents who do not believe one part of the Bible and they just take it one step further and disregard the entire Bible.

This breaks my heart because I love God and His Word, and I want Christians to honor and respect the Word of the Lord over all other belief systems, including the GTE and an old earth, which are parts of secular humanism. Is neglecting the Word of God expressing love to God?

> "Teacher, which is the great commandment in the law?" Jesus said to him, " 'You shall love the Lord your God with all your heart, with all your soul, and with all your mind.' This is the first and great commandment. And the second is like it: 'You shall love your neighbor as yourself.' On these two commandments hang all the Law and the Prophets" (Matthew 22:36–40).

With kindness in Christ and love for His Word.

## Chapter 17

# ᗺNOAH, A GLOBAL ℱLOOD, AND THE ᗢ℃ASE AℊAINᏠT RACISᎷ

Letter, unedited:

> The Bible does not say that all races came from Noah and his three sons. Noah was white, he was perfect in his generation, he was a direct descendant of Adam. In Hebrew Adam literally means white man blood in the face red. Adam is the father of the white race, no other. Noah's flood was local. If everybody came from Noah than why did God condemn interracial relations and marriage. It shouldn't make a difference. Ask a doctor if you can receive a blood transfusion from a black man. He will say no because the blood types are not related. You could get very sick and die. All the races made it through the flood. This is an archeological, anthropological, and historical fact. Noah was a white man, and his sons were white. They cannot produce black children, asian children, or children of any other race.
>
> T.G., U.S.

Response: [This response was coauthored with Dr. Tommy Mitchell, a friend and colleague at Answers in Genesis who is a medical doctor.]

Thank you for contacting Answers in Genesis. We often receive correspondence such as this, and we are taking the opportunity to respond to this one in kindness to help correct the false theology in this letter.

> The Bible does not say that all races came from Noah and his three sons.

There are two things wrong right from the start. First, the Bible doesn't lump people into multiple "races."

Second, the Bible does teach that people throughout the entire earth are descendants of Noah.

> Now the sons of Noah who went out of the ark were Shem, Ham, and Japheth. And Ham was the father of Canaan. These

three were the sons of Noah, and from these the whole earth was populated (Genesis 9:18–19).

The Bible indicates that all people came through Noah and his sons since all other humans and land animals died in the Flood (Genesis 7:21–23). But let's back up even further. On the sixth day of creation, God made the land animals and man. Thus, Adam and the woman were made on that day. Genesis 3:20 says "And Adam called his wife's name Eve, because she was the mother of all living."

Note that Scripture indicates that Eve was mother of *all*, not *some*, of the living. Obviously, this is referring to humans; otherwise, other so-called races of humans weren't living! Therefore, all humans trace their ancestry back to these two people, Adam and Eve.

Different people groups developed after the Flood from the descendants of Noah. After the Flood, all people spoke the same language. Genesis 11 explains that God confused their languages at the Tower of Babel to force them to scatter over the earth. This scattering isolated portions of the human gene pool geographically.

The physical characteristics of various ethnic groups developed in these isolated groups due to the sorting and isolation of genetic information already present in man's DNA. The information in that DNA was originally present in Adam's DNA and has just been shuffled and sorted. Therefore, the development of so-called races has nothing to do with molecules-to-man evolution. All people groups are still humans, descended from one original human. The Book of Acts confirms that humans are all related:

> And He has made from one blood every nation of men to dwell on all the face of the earth, and has determined their preappointed times and the boundaries of their dwellings (Acts 17:26).

All men are related and of "one blood" through Noah and, ultimately, Adam and Eve. Even secular scientists are finally realizing that all the so-called races are, indeed, one blood.[1]

**Noah was white,**

The Bible does not say that Noah was "white." In fact, no one is "white"; we are all brownish in tone — some more, some less. The Bible never describes

---

1. "Dr. Venter (head of the Celera Genomics Corporation, Rockville, MD) and scientists at the National Institutes of Health recently announced that they had put together a draft of the entire sequence of the human genome, and the researchers had unanimously declared, there is only one race — the human race." (Natalie Angier, "Do Races Differ? Not Really, DNA Shows," *New York Times*, Aug. 22, 2000).

Noah's physical appearance. He could have just as easily had a variety of features. To make such a dogmatic claim without a scriptural basis would imply that you are omnipresent and omniscient.

### he was perfect in his generation, he was a direct descendant of Adam.

Everyone, including Noah, was a direct descendent of Adam, but that didn't make them perfect in their generation. Everyone, including Noah and Adam, was a sinner. Noah was called perfect in his generation because he found grace in the eyes of the Lord (Genesis 6:8–9). Hebrews 11:7 explains that Noah's righteousness was by faith. In other words, like all people in his generation, Noah was a sinner. But unlike the other people, Noah trusted in God's forgiving grace. As a result, as Genesis 6:9 says, Noah walked with God. Noah was even a preacher of righteousness (2 Peter 2:5). Noah escaped death in the worldwide Flood because of his faith in God's grace, not because he was a white man, directly descended from Adam.

### In Hebrew Adam literally means white man blood in the face red.

Strong's Concordance says that Adam's name in Hebrew means "to show blood in the face, red, ruddy, rosy, a human being." This Hebrew word has nothing to do with being white.

According to the Bible, the life of the flesh is in the blood. When God breathed life into Adam, Adam became a living soul. Perhaps the association of life with blood explains God's name for Adam. Some have tried to make the assertion that Adam was red-skinned or red-haired, but there is no reason to think his name referred to these features over the red lifeblood. God's name for the first man implied nothing about white skin.

### Adam is the father of the white race, no other.

What do you mean by "white"? Irish? Russians? The claim that Adam was "white" is pure conjecture and totally unsupportable. Nothing in Scripture suggests that Adam was "white" or that Adam was the father of only "white" people.

Adam and Eve, and later Noah and his wife, probably had skin tones closer to middle brown. Adam's DNA had to contain information for a wide variety of skin tones. Only in this way could human DNA possess the genetic variability to produce the many skin tones we now see. Shuffling and sorting of this genetic information produces a variety of skin tones.

After the scattering of people from the Tower of Babel, genetic information was sorted and isolated into many geographic areas. Certain groups lost the ability to produce children of other skin shades because the genetic information for those skin shades was not present in their population group.

### Noah's flood was local.

Noah's flood was global, not local. But don't take our word for it; let's see what the Bible has to say.

> The waters prevailed and greatly increased on the earth, and the ark moved about on the surface of the waters. And the waters prevailed exceedingly on the earth, and all the high hills under the whole heaven were covered. The waters prevailed fifteen cubits upward, and the mountains were covered (Genesis 7:18–20).

©2004 Answers in Genesis

Additionally, there are many problems with the claim that Noah's Flood was local. For instance:

1. Why did God tell Noah to build an ark? If the Flood had been only local, Noah and his family could have just moved to higher ground or over the mountain to avoid the floodwaters.

2. The wicked people that the Flood was intended to destroy could have escaped God's judgment in the same manner.

3. Why take all the birds on the ark when they could have flown over the hill!

4. If the Flood were local, then God would be a liar, for God promised in Genesis 9:11 never to send a flood to destroy the earth again. Yet the world has seen many local floods.

Over the years, we have found that there are primarily two groups of people who promote a local flood for Noah's day:

1.  those who believe that the geologic layers represent millions of years instead of a global Flood

2.  those who are "racist" and insist that people of a particular shade of skin are not Adam and Noah's kin, and survived outside the ark

Why take such preconceived beliefs to the Bible to try to twist Genesis 6–9? I want to encourage readers to read these passages and then ask: *how, biblically, can people get a local flood out of these chapters?* The Bible should be the starting point for our theology, not an afterthought.

> **If everybody came from Noah than why did God condemn interracial relations and marriage. It shouldn't make a difference.**

Where did God condemn "interracial" marriage? He didn't. God doesn't lump people into multiple "races" anyway. The concept of "races" is a man-made idea.

Since there is only one race of humans, "interracial relations" makes no difference from a biological point of view.[2] However, from a spiritual point of view, marriages make a huge difference. God told the children of Israel not to intermarry with people from other cultures who were not godly (Deuteronomy 7:3–4). These were pagan cultures with their own customs and their own gods and would lead people astray. God knew that intermarrying with these people would soon lead them away from the worship of the one true God.

One only need look to the life of Solomon, who far exceeded others in wisdom (1 Kings 4:29–32), to see the effect that taking strange wives had on his life and his descendants. To maintain Israel as a peculiar people, God wanted separation from pagan cultures, but not by "racial" division. After all, Rahab (Canaanite) and Ruth (Moabite), who were not Israelites, were incorporated when they changed to serve the true God.

In the Bible, there is only one type of marriage that is forbidden. That is a marriage between a saved and an unsaved person:

> Do not be unequally yoked together with unbelievers. For what fellowship has righteousness with lawlessness? And what communion has light with darkness? (2 Corinthians 6:14).

---

2. In Leviticus 18, God forbade marriage between close relations. He knew, as one reason, that at that point, due to mutations in the gene pool, the risk of birth defects would be greatly increased. Even though we all still marry a relative (as we all are related as descendants of Adam and Eve), a union between more distantly related people would be less likely to produce problems in offspring. This instruction from God has nothing to do with race.

Again, this mimicked the command to the Israelites to not marry people who were not seeking after God and would lead both the person and his children astray.

> **Ask a doctor if you can receive a blood transfusion from a black man. He will say no because the blood types are not related. You could get very sick and die.**

I (Dr. Tommy Mitchell, a medical internist) don't have to ask a doctor. I *am* a doctor. What you state is absolutely incorrect. Blood is not typed on the basis of race. It is typed on the basis of antigens found on the red blood cells. It is ultimately more complicated than this. This is the basis for the ABO blood grouping and the Rh antigen typing classifications. When one needs a blood transfusion, the donor blood is checked for these various antigens to determine if it is compatible with the recipient's immune system.

A transfusion of improperly matched blood can lead to a serious reaction (and sometimes even death) for the person receiving the blood. However, this has absolutely nothing to do with "race."

> **All the races made it through the Flood. This is an archeological, anthropological, and historical fact. Noah was a white man, and his sons were white.**

I agree that all the "races," if such a term could even be used, made it through the Flood, but not at the sake of forsaking Genesis 6–9 as a local flood. The author's term here would be "people groups," not "races," anyway. All people groups are the descendants of Noah and his family. These eight people ultimately gave rise to all people groups on earth. Thus, we would agree that it is an anthropological and historical fact.

But we will go one step further. Archaeologically and anthropologically, most of the people in Africa are descendants of Cush, Mizraim, and Phut, three of Noah's great-grandsons. *Mizraim* is still the Hebrew name for Egypt. Parts of modern-day Libya and Morocco are the land of Phut, and Libya was renamed for one of Mizraim's sons named Lybyos (Lehabites). Ethiopians still call themselves Cushites today! The indigenous African continent is primarily inhabited by people who go back to Noah's son Ham, outside some places on the Mediterranean coast. This has rarely been disputed in history, and even Josephus, writing nearly 2,000 years ago, confirms this.[3] In fact, Noah's descendants' names can be found in many parts of the world, if one takes the time to look. The following chart shows a few:

---

3. Josephus, *The Antiquity of the Jews*, 1st Century A.D. in William Whiston, *The Works of Josephus Complete and Unabridged* (Peabody, MA: Hendrickson Publishers, 1987), p. 36–37.

| | Early Descendant of Noah | What is it?* |
|---|---|---|
| Aramaic | Aram | This language came out of Babel and still survives, likely with changes down the ages. Some short parts of the Bible are written in Aramaic. Jesus spoke it on the Cross when He said: "ELOI, ELOI, LAMA SABACHTHANI?" (Mark 15:34). |
| Cush | Cush | Ancient name of Ethiopia. In fact, people of Ethiopia still call themselves Cushites. |
| Medes | Madai | People group often associated with the Persians |
| Ashkenaz | Ashkenaz | This is still the Hebrew name for Germany. |
| Galacia, Gaul, and Galicia | Gomer | These regions are the old names for an area in modern Turkey, France, and northwestern Spain, respectively, where Gomer was said to have lived. His family lines continued to spread about across southern Europe. The Book of Galatians by Paul was written to the church at Galatia. |
| Gomeraeg | Gomer | This is the old name for the Welsh language on the British Isles from their ancestor, Gomer, whose ancestors began to populate the Isle from the mainland. |
| Javan | Javan | This is still the Hebrew name for Greece. His sons, Elishah, Tarshish, Kittim (Chittim), and Dodanim still have reference to places in Greece. For example, Paul, the author who penned much of the New Testament, was from the region of Tarshish (Acts 21:39) and a city called Tarsus. Jeremiah mentions Kittim in Jeremiah 2:10. It is modern-day Cyprus (and other nearby ancient regions that now have varied names such as Cethim, Citius, and Cethima Cilicia). The Greeks worshiped Jupiter Dodanaeus from Japheth/Dodanim. The Elysians were ancient Greek people. |
| Meshech/ Moscow | Mechech | Mechech is the old name for Moscow, Russia, and one region called the Mechech Lowland still holds the original name today, as does a state park. |
| Canaan | Canaan | The region of Palestine that God removed from the Canaanites for their sin and gave as an inheritance to the Israelites beginning with the conquest of Joshua. It is often termed the Holy Land and is the site of modern-day Israel. |

| Elamites | Elam | This was the old name for the Persians prior to Cyrus. |
|---|---|---|
| Assyria | Asshur | Asshur is still the Hebrew name for Assyria. |
| Hebrew | Eber | This people group and language was named for Eber. Abraham was a Hebrew, and the bulk of the Old Testament is written in Hebrew. |
| Libya | Lybyos | Mizraim's son and modern-day Libya; the same region is also known as the land of Phut, one of Noah's grandsons. |
| Taurus/Toros | Tarshish | A mountain range in Turkey |
| Tanais | Tarshish | The old name of the Don River flowing into the Black Sea. |
| Mizraim | Mizraim | This is still the Hebrew name for Egypt. |

\* Josephus, *The Antiquity of the Jews*, 1st Century A.D. in Whiston, *The Works of Josephus Complete and Unabridged*, p. 36–37; Bill Cooper, *After the Flood* (Chichester, England: New Wine Press, 1995), p. 170–208; Harold Hunt with Russell Grigg, "The Sixteen Grandsons of Noah," *Creation* 20(4) (September 1998): pages 22-25; there are many other references to these as well, but this should suffice to get you started, including James Anderson's *Royal Genealogies*.

### They cannot produce black children, asian children, or children of any other race.

Since the sorting of genetic material that occurred after the Tower of Babel, many darker-skinned peoples have lost the ability to have light-skinned children. By the same token, many light-skinned peoples have lost the variability needed to produce darker-skinned offspring.[4] Perhaps you did not know what the Bible teaches, or perhaps you have been taught these beliefs and didn't test them against the Scriptures. I pray that you would consider what is written here in response and be like the Bereans, who "searched the Scriptures daily, whether those things were so" (Acts 17:11).

In kindness with Christ,

Dr. Tommy Mitchell and Bodie Hodge

---

4. This is assuming they marry within their own ethnic/people group and little genetic material that had been lost is reintroduced into the gene pool.

## Chapter 18

# WHAT ABOUT THE ARK DESIGN?

Letter, unedited:

> Hi Bodie, read your article on the shape of the Noah's Ark on A/I/Genesis today.
>
> May I just make a small comment on said paper, and please this is just not to be argumentative in any way. Re the thought behind the reason for the Ark to have a pointed end, bow, and stub end stern. Unless the vessel had some means of forward propulsion it would make absolutely NO difference to the stability of the vessel.
>
> In fact the difference in the ends would, being unequal, give reason to cause the vessel to in effect spin due to the difference in resistance to the flow of the waters brought to bear on the unequal ends. The thought of losing forward power drive in large waves or winds or storms is a nightmare scenario for all mariners. The Ark didn't even have sail power.
>
> And no doubt God was exercising a protecting hand all thru the process of the flood and could have had a calm around the Ark to ensure its safety. Just as our Lord calmed the storm when crossing the Sea of Galilee. I may be missing something of course here and would welcome your kind response if possible. Keep up the good work of defending and championing the truths of Gods word.
>
> May God bless your ministry . . . R.

Response: [With the help of friend and leading ark researcher from Australia, Tim Lovett, we formulated a response. Keep in mind this inquirer is on-side but disagreed on a particular point.]

It is nice to hear from you, and no argumentative tone taken. Christians should be able to talk and discuss these things as iron sharpens iron (Proverbs 27:17). We would agree that it is a reasonable assumption that there was no propulsion system on the ark. This is likely why the word for ark (*tebah*) is used as opposed to ship (*'oniyah*), a common word for a boat that usually had a form of propulsion (oars, sails, etc.). Moses was also placed in an ark (*tebah*), likely a simple tiny floating vessel, rather than a boat with propulsion.

However, with large wind-driven waves, turning sideways is the natural position for any long vessel, which is exactly why "losing forward power drive in large waves or winds or storms is a nightmare scenario for all mariners." Sideways is bad and this is called "beam sea."

If the ark had features like we have added (i.e., a wind-catching fin on the bow and the stern extension), then the ark would have turned *into* the wind and waves for much better stability. These features make sense because they would make the ark align with the wind and waves. Note that the fin at the bow is aligned downwind, and the stern (resembling a modern bulbous bow) is designed to face the waves. So it seems to run backward compared to a modern ship. Also, the dimensions given in Scripture (300 cubits long by 50 cubits wide) are far more slender than a modern lifeboat designed for random orientation in the sea.

You point out that these features appear to be designed for propulsion. This is partly true; some limited propulsion is achieved by the forecastle superstructure and fin aligned with the wind (i.e., the vessel has waves at the stern). It is estimated that this design would travel at only a few knots, enough to gain directional stability afforded by keel and skeg, but not fast enough to introduce a broaching risk in a quartering sea.

Furthermore, I would be cautious of making statements such as, **"And no doubt God was exercising a protecting hand all thru the process of the flood and could have had a calm around the Ark to ensure its safety."** The Bible doesn't say this, and these types of claims could render the ark almost pointless. We need to keep in mind that the ark *was* the "protective hand" given by God. Of course, God upholds all things, but thinking that God miraculously protected the ark throughout the Flood could open a door for other ideas that are not recorded in Scripture. Please don't take this as a criticism but as a teaching point, as we have all probably made mistakes like this before.

The ark certainly served its purpose to stay afloat during the Flood to preserve life. The Bible indicates that the ark floated on the waters of the Flood until it came to rest "in the seventh month, the seventeenth day of the month, on the mountains of Ararat" (Genesis 8:4). I hope this helps.

With kindness in Christ, God bless.

Bodie Hodge and Tim Lovett

## Chapter 19

# TOO MANY THEORIES?

Letter, unedited:

> I have been visiting your website pretty regularly for about a year. I am amazed by the time and energy you put in attempting to refute common scientific facts. Over the last year I have read no less than three contrived theories dealing with the speed of light and how gravity can explain a 6000 year old universe. If I understand you correctly, light was faster, created already on its way or we are sitting in a gravity well causing a time dilation.
>
> It appears that you skew science to fit into what you think is true. It seems that the body of evidence for evolutionary biology is at a minimum overwhelming. The evidence agrees with all the observations from the different sects of science. Molecular biology confirms that DNA is the building blocks of life. Quantum physics explains the interactions of particles and justifies changes (mutations) within DNA. Archeology illustrates the layering of the fossil record exactly as we would expect, but you guys don't want to see or believe what is.
>
> J.P., U.S.

Response:

Thank you for contacting Answers in Genesis. Please see my comments below and note that they are said with sincerity and respect.

**I have been visiting your website pretty regularly for about a year.**

Thanks, I hope it has been challenging you.

**I am amazed by the time and energy you put in attempting to refute common scientific facts.**

The reason some people say this is usually that they fail to understand the difference between a "fact" and an "interpretation of a fact." For example, a fact would be that a cow has DNA. A [false] interpretation is that "the cow evolved from a microbe a long time ago when no one was there to observe the process because it has DNA."

**Over the last year I have read no less than three contrived theories dealing with the speed of light and how gravity can explain a 6000 year old universe. If I understand you correctly, light was faster, created already on its way or we are sitting in a gravity well causing a time dilation.**

Scientific thought thrives on competing models. So I'm not certain why this would bother you. It seems strange that of the "no less than three" models, only one of the three models that were listed is given much credence on the Answers in Genesis website. Perhaps you have confused this with things that you have read elsewhere.

But on the subject of distant starlight, those who often ask this question are rarely aware that in a big bang, they also have a light travel–time problem (horizon problem).[1] The visible universe is estimated at about 46 billion light years across, based on the cosmic light horizon. Yet the universe is only supposed to be about 13–15 billion years old. So, how could distant starlight exchange in such a short time in a uniformitarian framework to make a uniform temperature in the universe?[2]

Starting from the Bible, there are several potential solutions to the problem.

1. Speed of Light decay (e.g., researched by Mr. Barry Setterfield): Most creationists reject this now, but we encourage researchers to keep working on it. It ends up with too many problems with all other contestants of the universe changing, but the evidence of this is lacking. Furthermore, as people really researched the speed of light over the past three centuries, they found it really hasn't been changing as previously thought but has remained largely the same. Though the CDK model has problems, even some secular physicists have appealed to a changing speed of light to ameliorate problems with their own models.

2. Light in Transit (most reject this as well): This is the idea that the starlight was already in transit when God created the stars. However,

---

1. Robert Newton, "Light-Travel Time: A Problem for the Big Bang," September 1, 2003, http://www.answersingenesis.org/articles/cm/v25/n4/light-travel-time.

2. Some may appeal to an *ad hoc* solution such as "inflation" where the universe rapidly expands for no reason, then suddenly slows for no reason, but this still doesn't solve the horizon problem.

stars blow up into supernovas like SN 1987a, etc., and none of this would be real but merely starlight made to appear like a star and a supernova, etc. This seems far too deceptive, so most creationists have rejected this idea.

3. Relativistic models:

   a. Dr. Russell Humphreys: White hole cosmology based on God stretching the heavens. According to Einstein, if you stretch the fabric of space, you get a time change. Many passages mention this: Job 26:7, Isaiah 40:22, Zechariah 12:1, etc. This model works well with distant objects, but for things closer to our galaxy, it doesn't seem to work well.[3]

   b. Dr. John Hartnett: Similar to Humphreys' relativistic model with a bit more miraculous attributed to it during creation week.[4] He utilizes Carmellian physics. But this model actually assumes Dr. Jason Lisle's model (below) to work it out. Dr. Lisle first submitted this in the peer review, years ago.[5]

4. Lisle-Einstein Synchrony Convention Model or ASC (Anisotropic Synchrony Convention): This is based on an alternative convention that is *position based* physics (think time zones) as opposed to *velocity based* physics. Einstein left open both options but did most of his work based on velocity, and so have most physicists since him.

   Dr. Jason Lisle built on this position-based physics and the one direction speed of light that cannot be known, and it solves distant starlight. Einstein pointed out that time is not constant in the universe, so our simple equation [Speed = Distance X Time] is not so simple anymore. But this model is based on something quite "simple." Think of it like this: You leave on a plane in New York at 1 p.m. and you land in Los Angeles at 1 p.m. But you might say, "The flight took about 5 hours when you rode on the plane."

   Here is the difference: according to Einstein, when you approach the speed of light, time goes to zero. So if you rode on

---

3. See Dr. Humphreys' book *Starlight and Time* for more details (Green Forest, AR: Master Books, 1994).

4. See Dr. John Hartnett, "A New Cosmology: Solution to the Starlight Travel Time Problem," *TJ* 17(2):98–102, 2003.

5. Hartnett's was presented at the ICC (International Creation on Creationism) in 2008; see "Starlight, Time, and the New Physics" in the 2008 *Proceedings of the International Conference on Creationism*, Ed. Dr. Andrew Snelling, 2008.

top of a light beam from a star that was billions of light years away from earth, it took no time for you to get here. So that five-hour flight was a "no hour" flight for light. Based on this convention-based model, light left distant stars and arrived on earth in no time, and this fulfills God's statement that these lights were to give light on the earth in Genesis 1:14. Of course, the physics is more complicated than this, but this analogy should give you an idea of how the model works.[6]

5.  Miraculous/Future models (we would leave open miracles or future models as well.)[7]

Although the question of distance has been argued for many years, few today argue along the lines of distance being the only reason for alleged long ages:

1.  Parallax: Earth is on one side of sun; view stars. Then when earth is on the other side of the sun, view stars. It makes a very small triangle and we can calculate the distances. This is called parallax.

2.  Red Shift: Some stars are so far away that the triangle of parallax does not solve it. So then we move to "red shift" to calculate the distance. Not as accurate, but seems to do the job. Some objects, like many quasars, do not work properly with red shift. But these are assumed to be accurate for long distances.

The actual relevant equation is ds = c x dt.

Here, c is the speed of light, which is constant in vacuum (with respect to any observer) according to relativity, ds represents distance, and dt represents time. Many fail to realize that the flow of time is not constant in the universe but can change due to different circumstances, such as velocity frame dilation or the presence of a gravitational field. When the fabric of space is stretched, the differential for time must also change, as c is constant. Interesting that God often stated that He stretched or stretches out the heavens:

---

6. For more, see http://www.answersingenesis.org/articles/am/v6/n1/distant-starlight (Distant Starlight: Anisotropic Synchrony Convention) and the technical journal article "ASC — A Solution to the Distant Starlight Problem," http://www.answersingenesis.org/articles/arj/v3/n1/anisotropic-synchrony-convention.

7. Editorial Note: Since the writing of this, Dr. Danny Faulkner has put forth a model that is dubbed the "Dasha Solution." Basically, it says light was rapidly accelerated during creation week to get light to earth on day 6 for Adam to see. This solves distant starlight for creation week, but still falls short of getting light to earth since that time. For more, please see: D. Faulkner, "Astronomical Distance Determination Methods and the Light Travel Time Problem," *Answers Research Journal* 6 (2013): 211-229, http://www.answersingenesis.org/articles/arj/v6/n1/astronomical-distance-light-travel-problem.

Job 26:7; Isaiah 40:22, 42:5, 44:24, 45:12, 48:13, 51:13; Zechariah 12:1; and Jeremiah 10:12.

The relativistic models are working with this concept. Interestingly, the secular models often appeal to inflation of the universe as a conjecture to try to solve their starlight problem. It is puzzling why we get criticized for discussing the stretching of space, when secular scientists do the same thing.

Then there is cosmological time zone conventions, which use an entirely different perspective from the time dilation models. And this solves distant starlight.

But as biblical Christians, we also leave open the possibility for miraculous events, considering this was done during creation week. God can create stars on day 4 and have the light arrive at earth using miraculous means. This is not to be confused with light-created-in-transit, which we reject, as the light we would see if such an idea were true would not actually be from a star. God is not deceptive in any way, and God saying these things were to put light on the earth would not necessarily be true.

**It appears that you skew science to fit into what you think is true.**

Many creationists would argue the same about evolutionists. However, the concepts of "science" and "truth" are really only meaningful in a biblical creation worldview. Apart from the biblical God, what would be the objective basis for such things? Jesus even said:

> Jesus said to him, "I am the way, the truth, and the life. No one comes to the Father except through Me" (John 14:6).

Science, which came out of a Christian worldview, is an excellent methodology that confirms the Bible's teachings. For example, the law of biogenesis says that life comes from life. We expect this, since all animals today are descended from the originals that were created by God. It is the same with humans. My life came from my parents, who in turn came from their parents, back to the first parents, Adam and Eve (Hebrews 7:9–10). Eve's life came from Adam, and Adam's came from God, who is the ultimate life-giving source.

In an evolutionary worldview, life ultimately arose from nonlife. This has never been repeated and violates the law of biogenesis.

**It seems that the body of evidence for evolutionary biology is at a minimum overwhelming.**

Such as? Besides, all evidence is interpreted in light of a worldview. It's hardly surprising that evolutionists think that the evidence supports their position, and creationists think the evidence confirms creation. So, the real question is, "Which worldview can make sense of science at all?" We have shown that only the Bible can.

**The evidence agrees with all the observations from the different sects of science.**

Evidence doesn't agree or disagree or draw conclusions. You are falsely giving human qualities to things that don't have them. This is called the fallacy of reification. People interpret facts and observations as evidence. Such inanimate things simply can't do that.

**Molecular biology confirms that DNA is the building blocks of life.**

DNA does contain information that generates the proteins of organisms and is essential to life. I fail, however, to see how this necessarily supports molecules-to-man evolution. This is what is expected from an intelligent Creator God.

**Quantum physics explains the interactions of particles and justifies changes (mutations) within DNA.**

We agree that quantum physics explains the interactions of (subatomic) particles, but what does that have to do with errors in the copies of the DNA during the replication process at the molecular level? Since mutations are allegedly random (outside of programmed mutations, which is a design feature in some critters), they cannot generate the information necessary to drive particles-to-people evolution.

**Archeology illustrates the layering of the fossil record exactly as we would expect, but you guys don't want to see or believe what is.**

Since archaeology is the study of the remains/artifacts of peoples and their culture, then are you agreeing with Answers in Genesis that people have been around throughout the duration of time that the fossil layers have been laid down? Perhaps you mean that geologists illustrate your point, though the fossil record is not as "supportive" of evolution as many seem to think. In fact, creation geologists see quite well that the fossil record (layering and all) is excellent evidence for the worldwide Flood of Noah's day. Geological layers don't speak for themselves.

I encourage you to carefully consider the implications of the position you are espousing. Life has never been observed to come from nonlife; no one has ever observed millions of years of progress; no one has even observed a single-celled organism, such as a protozoa, evolve into a zebra. When you realize how bankrupt the view of molecules-to-man evolution is, consider the claims in the Bible. An encouraging passage is Jesus's statement about the joy among angels when people accept His free gift of salvation and repent:

> "Likewise, I say to you, there is joy in the presence of the angels of God over one sinner who repents" (Luke 15:10).

It doesn't matter how many steps in the wrong direction you have taken, it is only one step back to receive Christ as Lord of your life.

With kindness, God bless.

*Chapter 20*

# ℋUMANS AND DINOSAURS BURIED TOGETHER?

Letter unedited:

> You assumptions are quite inaccurate. We should have human remains with dinosaur remains, but you reject this illogically. We have human remains in the fossile recirds whenever there were other beasts with us at the time. To call out some immacualte exception to this with respect to dinosaurs is incredulous, at best.
>
> M.D., U.S.

Response:

> You assumptions are quite inaccurate. We should have human remains with dinosaur remains, but you reject this illogically.

I deny the assertion that humans and dinosaurs should be buried and fossilized together. This is actually a fallacy of denying the antecedent that says if humans and dinosaurs lived together they should be found buried together: we don't find them buried together so therefore they didn't live together. But there are other reasons that humans and dinosaurs may not be buried together.

For the sake of understanding, let's think about this logically for a moment. If there were a worldwide flood today (that is, a marine catastrophe that overtakes the land), what are the odds of the few emperor penguins that would get fossilized in Antarctica being buried with the few humans that would get fossilized around the rest of the world? Pretty slim.

If the two aren't buried together, this in no way indicates that humans and penguins didn't live at the same time. There are many possible reasons for humans and dinosaurs not to be buried together:

(1) We know that both dinosaurs and humans were vegetarian in the beginning. However, after the Fall, behaviors changed. Some dinosaurs may have developed carnivorous diets (as evidenced in

the fossil record by fossilized dinosaurs found with other animals in their stomachs), and therefore humans may have not have lived near them. Of course, there could be other reasons they didn't live near each other. But the odds would be low of being buried together if they didn't live near each other.

(2) Humans are very resourceful and may have been able to survive longer by hanging on floating debris, swimming, or other means to keep from being buried as easily as animals, which would keep their burial separate.

(3) Most people today live within about 100 miles of a coast. If the bulk of the pre-Flood population were living near coasts, then initial tsunamis would destroy and drag people out to sea. Hence, they would not be candidates for fossilization. They would be more apt to rot and decay instead of be buried and fossilized. These initial tsunamis would be one of the mechanisms to churn up the waters to more sediment rich for later burial and fossilization.

(4) Lower population would naturally reduce the possibility of humans even being found, let alone buried with dinosaurs.

(5) Given the amount of sedimentary rock, we still have a great deal to explore before we could say with any confidence that the two aren't found together. Not finding the two co-fossilized doesn't support or detract from either biblical or evolutionary viewpoints — it is not "proof" of much of anything — it only proves that at that specific time, in that specific place, under those specific conditions, the two weren't together.

**We have human remains in the fossile recirds whenever there were other beasts with us at the time.**

Perhaps some, but coelacanths, ginkgo trees, Laotian rock rat, and so on aren't buried with humans, and yet we live together today. The problem is the way you are looking at the fossil layers. Don't be afraid to question what you think (or perhaps what you were taught in school) about the fossil record: that there are no other possible (and, we would submit, more plausible) explanations.

In light of the biblical account of a worldwide Flood about 4,400 years ago, we can offer another interpretation of the physical evidence. The bulk of the fossiliferous layers are really an order of burial, not a record of millions of years. So the fossil layers often called the Jurassic, Cretaceous, and so on that contain dinosaur fossils were laid down over the course of a year about 4,400 years ago, during the lifetime of Noah.

Human fossils have been found in the layers often called the lower Pleistocene and Pliocene (which most creationists consider post-Flood, probably during the dispersion from Babel less than 4,200 years ago)![1] So looking at the layers from a biblical perspective, fossils of man and dinosaurs were formed within 200–500 years of each other!

**To call out some immacualte exception to this with respect to dinosaurs is incredulous, at best.**

I have a chapter that dives into this topic in more detail in the *New Answers Book 1*.[2] I want to encourage you to get a copy and read it. I also want to encourage you to read and trust what God says in His Word. The history in the Bible is true and explains the world, and because its history is true, the message of the gospel is also true.

In kindness.

---

1. Marvin Lubenow, *Bones of Contention* (Grand Rapids, MI: Baker Books, 1992), chapters 12 and 13.
2. Ken Ham, gen. ed., *The New Answers Book 1* (Green Forest, AR: Master Books, 2006).

*Chapter 21*

# HUMANS AND DINOSAURS...
# ANY EVIDENCE?

Letter, unedited:

**If man and Dinosaurs lived at the same time why do we not [find] evidence of it?**

**D., U.S.**

Response:

Thank you for contacting Answers in Genesis.

We do find evidence of man and dinosaurs living at the same time. First, there is the biblical evidence:

1.  Genesis 1:24–31 clearly reveals that man and dinosaurs, which are land animals, were created on the same day. Water dragons were created one day before.

2.  Job 40 discusses a creature that is most likely a sauropod type of dinosaur.

3.  Numerous passages that discuss dragons in the Old Testament. (Dragon is the old name for dinosaurs; "dinosaur" is a relatively new word that was coined in 1841. Dragons included both land- and water-dwelling reptiles.)

Second, there is ancient literature that reveals such things. For example, writings by historians such as Athanasius Kircher, John of Damascus, Beowulf, Marco Polo, Herodotus, John Gill, John Calvin, *The Golden Legend* (*Legenda Aurea*) by Jacobus de Voragine, and even a fairly modern newspaper, the *Tombstone Epitaph,* recorded the killing in 1890 of a large winged reptile whose description was similar to the pteranodon or pterodactyl!

Finally, there are petroglyphs — which are cave paintings, etchings, and the like. These are found all over the world, such as the Ishtar Gate in Babylon that was made by order of Nebuchadnezzar. It includes a dinosaur on it. There is one that looks like a dinosaur at Natural Bridges National Monument that stirred up some controversy recently. There are some creatures that look like dinosaurs on Bishop Bell's grave in Carlisle Cathedral in

Northern England. Also, there is a relief in a temple of the Ancient Khmer at Angkor, Cambodia, that has a stegosaur with other animals.[1]

We have also found dinosaur remains within 500 years of human remains. Let me explain. The vast majority of the fossil record was laid down about 4,300 years ago during the Flood of Noah. Of the small amount of Flood sediment actually sifted through (about 2 percent), many dinosaur fossils have been unearthed, particularly in the Flood layers called Triassic, Jurassic, and Cretaceous.

After the Flood, we wouldn't expect too many human fossils until the population started to re-grow and people began spreading across the earth. In fact, the Bible records that the first post-Flood death was that of Peleg about 340 years after the Flood.[2]

Early in Peleg's life, the people groups were separated at Babel, and people migrated to all parts of the globe. From this time on, we would expect people to have died in a few catastrophes or been buried along their routes of migration or in the areas where they settled. This is exactly what we do find. Human fossils (like *Homo erectus,* Neanderthals, and modern *Homo sapiens*) begin popping up in post-Flood sediments in burial forms, in caves, areas of volcanic disturbances, etc.

Some of these fossils could be from as early as the migration from Babel (100–200 years after the Flood), but others could be from a few hundred years later. Either way, at least some of these humans are within 500 years or so of the Flood, in which layers most of the dinosaur fossils were laid down.

Christians need to think biblically about dinosaurs as well as the rock layers. I still find it strange how humanists attempt to take the Flood sediment that was laid down over the course of about a year and stretch it out to millions and billions of years. Thinking biblically, though, how could dinosaurs, which are found buried in Flood sediments, have evolved into birds when birds like doves (Genesis 8:8–12) and ravens (Genesis 8:7) were aboard the ark with Noah at the same time the dinosaurs were dying? The secular position falls into shambles in light of the Bible

As for evidence of dinosaur and human coexistence after the Flood, there is plenty, and it is consistent with a biblical worldview. One just needs to do some research. God bless.

---

1. Much of the information in the last three paragraphs can be found in the book I coauthored with Laura Welch called *Dragons: Legend and Lore of Dinosaurs* (Green Forest, AR: Master Books, 2011). See also "Evidence of Dinosaurs at Angkor," Kenneth Cole, Answers in Genesis website, January 15, 2007, http://www.answersingenesis.org/articles/2007/01/15/evidence-dinosaurs-angkor.

2. Bodie Hodge, "Ancient Patriarchs in Genesis," Answers in Genesis website, January 20, 2009, http://www.answersingenesis.org/articles/2009/01/20/ancient-patriarchs-in-genesis.

## Chapter 22

# EVOLUTIONISTS AND THEIR CLAIMS

Letter, unedited:

> Crackpots are a hobby of mine, and AIG has provided me with much amusement, although most AIG fantasies are standard creationist nonsense. But there are occasional novelties. In his June 4 Feedback article, Jason Lisle asserts that "all nonbiblical worldviews are irrational". He often makes statements along these lines. He apparently believes, or pretends to believe, that, if the Bible says one thing that is true, then everything it says is true. Never mind all the childish myths, such as Genesis 1-11, all of Daniel, and so on. I say "pretends to believe" because I'm pretty sure that he isn't stupid enough to actually believe this. If he were, how could he cope with daily life? Presumably he thinks, perhaps correctly, that most of his readers are that stupid, or will pretend to be. Of course, such dishonesty is customary for creationists. But I'm not mad at Lisle. Far from it; I'm grateful to him for the laughs.
>
> Dr. C.P., U.S.

Response:

It is nice to hear from you. Please see my comments below and note they are said with sincerity and respect.

**Crackpots are a hobby of mine,**

So, do you study a number of evolutionists like Hitler, Stalin, Pol Pot, etc.?

**and AIG has provided me with much amusement,**

Such as?

**although most AIG fantasies**

And what fantasies are these?

**are standard creationist nonsense.**

Such as? Dr. P., why not send substantiation for such claims. Here are three unsubstantiated claims in a row. If you expected me to trust your arbitrary claims and mere opinions, I will not; such arbitrariness is revealing though.

> But there are occasional novelties. In his June 4 Feedback article, Jason Lisle asserts that "all nonbiblical worldviews are irrational".

This is true.[1]

> He often makes statements along these lines. He apparently believes, or pretends to believe, that, if the Bible says one thing that is true, then everything it says is true.

Dr. Lisle believes the Bible to be true, not because one thing it says is true, but because it is the Word of God, and God cannot lie (Hebrews 6:18). If it isn't true, then what makes you think truth *exists*? Truth exists because God exists and God is truth (John 14:6). If you deny God's Word, which comes with the authority of God Himself, then truth (and for that matter logic, science, morality, knowledge, etc.) would become meaningless, which would mean your email is meaningless — by your own standard.

> Never mind all the childish myths, such as Genesis 1-11,

This is *question begging epithet* fallacy. I still find it fascinating that evolutionists think Genesis is a myth (which teaches that people come from people), and all the while they proclaim that people came from rocks that came from nothing. One of these two views is demonstrated every time a child is born.

> all of Daniel, and so on.

So you must deny the existence of Nebuchadnezzar, Belshazzar, the Babylonian siege of Jerusalem, and that the city of Babylon was conquered in one night by the Medo-Persian Empire — all of which are discussed in Daniel and supported by historians.

> I say "pretends to believe" because I'm pretty sure that he isn't stupid enough to actually believe this.

---

1. See Feedback: "Testing Worldviews, the Bible and Doctrine," Dr. Jason Lisle, Answers in Genesis website, June 4, 2010, http://www.answersingenesis.org/articles/2010/06/04/feedback-testing-worldviews-bible-doctrine.

This is an *ad hominem* fallacy. Dr. Lisle is consistent in the logic previously provided. But I ask, what *basis* does the atheistic evolutionist have for logic, truth, or knowledge?

**If he were, how could he cope with daily life?**

After reading the many fallacies in your email, how do you, knowing that your (anti-biblical) worldview is irrational? The answer is simple: in your worldview you must appeal to illogical comments (e.g., *question begging epithet* fallacies and *ad hominem* fallacies) to attack the truth and those who believe it. But does this actually help? Not at all. The atheistic worldview still falls short.

**Presumably he thinks, perhaps correctly,**

So you *agree* that logic exists? That is biblical (being made in the image of a logical God), which is one of the preconditions for intelligibility. Why would you assume the Bible to be correct to argue against it? In an atheistic, evolutionary mindset, nothing immaterial exists, like logic and truth, so you have just refuted yourself.

**that most of his readers are that stupid, or will pretend to be.**

More *epithet* fallacies.

**Of course, such dishonesty is customary for creationists.**

*Au contraire*, being *honest* is a virtue from the Bible, which you *must* appeal to if you think morality exists. From an anti-Bible perspective, what makes you think morality — such as honesty — even exists? Are animals immoral when they rape or cannibalize their own kind? When dogs steal food, etc., do they apologize and give it back? No. Did famous evolutionist Hitler say "sorry" to the Jews, Poles, etc.? Did Darwin ever apologize for saying that all non-Caucasians people should be exterminated (Darwin says this in his book *The Descent of Man*)?

**But I'm not mad at Lisle.**

There is no reason to be mad, or even consider it, if you are consistent with your worldview. If an atheistic, evolutionary worldview were "true," then people would be merely chemicals reacting with each other. Would you be mad at titanium for reacting with carbon? Again, moral arguments have already been addressed by Dr. Lisle and Dr. Greg Bahnsen in their books *The Ultimate Proof of Creation* and *Always Ready*, respectively.

**Far from it; I'm grateful to him for the laughs.**

Dr. Lisle took the time to look over this and he returned the same response. But Dr. P., the issue is more than laughs and debating morality, truth, and logic. Are you saved? Do you even know what it means to be saved? I've seen far too many people attack the Bible and the character of God without knowing much about the Bible or God. To get the true big picture, I encourage you to read the Bible or perhaps start with the book *Begin* that gives you a good big picture and gets you started with selected Scriptures.[2]

With kindness in Christ.

---

2. *Begin*, compiled and edited by Ken Ham and Bodie Hodge (Green Forest, AR: Master Books, 2011).

## Chapter 23

# COLLAPSE OF THE CANOPY MODEL

Letter, unedited:

> **I know that most Creation Scientists are now shying away from teaching the "Canopy Theory." What I seem to mostly read is that they can't make a "computer model" work. 2 questions. 1. Isn't it somewhat arrogant (for lack of a better word) to think that we know all of the variables involved with something like this, and to be able to input it all into a computer? I can't help but think about something like the bumblebee, that science still says "shouldn't be able to fly," but yet there they are in my back yard. 2. The fact that 70% of the earth's surface is water helps the earth to maintain a more consistant temperature, which in turn allows us to survive here. Before the flood, most of this water was deep under ground. What mechanism (or system) do you propose to help the earth maintain it's temperatures without all that water, if not a canopy? Thank you all so much for your ministry, and keep up the good work! God Bless you.**
>
> **J.M., U.S.**

Response:

Thank you for contacting Answers in Genesis. I understand your concerns regarding the traditional canopy model, and when it comes to all the variables you are absolutely right.[1] The canopy models had some problems (for example, solar radiation would have to decrease by around 25 percent).[2] But first, let's look at some history and then biblical aspects.

---

1. This is not to be confused with canopy models that have the edge of water at or near the end of the universe (e.g., white hole cosmology), but instead the models that have water canopy in the atmosphere, e.g., like those mentioned in *The Genesis Flood* or *The World that Perished*.

2. For more on this see "Temperature Profiles for an Optimized Water Vapor Canopy" [PDF] by Dr. Larry Vardiman, a researcher on this subject for over 25 years at the time of writing that paper, ICR website, http://static.icr.org/i/pdf/technical/Temperature-Profiles-for-an-Optimized-Water-Vapor-Canopy.pdf.

## History of the model

The idea of a canopy was brought forth by respected men of God, Drs. Henry Morris and John Whitcomb. In brief, the canopy models gained popularity thanks to the work of Joseph Dillow, Dr. Larry Vardiman, and many creationists who have since researched various aspects of this scientific model. The canopy model was developed from an interpretation of the "waters above" in Genesis 1:6–7 when discussing the firmament (or expanse).

> Then God said, "Let there be a firmament [expanse] in the midst of the waters, and let it divide the waters from the waters." Thus God made the firmament [expanse], and divided the waters which were under the firmament [expanse] from the waters which were above the firmament [expanse]; and it was so (Genesis 1:6–7).

From these verses, scientific models were developed and modified to help deal with problems that arose. These models included ideas about the earth's temperature and atmospheric color, as well as oxygen concentration (to attempt to explain ancient man's longevity).

The proposed models have this canopy fading into history at the time of the Flood. Researchers thought it could have provided at least some of the water for the Flood and was associated with the "windows of heaven" mentioned along with the fountains of the great deep at the onset of the Flood (Genesis 7:11).

Currently, the pitfalls of the canopy model have grown to such an extent that most researchers have abandoned the model. Today, few believe the canopy models "as is," and there are biblical and scientific reasons for it. For example, if a canopy existed and collapsed at the time of the Flood to supply the rainfall, the latent heat of condensation would have boiled the atmosphere! And a viable canopy would not have had enough water vapor in it to sustain 40 days and nights of torrential global rain. But I prefer to begin with biblical problems.

## Biblical problems

With the Bible, there may be a much bigger issue at play: if the canopy really was part of earth's atmosphere, then all the stars, sun, and moon would have been created within the earth's atmosphere.

Why is this? A closer look at Genesis 1:14 reveals that the "waters above" may very well be much farther out — if they still exist today. The entirety of the stars, including our own sun (the greater light) and moon (lesser light) could not possibly be in our atmosphere, since they were made "in the expanse."[3]

> Then God said, "Let there be lights in the expanse of the heavens to separate the day from the night, and let them be for signs and for seasons and for days and years (Genesis 1:14; NASB).

In Genesis 1, some have made distinction between the expanse in which the birds fly (Genesis 1:20) and the expanse in which the sun, moon, and stars were placed (Genesis 1:7). This is not a distinction that is necessary from the text. From the Hebrew, the birds are said to fly "across the face of the firmament of the heavens." Looking up at a bird flying across the sky, it would be seen against the face of both the atmosphere and the space beyond the atmosphere — the "heavens." The proponents of the canopy model must make a distinction between these two expanses to support their position, but this is an arbitrary assertion that is only necessary to support the model and is not described elsewhere in Scripture.

Some have argued that the prepositions in, under, above, etc., are not in the Hebrew text but are determined from the context, so the meaning is vague. It is true that the prepositions are determined by the context, so we must rely on a proper translation of Genesis 1:14. Virtually all translations have the sun, moon, and stars being created in the expanse, not above as the canopy model would require. So we need to be careful with this. There is also another problem.

> Praise Him, you heavens of heavens, and you waters above the heavens! (Psalm 148:4).

The Psalmist wrote this in a post-Flood world in the context of other post-Flood aspects. So it appears that the windows of heaven still exist at this point (see also 2 Kings 7:2, 19 and Malachi 3:10), and this is complemented by the following verse:

---

3. The winged creatures were flying in the face of the expanse (Genesis 1:20; the NKJV accurately translates the Hebrew), and this helps reveal the extent of the expanse. It would likely include aspects of the atmosphere as well as space. The Bible calls the firmament "heaven" in Genesis 1:8, which would include some of both. Perhaps our understanding of "sky" is similar to this as well. Regardless, this does not affect the fact that the stars are in the expanse, and this means that any canopy, which is beyond the stars, is not limited to being in the atmosphere. Also, 2 Corinthians 12:2 discusses three heavens, which are likely the atmosphere (airy heavens), space (starry heavens), and the heaven of heavens (Nehemiah 9:6).

> The fountains of the deep and the windows of heaven were also stopped, and the rain from heaven was restrained (Genesis 8:2).

This verse merely points out that the two sources were stopped and restrained, not necessarily done away with. These two verses suggest that the windows of heaven remained after the Flood. The canopy model would have to explain when and how they suddenly dissipated, without any basis for this in Scripture. It makes more sense that "windows of heaven" is more of a Hebrew idiom as used elsewhere in Scripture.

Another biblical problem seems insurmountable, too. That is the issue of the being able to see the stars.

> Then God said, "Let there be lights in the firmament [expanse] of the heavens to divide the day from the night; and let them be for signs and seasons, and for days and years; and let them be for lights in the firmament [expanse] of the heavens to give light on the earth"; and it was so (Genesis 1:14–15).[4]

The stars were to be seen to give light on the earth and used to monitor seasons. If there is a vapor canopy, water, or ice canopies, be it thin or thick, then man cannot see such things in the heavens. This is a major problem.

## Scientific problems: temperatures

A canopy has a scientific issue; it would cause major problems for the regulation of earth's temperature. A canopy would trap and retain heat that would normally radiate to space. Most calculations would require the sun to have much less output, by nearly 25 percent. Otherwise, the earth would overheat. Even with variant forms of the canopy model, it is still an issue.

To answer the question about how the earth regulates its temperature without a canopy, consider that it may not have been that much different than the way it regulates it today — through the atmosphere and oceans. Although there may have been much water underground prior to the Flood, there was obviously enough at or near the surface to sustain immense amounts of sea life.

We know this because nearly 95 percent of the fossil record consists of marine organisms. Was the earth's surface around 70 percent water before the Flood? That is a question researchers still debate over. Was it more like shallow seas? It is possible. But continental and mountainous arrangements

---

4. See also Genesis 1:17.

could easily have helped regulate a global temperature and weather patterns prior to the Flood without the need of a canopy.

## Biblical models

Answers in Genesis continues to encourage research and the development of scientific models.[5] However, a good grasp of all biblical passages that are relevant to the topic must precede the scientific research and model. The canopy model may have a glimmer of hope still remaining, and I will leave that to the researchers, but both the biblical and scientific difficulties need to be addressed thoroughly.

I pray this helps clarify. God bless.

---

5. There is an expanded chapter by Bodie Hodge on this subject in the *The New Answers Book 4* (Green Forest, AR: Master Books, 2013).

*Chapter 24*

# LISTEN TO THE ROCKS?

Letter, unedited:

> **Ref Feedback: So Old You Can See It**
>
> **I cant speak for creationists, but Im sure I speak for scientifically-minded Christians when I say that, yes, we do groan when you publish well-meaning but inaccurate emails. Of course the main problem is that you rarely, if ever, publish accurate emails.**
>
> **For example, I could draw your attention to the rock formations at Siccar Point in Scotland, which inspired James Hutton. These conclusively show, along with thousands of other features on every continent, that the worldwide flood theory is false.**
>
> **I could further point out that geologists had established that the Earth is millions of years old before Darwin published his theory, and long before radioactivity was discovered. However, if I did that, you wouldnt publish my email.**
>
> **D.E., England**

Response:

Thanks for writing. Please note that my comments below are said in kindness.

> **I cant speak for creationists, but Im sure I speak for scientifically-minded Christians**

Why do you assume that creationists are not scientifically minded Christians? As a scientifically minded Christian who developed a new method of production of submicron titanium diboride, I am a Christian and a creationist. I believe in Jesus Christ as my Lord and Savior. Such are not mutually exclusive (this is a false dichotomy).

And further, who are you to elevate yourself above other "scientifically minded Christians" to speak for them? Essentially, you have appealed to yourself as an authority over these others. What makes you think you are greater than these others?

**when I say that, yes, we do groan when you publish well-meaning but inaccurate emails.**

Sadly, these are representative of real emails that we get, and many do show a lack of knowledge, civility, etc., of many who argue against a biblical position. Considering the tens of thousands of emails we get a year, imagine the number of these emails we get and have to groan over when reading them.

**Of course the main problem is that you rarely, if ever, publish accurate emails.**

Such as this one? Consider the false dichotomy (stated already) that creationists cannot equal scientifically minded Christians as well as the fallacies below. Consider also the implication that we are *dishonest* in what we choose to publish as not being representative of our email pool.

**For example, I could draw your attention to the rock formations at Siccar Point in Scotland, which inspired James Hutton. These conclusively show,**

This is the fallacy of personification. Rock formations do not "conclude and show," nor do they "refute" (i.e., they cannot think). This is falsely applying human-like attributes to something inanimate. From a logical perspective, this is absurd and fallacious.

James Hutton mistakenly interpreted these formations as evidence of long ages. However, others, such as creationists, have interpreted them from a different perspective — the Flood — in light of what God says on the subject in Genesis 6–8, and they are a good confirmation of what we expect from a global Flood. Such rock layers were formed, deformed, tilted, and eroded, and more sediment came and covered them. Such can easily be explained by the catastrophic Flood without appealing to millions of years of slow processes.

Keep in mind that not a single experiment has been run over the course of these alleged "millions of years." But there are observable scientific examples of rapidly formed rock layers and sedimentation, rapid rock cementation, rapid canyon formation, etc. within short periods of time such as the event at Mount St. Helens. That event shows how catastrophes can shape the geology of an area quickly.

So this becomes a question of authority — is a fallible, sinful James Hutton's interpretation correct, or is a perfect, infallible God wrong about a global Flood? To anyone claiming to be a Christian, there should be no question — God is correct about a worldwide Flood.

**along with thousands of other features on every continent,**

This is an elephant hurl — another logical fallacy. I could make the same statement about thousands of other features as evidence *of* a global Flood. But the fact remains: the evidence isn't the issue; it is the *interpretation* of the evidence that matters.

**that the worldwide flood theory is false.**

Let me get this straight: as one who claimed above to be a Christian, are you really saying that God was in error here? He's the one who said it was worldwide in His own inspired Word. Look for yourself:

> And the waters prevailed exceedingly on the earth, and all the high hills under the whole heaven were covered. The waters prevailed fifteen cubits upward, and the mountains were covered (Genesis 7:19–20).

So this cannot be a local flood. The Bible says in Hebrews 6:18 that it is impossible for Him to lie. Paul says:

> Certainly not! Indeed, let God be true but every man a liar. As it is written: "That You may be justified in Your words, and may overcome when You are judged" (Romans 3:4).

**I could further point out that geologists had established that the Earth is millions of years old before Darwin published his theory, and long before radioactivity was discovered. However, if I did that, you wouldnt publish my email.**

How do you *know* for an absolute fact that it is that age? Were you there — did you observe it? In fact, I like the way God says it:

> "Who is this who darkens counsel by words without knowledge? Now prepare yourself like a man; I will question you, and you shall answer Me. Where were you when I laid the foundations of the earth? Tell Me, if you have understanding. Who determined its measurements? Surely you know! Or who stretched the line

upon it? To what were its foundations fastened? Or who laid its cornerstone?" (Job 38:2–6).

In fact, God continues to put Job in his place. And we should be no different. We certainly agree that many secular geologists *believed* the earth was millions of years old long before Darwin and his ideas (such as Lyell), and long before Arthur Holmes used radiometric dating in 1916. In fact, we have published this on our website, in books, and in other resources. But who are these people to claim to be greater than God on this subject?

"You shall have no other gods before Me" (Exodus 20:3).

I really want to encourage you to trust God's Word over the fallible, sinful ideas of man. God was there, He eyewitnessed what He did, cannot lie, and knows all things. Why not trust Him? In Christ.

## Chapter 25

# SAVED BY GRACE... AND EVOLUTION?

Letter, unedited:

> I am a Christian, and so I do not mislead you I disagree scientifically with your beliefs. However, I don't care if you think the earth is a few thousand years old. I don't care if you reject evolution. We are both saved by the grace of God. However, I cannot help but feel that this movement is based on one giant sin. It is clear, very clear, especially in Paul's epistles, that the entire purpose of the Church is to spread the word, to bring people to God, to give Him glory. First, who gets glory out of this grand theory? Not God. No, rejecting evolution does not give glory to God, because evolution IS COMPATIBLE with God, even if you believe it to be wrong. Secondly, I am witnessing to people in pain, people who NEED Christ, but these people are thinkers, and they have been presented the face of Christianity that YOU PRESENT. They are disgusted! Why should we be hindering the spread of the Gospel over a LESS THAN FUNDAMENTAL TRUTH? Teach God's love, the cross, mercy- those are TRUE
>
> K.N., U.S.

Response:

> **I am a Christian, and so I do not mislead you I disagree scientifically with your beliefs.**

Thanks for being upfront about your belief system (i.e., theistic evolution as can be determined in your email). Please see my comments done by point-by-point style below. I pray this response will help you realize the importance of accepting *all* of God's Word — including the Book of Genesis. My comments are said with sincerity.

> **However, I don't care if you think the earth is a few thousand years old. I don't care if you reject evolution.**

Then why send the email if you don't care?

**We are both saved by the grace of God.**

Of course we are both saved if we've called upon Christ in the Bible to be our Savior.[1] But what are you saved from? I assume you would say "sin." But what is sin? The Book of Genesis provides the definition: disobedience to God's commands. A literal man (Adam) disobeyed a literal command of God (Genesis 2:15–17) and suffered the consequences (Genesis 3). And we all sin, too, because we all sinned in Adam and continue to sin.

Within the evolutionary, millions-of-years paradigm, there is no Adam and thus no first sin. Death is not the punishment for sin (contrary to Genesis 3:19) but has existed for millions of years. In this scenario, why do you need Christ to save you from sin and death, as that would be a natural part of creation? Such a position undermines the gospel. Even atheists understand this point:

> Christianity has fought, still fights, and will continue to fight science to the desperate end over evolution, because evolution destroys utterly and finally the very reason Jesus' earthly life was supposedly made necessary. Destroy Adam and Eve and the original sin, and in the rubble you will find the sorry remains of the Son of God. If Jesus was not the redeemer who died for our sins, and this is what evolution means, then Christianity is nothing.[2]

**However, I cannot help but feel that this movement is based on one giant sin.**

Feelings are not the measure of truth or the standard that determines what sin is. God's Word is.

**It is clear, very clear, especially in Paul's epistles, that the entire purpose of the Church**

But these three purposes mentioned below do not comprise the entire purpose of the Church. I suggest a search for the word "church" in the Bible to give you an idea of a few other important roles. For example, the Church is to pray (Acts 12:5) and settle disputes (Matthew 18:17; 1 Corinthians 6:4).

**is to spread the word,**

---

1. Note that if someone refers to a Christ other than He who is described in the Bible, then it is a false Christ and a false gospel, and they would not be saved. A false Christ cannot save you.

2. G. Richard Bozarth, "The Meaning of Evolution," *American Atheist* (September 20, 1979): p. 30.

Why spread the Word if you don't even believe it in the first place?

Since you brought up Paul, then consider that he used a creation-evangelism message when he preached on Mars Hill (Acts 17:22–31). The concept isn't original to us: we follow his example and spread God's Word and the good news of Jesus Christ beginning in Genesis. If you are familiar with the Creation Museum, you know that the whole experience culminates in presenting the glorious gospel of Jesus Christ. Christ first (the Creator — Colossians 1:16); Christ last and throughout (Savior, Ruler, and Sustainer of His creation).

A theistic evolutionist has no choice but to reject the plain teachings in Genesis 1–11, as these chapters clearly stand opposed to molecules-to-man evolution. When Genesis 1–11 is deemed myth or allegorized, what happens? In addition to there being no basis for the gospel, there is also no basis for clothing (Genesis 3), for death being an enemy (Genesis 3; 1 Corinthians 15:26), for marriage (Genesis 1–2; Matthew 19:4–5), and so on.

If we are being chastised for preaching the Word in Genesis and not going along with the world when it rejects Genesis, well then, thanks for the compliment! We would rather trust what God said He did and encourage others to do the same.

### to bring people to God,

One thing should be noted — we don't bring people to the Lord. In fact, no human does. We provide witness, testimonies, and answers, but only the Spirit can convict and regenerate the sinner (1 Corinthians 12:3; Romans 10:17). We are working to help people come to know the Lord, but it is the work of the Lord that really saves.

So there is a difference: we can't force people into believing (John 6:44). The gospel is the primary reason for why we minister as we do. And we have seen many people come to Christ because they discover that the Bible can be trusted from the very first verse.

### to give Him glory.

Our hope is to always give glory to God in all that we do. We would not do what we do if that weren't our goal. But what about the other goals of the Church — and there are too many to list — but one is to teach people to believe what is set forth in the Bible . . . every thought included (Matthew 28:20; 2 Corinthians 10:5).

**First, who gets glory out of this grand theory? Not God.**

I take it that this "grand theory" that you are referring to is biblical creation (God created supernaturally, made man from dust, made woman from man, made a "very good" world without death or suffering; man sins, and death and suffering enter the creation [hence we need a Savior]; a worldwide Flood destroys the wicked, and Noah, his wife, and his three sons and their wives were saved on an ark to repopulate the earth, etc.). Such teachings simply come from Genesis, God's Word. This is not a theory; this is what God said happened, an eyewitness account. Who is anyone to question what God said and put their trust in imperfect human speculations about the past?

Certainly there are creationist models that we base on the biblical *account*, such as catastrophic plate tectonics, but you'll notice that we don't take a firm stance on any model — even creationist ones. The only thing we stand on is the *account* (not theory) of Genesis 1–11, and the authority of Scripture as a whole. How can teaching others to trust God's Word *not* be honoring to Him and bring Him glory?

**No, rejecting evolution does not give glory to God,**

Perhaps I don't follow your logic: telling people that God was wrong in Genesis somehow gives God glory, but telling people that God is correct in Genesis doesn't give Him glory? This is illogical. David presented this psalm:

> Declare His glory among the nations, His wonders among all peoples (1 Chronicles 16:24).

Declaring God's glory and His marvelous deeds doesn't entail pretending God did something other than what He recorded in Genesis. God is correct in all things that He speaks, including origins. In fact, throughout the psalms David worshiped God and gave Him glory specifically because of His deeds of creation (as Job did).

**because evolution IS COMPATIBLE with God,**

Which "god" are you referring to here? The God of the Bible, who says what He did in Genesis, openly disagrees with molecules-to-man evolution. A god of a millions-of-years-old earth is a god of death, not the God of life and God of love that Scripture teaches. Applying attributes of such a false god to the God of the Bible demeans the character and nature of God. It would also mean that an all-good, all-powerful, truthful God deceived Israelites and Christians, who loved and trusted Him for thousands of years, all the while waiting for *atheists* to "interpret" Genesis properly for us. It is better to trust God than men (Psalm 118:8).

I understand that you, like most of us who work in ministry, have been taught evolution, whether in public schools or the media. But holding it in such high regard over the Word of God is not good theology. The false belief system of evolution that has been promoted for 150 years has subtly crept into many Christians' thinking, and it is time to get back to God's Word and not be deceived. God's Word is sufficient.

In these past 150 years, many once-Christian universities have become atheistic upon the acceptance of evolution. Public schools have become atheistic upon acceptance of evolution, with prayer, the Ten Commandments, and the Bible removed from the classroom. Nations that were largely Christian have become largely atheistic upon acceptance of evolution (England, for example). Evolution was a driving force in the actions of Hitler, Stalin, and other mass murderers. After such a history, what would possibly make someone think that evolution provides a foundation to lead people to Christ?

**even if you believe it to be wrong.**

It is not a matter of what I believe, but a matter of what God says.

**Secondly, I am witnessing to people in pain, people who NEED Christ,**

As do we. And we have many resources on the subject to give people answers. In an evolutionary perspective, death, pain, and suffering existed long before man, was a tool God used, and was something God would have called "very good" (if one allegorizes Genesis): so God would be responsible for it or perhaps powerless to do anything about it in a theistic evolutionary view. So why are you spending time dealing with people in pain if pain, suffering, and death are good from your perspective?

However, in Genesis 3, we find that man's sin is responsible for death entering the creation (Genesis 3; Romans 5:12). God is not to blame but man's actions are. Death (and all that accompanies it — pain, suffering, disease, sickness, cancer, tears, heartbreak) is an *intrusion* into God's creation; death is described as an enemy (1 Corinthians 15:26) that will be removed (Revelation 21:4).

This is all the more reason to realize that Jesus came to save us from the problem we, as mankind, caused in the first place. The beautiful hope is that through receiving the free gift of eternal life provided for by the death and Resurrection of Jesus Christ (our Creator!), we can look forward to a time when the Curse God placed on His creation (Genesis 3; Romans 8:18–21) is no more. To a time when there will be no more pain, tears, heartbreak, or death (Revelation 21:1–5, 22:3), as it was in the beginning.

If Genesis isn't true, then what answers can you give them for people's pain? "That's the way God created things"? "Pain is a part of the process that God used to bring about His creation"? "Death is a very natural and good part of God's creation"? "Tears are part of the evolutionary process as we struggle to survive in this dog-eat-dog world that God created"? If you're consistent with the "millions of years" mindset, this is what you *must* say to them. How sad and hurtful.

**but these people are thinkers,**

What do you mean by "thinkers"? As opposed to our scientists and those with advanced degrees? Or general creationists, which, statistically speaking, run the gamut of intellectual prowess, as any subset of society does? The Bible says all the treasures of wisdom and knowledge are in Christ (Colossians 2:2–3). Jesus quoted Genesis 1 and Genesis 2 when explaining the basis of marriage (Mathew 19 and Mark 10). Jesus pointed out that marriage between a male and female has been around since the *beginning* of creation. This is obviously in contradiction with theistic evolution that doesn't have man on the scene until billions of years after "the beginning." Have these "thinkers" thought through that?

**and they have been presented the face of Christianity that YOU PRESENT.**

So they've been presented with the biblical view that an all-good God made everything "very good" (Genesis 1:3; Deuteronomy 32:4) and justly cursed His creation as He said He would because of man's sin (Genesis 3), which caused death and suffering to come into the world (Genesis 2:17; Genesis 3; 1 Corinthians 15:21–22). And that a loving Savior stepped into history to save us from that sin, death, and suffering (John 3:16; Revelation 21:4). Good. This is the gospel.

**They are disgusted!**

What face of Christianity would they like, then? One that isn't real? One with a sadistic, sloppy god who uses the process that kills the undesirables, helpless, old, and feeble? And what of those who have been presented with theistic evolution who have thereafter left the Church? Compromising the Word of God to try to win the unsaved is a dangerous way to go. They are being sold, not converted, by tickling ears (2 Timothy 4:3). Paul became all things to all people, but he did not give up his foundation, rooted in the Old Testament.

Why would they be disgusted with a perfect God who loves us enough to take the punishment we deserve upon Himself and who offers a free gift of salvation? One reason they are disgusted may be because the gospel doesn't "fit" with their current preconceived belief system. They are challenged. They would have to repent and change their beliefs and possibly their way of life. Although they may believe they would be committing intellectual suicide, that simply is not so. Paul often encountered people who also didn't like biblical teachings, but he didn't water down or change his message. For example, he didn't tell the Greeks to just add Christ to the multitudes of mythological gods they already worshiped. On the contrary, Paul said:

> We destroy arguments and every lofty opinion raised against the knowledge of God, and take every thought captive to obey Christ, being ready to punish every disobedience, when your obedience is complete (2 Corinthians 10:5–6; ESV).

### Why should we be hindering the spread of the Gospel over a LESS THAN FUNDAMENTAL TRUTH?

You have it the wrong way around. You are telling people that God is wrong in Genesis and that God is a god of death with tumors, carnivory, thorns, pain, and suffering in the fossil record, and then you try to tell people that God is love? This is inconsistent within itself, and certainly with Scripture, and is, in fact, hindering the gospel, since billions-of-years thinking is a stumbling block for many.

You completely remove the foundation for the gospel and want people to believe it anyway. If a builder came to me and tried to get me to buy a house, and I asked, "What foundation does the house have, brick or block?" How do you think I would react if the builder said: "Neither, I'll build it on sand on the beach for you." This is essentially the warning that Jesus gave in the parable of the man building a house on shifting sand. If we don't put our trust in God's Word — all of it — what basis do we have for our belief? Man's ideas about the past are shifting sand. They have changed. God's Word has not. And as the Church has moved with the shifting sand, it has lost its credibility. That is a face of Christianity that is harmful.

The foundation for the gospel is Genesis. The good news of Jesus Christ goes back to the bad news in Genesis. This is why Paul, when discussing the gospel, relates Christ as the Last Adam, comparing Him to the first Adam in Genesis:

> And so it is written, "The first man Adam became a living being." The last Adam became a life-giving spirit (1 Corinthians 15:45).

This is why Paul relates the doctrine of the sin-death relationship back to the first man in Genesis:

> Therefore, just as through one man sin entered the world, and death through sin, and thus death spread to all men, because all sinned (Romans 5:12).

### Teach God's love, the cross, mercy- those are TRUE

Yes, those are. But are you saying that the rest of God's Word isn't true or worthwhile? God is the truth (John 14:6), and His Word is truth (John 17:17). If you really love God, then love His Word. When you love His Word, then you have a basis for the Cross and for mercy. God mercifully offers us what we don't deserve: salvation through His Son Jesus Christ, the perfect sacrifice for sin, and the hope that our bodies will be glorified and curse-free in the future.

What basis do you use for deciding which part is to be read as is and which part is to be glossed over? If that is what you teach others, I would expect them to *further* question the parts that *you* say are essential. For example, why believe in the virginal conception? Or the sinless life of Christ? Or His Resurrection? After all, any "thinking" person knows these things can't happen. And down the slippery slope we continue.

There is no need to combine the false religion of evolution with God's Word. Was Aaron praised for making a calf that was intended to represent the true God? Did Paul allow the early Church to enforce the Hebrew practice of circumcision? Were the Israelites praised for worshiping Baal rather than or even in addition to God? I see the same relationship here. You are holding on to the false religion of our day (molecules-to-man evolution), and then you are disbelieving or trying to add to what God says in Genesis. It is time to return to the authority of the Word of God:

Professing to be wise, they became fools, and changed the glory of the incorruptible God into an image made like corruptible man — and birds and four-footed animals and creeping things. Therefore God also gave them up to uncleanness, in the lusts of their hearts, to dishonor their bodies among themselves, who exchanged the truth of God for the lie, and worshiped and served the creature rather than the Creator, who is blessed forever. Amen (Romans 1:22–25).

In kindness in Christ.

*Chapter 26*

# A GOOD DAY RUINED?

Letter, unedited:

> Wow . . . Just when I got that really happy feeling because I'm
> done with work . . . I saw you website and [got sick]. The fact
> that you would call someone a creation scientist is ridiculous to
> say the least. What science are you doing? Where do you publish
> your works? How often are your results put up against an un-
> biased peer-review board? And how in, dare i say, "god's name"
> do you get off at brainwashing children to believe your supersti-
> tious, astrological, irrational, primitive belief systems? Just when
> I thought I was having a good day. Get educated and EVOLVE!

> K., U.S.

Response:

Thank you for contacting Answers in Genesis. I was saddened to read
your email, as there is really no argument but merely attacks to degrade. I
pray this response will help you realize that such an attack has no merit, and
that these types of questions can easily be answered. My hope is that you will
take them to heart and realize the error of the humanistic worldview. This
response is intended with sincerity and kindness.

> Wow . . . Just when I got that really happy feeling because I'm
> done with work . . . I saw you website and [got sick]. The fact
> that you would call someone a creation scientist is ridiculous to
> say the least.

Why is it ridiculous? Most fields of science were developed by creation-be-
lieving scientists of the past, such as Isaac Newton, Gregor Mendel, Louis
Pasteur, and many others. They realized that an orderly God would create
an orderly universe that made repeatable scientific testing possible. In fact,
Francis Bacon, a creationist, developed the scientific method based on the
idea of a God-made universe. But why, in a big bang, no-God, universe,
would things be orderly?

### What science are you doing?

Real science, unlike molecules-to-man evolution, which cannot be repeated or observed; for example, friends of ours have invented the MRI (Dr. Raymond Damadian) and the gene gun (Dr. John Sanford). Evolution, on the other hand, is far from scientific:

1. No one has been able to make life from nonlife (matter giving rise to life, which is foundational to molecules-to-man evolution).

2. No one has been able to change a single-celled life form like an amoeba into a cow or goat.

3. No one has been able to repeat the big bang (which is foundational to molecules-to-man evolution).

4. We haven't observed billions of new information-gaining mutations required to build the DNA strand and give rise to new kinds of life forms.

5. Matter has never been observed to give rise to new information.

6. No one has observed millions of years of time progressing.

7. No one has found the billions of transitional fossils needed to help show the changes of one kind into another.

This isn't to say that non-Christians can't do science, but they are assuming the truthfulness of the Bible, perhaps even inadvertently, to do science. And, of course, it's silly to assume that all science is hinged to evolution. Data collection and analysis have nothing to do with origins and the inherent presuppositions of origins science.

### Where do you publish your works?

With kindness, apparently you did not spend much time researching before asking such a question. We publish peer-reviewed, technical papers (*Answers Research Journal*), peer-reviewed, semi-technical articles (*Answers In-Depth*), and, naturally, peer-reviewed lay articles in *Answers* magazine and the website.

But beyond Answers in Genesis, there are other places for technical discussion, such as the International Conference on Creationism, the *CRS Quarterly*, and many others. But many creation scientists have also published in secular journals — even I have.

### How often are your results put up against an unbiased peer-review board?

If there were such a thing as unbiased, this would surely be an option. However, if you possibly think *Science, Nature,* and so on are unbiased, you have not done your research. These journals are obviously pushing for the religion of humanism. All review boards are biased because all review boards are made up of human beings.

All the papers in *Answers Research Journal,* for example, go through a gauntlet of reviewers, most of whom are biased by their belief in the God of the Bible. We certainly don't hide that. And many creation scientists *have* published in secular journals on non-origins-related topics. But secular journals refuse to allow any research that does not affirm naturalistic explanations. It is common to find articles supporting tenets of the Humanist Manifestos and authors and editors who have signed the Humanist Manifestos within their pages. Since biblical creationists do not accept naturalistic explanations, it seems absurd to think that they would write as if they did — just to be published.

**And how in, dare i say, "god's name"**

Your saying this is fascinating and confirms two things. First, Romans 1 reveals that everyone knows God exists based on your letter, why not say in the name of Darwin, evolution, or mother nature, etc.?

Why is this important? Because man realizes that deep down there is a God, and He is the highest authority. In light of this, I want to ask you to reconsider the evolutionary ideas that you may not realize have been forced on you from a very early age. Note J. Dunphy's words in the early 1980s:

> I am convinced that the battle for humankind's future must be waged and won in the public school classroom by teachers who correctly perceive their role as the proselytizers of a new faith: a religion of humanity that recognizes and respects the spark of what theologians call divinity in every human being. These teachers must embody the same selfless dedication as the most rabid fundamentalist preachers, for they will be ministers of another sort, utilizing a classroom instead of a pulpit to convey humanist values in whatever subject they teach, regardless of the educational level — preschool day care or large state university. The classroom must and will become an arena of conflict between the old and the new — the rotting corpse of Christianity, together with all its adjacent evils and misery, and the new faith of humanism.[1]

---

1. J. Dunphy, "A Religion for a New Age," *The Humanist* (January–February 1983): p. 23, 26.

Please consider this and reevaluate the atheistic ideas that were forced on you by humanists who still hold you captive to their false philosophy.

### do you get off at brainwashing children to believe your superstitious,

This is called projection — ironic, when humanists have been teaching their superstitions, such as asserting that single-celled organisms became dinosaurs and then chickens over millions of years, that truth doesn't exist, that people are animals, etc. I doubt you've questioned their dogma. We do not want anyone who reads our materials to be brainwashed or to unquestioningly accept what *we* say. God doesn't really need our help or for people to be brainwashed to believe in Him. It's the opposite: one has to be brainwashed to *not* believe (Romans 1:20–25). We simply point to what the Bible teaches and do our best to understand the world in light of what God says in His Word. Beyond that, children and adults should search the Scripture (which the Creator Himself is responsible for) for themselves to see if what we say lines up.

### astrological,

Perhaps there is some confusion here; we are not astrologers and would join in arguing against this religion. Astrology is the belief that stars and other heavenly bodies can reveal the future. The Bible condemns such practice.

### irrational,

How are we irrational? Besides, rationality comes from a biblical worldview. How can the materialistic evolutionist have a basis for the immaterial, such as logic and truth, in the first place? In fact, they borrow from a biblical worldview when they even try to use logic.

### primitive belief systems?

What do you mean by "primitive"? The Christian worldview has a basis for logic, truth, happiness, love, arts, and science. It also explains how death and suffering are an intrusion into God's originally perfect creation due to sin in Adam, and, mercifully, that God offers salvation and restoration through Christ. But what does an evolutionary worldview have to offer? The humanist religion teaches that you are rearranged pond scum, that lying and murder are neither right nor wrong, that we are likely headed for extinction, that life has no real meaning, and it gives a flawed basis for logic, truth, happiness, science, etc.

**Just when I thought I was having a good day.**

What do you mean by "good"? This is a Christian concept where God determines what is good. In an evolutionary worldview, there is no such thing as "good." But since you really seem to want goodness and happiness to exist (and I encourage this), then I suggest you find out more about God.

**Get educated and EVOLVE!**

Well, the use of "evolve" here is actually correct, but I would like to return this statement back to you in kindness. You have made several unresearched and incorrect statements and assume that we are ignorant simply because we do not share your false presuppositions and beliefs about how the world came to be and the origin of life. Most of those working at Answers in Genesis have college degrees — and many have advanced ones and from secular institutions. But true education starts with the right foundation — Jesus Christ (Colossians 2:3).

As a person made in the image of God, you can do so much better than simply believing you are an animal who has nothing to offer but ridicule. In fact, Jesus Christ, the Son of God, cared enough to step into history to die on a Cross for people like you and me — who deserve the death He died for us. So please take this to heart and reconsider the work of Christ, starting in Genesis.

## Chapter 27

# THE LIMITS OF SCIENCE

Letter, unedited:

> In response to "Dinosaurs and the Bible"
>
> I do not intend this as an attack on any of you, I simply wish to comment on many of the flawed accusations you throw at "evolutionary scientists" Evolution is not a belief . . . it is a fact. Religion is a belief. While good science offers us a way to study the natural world and our surroundings in an objective imperical way. . . religion is a great partner (not alternative) to explaining our lives spiritually. There is no need to attack evolution as false when the most well acclaimed scientists and associations such as the National Academy of Science is doing nothing to dismantle the foundations of religion. And the reason for that is because science is not able to enter the realm of the meta-physical and anyone who says they can is not practicing science. There is no conflict between science and religion. period. I would appreciate that you read more literature and get your information from less biased sources. Science will never be able to explain empirically religion. And on the other foot religion is not science and creationism is not science because it is not based on scientific fact. If you do not "believe" in evolution you should do some research on anti-biotic resistence and let me know how to explain what happens. I won't hold my breath.
>
> F.E.

Response:

With kindness, please see my comments below.

> I do not intend this as an attack on any of you, I simply wish to comment on many of the flawed accusations you throw at "evolutionary scientists"

Such as? What accusations are you referring to and where are the references?

**Evolution is not a belief . . . it is a fact. Religion is a belief.**

Considering that evolution is a subset of the religion of humanism, as clearly outlined in Humanist Manifestos, this puts you in a predicament. How can evolution be a belief and not a belief at the same time and reference? This violates basic logic and is a contradiction. But more importantly, your definitions are skewed. *Religion* is a system of practices based on beliefs about the world and the past. *Evolution* is a framework about the past that can never be repeated or tested and must be accepted by interpretation and authority. That is, by all measures, a belief.

It also seems that you labor under the misconception that beliefs cannot be facts. So if someone believes that computers exist, does that negate the existence of computers being a fact? Who determines what is "factual" and what is not? If something violates the laws of nature that we know, but is accepted by most people, does that make it factual or not? (Evolutionary belief violates some basic laws of nature.) Christians accept fact because they believe in an objective Creator who does not lie. Where, then, does the humanist find a basis for fact?

**While good science offers us a way to study the natural world and our surroundings**

Creationists agree here, and this methodology was developed by a creationist named Francis Bacon. But note that good science is observable and repeatable — unlike evolution and its historical postulates.

**in an objective imperical way**

But for objectiveness to be valid requires a correct worldview with which to interpret empirical facts. There are two worldviews competing here. Science is a useful tool for examining the universe, but humans are not objective. We all have basic foundational concepts through which we interpret evidence — some starting with the Bible and some assuming naturalism. Few realize that the evolutionary/humanistic worldview must borrow from the biblical worldview to even begin its case. So this undermines an evolutionary position right from the start.

Also empiricism (that all truth claims must be obtained by experience), is self-refuting, as that alleged truth claim cannot be experienced! In other words, empiricism can never be proven empirically.

**. . . religion is a great partner (not alternative) to explaining our lives spiritually.**

Creationists would agree as well, as correct religion is foundational to looking at any aspect of the world around us. Your argument here is self-refuting. That is, you define *science* naturalistically and then claim that naturalism and supernaturalism (religion) are partners. This is impossible, as naturalism does not allow supernatural beings or causes and supernaturalism requires them. On the other hand, science (as in observational science) is truly a partner in understanding the world — when we begin with God's Word, since science is predicated on Christianity. So for good science to even be a possibility is further confirmation of the truth of the Bible.

**There is no need to attack evolution as false**

But it *is* false. It contradicts Scripture in Genesis and Christ Himself and leads many astray from the truth of Scripture:

> "But from the beginning of the creation, God 'made them male and female' " (Mark 10:6).

See also Genesis 1 and Exodus 20:11. Also, Christians are commanded to demolish these false arguments:

> We destroy arguments and every lofty opinion raised against the knowledge of God, and take every thought captive to obey Christ, (2 Corinthians 10:5; ESV).

Third, we are warned not to succumb to such false beliefs:

> Beware lest anyone cheat you through philosophy and empty deceit, according to the tradition of men, according to the basic principles of the world, and not according to Christ (Colossians 2:8).

**when the most well acclaimed scientists and associations such as the National Academy of Science is doing nothing to dismantle the foundations of religion.**

First, this is the fallacy of appeal to majority. The majority of Germans during WWII either allowed or participated in the persecution of the Jews — but that doesn't make it right.

Second, the NAS has aligned itself with the religion of humanism and has a history of attacking the truthfulness of the Bible. Through numerous articles and publications they promote the religion of secular humanism and naturalistic philosophies that deny the power of God. This is hardly "nothing." In addition, the president of the NAS openly recommends a leading humanist organization called the NCSE.[1]

> **And the reason for that is because science is not able to enter the realm of the meta-physical and anyone who says they can is not practicing science.**

And yet, evolutionists claim to transcend the metaphysical millions of years in the past to know for a "fact" what happened? This means evolutionists are not practicing science according to their claimed worldview. Scientific methodology cannot repeat the past. Evolutionary thinking is unrepeatable historical science, not operational science.

Let's face it: there has never been a single experiment run over millions of years — not even one — nor is it possible. Where is the science here? And scientists look for "God spots" on the brain and alternate universes to explain away how finely tuned our universe is, and the "evolutionary history" of religion. All of these are attempts to explain the metaphysical aspects of the universe (poorly) using naturalistic assumptions.

> **There is no conflict between science and religion. period.**

You would be surprised to know that we agree, but I suggest you have tried to use a bait-and-switch fallacy here by calling science "evolution." This common mistake is equivocating on the word "science" to mean the worldview of naturalism that includes evolution. Evolution is not science in any observable or repeatable means (called "operational" or "experimental" or "observable" science). We all have the same observable and repeatable science. The difference is the worldview by which we interpret scientific facts.

> **I would appreciate that you read more literature and get your information from less biased sources.**

This is the pretended neutrality fallacy. You are assuming that you and other humanists are less biased, i.e., neutral, all the while trying to argue for the evolutionary worldview. By "less biased," do you mean scientific sources that agree with naturalism? We do, in fact, get a great deal of our news and information from mainstream journals and media sources. One of our goals is to reveal that there is no neutrality and that there are underlying assumptions upon which such papers and articles are written.

---

1. nasonline.org/site/PageServer?pagename=NEWS_letter_president_03042005_BA_evolution.

"He who is not with Me is against Me, and he who does not gather with Me scatters" (Luke 11:23).

God makes it clear in His Word there is no such thing as neutrality. You are either for Christ or against Him. I want to encourage you to reconsider the claims of Christ and what it means to be saved (see appendix 4).

**Science will never be able to explain empirically religion.**

Science doesn't explain things; this is the fallacy of reification. Science is a methodology to determine observable and repeatable facts and is predicated on biblical Christianity. In other words, it would be impossible to do science without the Bible being true.

**And on the other foot religion is not science**

With this statement, you have no choice but to agree that interrelated religions like humanism, naturalism, and evolutionism are not science. Additionally, belief in the One true God of the Bible who is logical and cannot lie means that scientific inquiry makes sense. Science is possible because the universe exhibits uniformity. There is no reason to divorce exploring the world around us from the eyewitness account of the Creator and Sustainer of all things.

**and creationism is not science because it is not based on scientific fact.**

Science in its strictest sense means knowledge. Creation and evolution have little to do with scientific facts because we all have the same scientific facts! Creation and evolution are both subsets of religions: biblical Christianity and secular humanism, respectively. The worldview of biblical Christianity, from which creation comes, is the same worldview by which science is possible. I suspect that what you mean is that creation science is not based on naturalistic assumptions about how the universe and life came to be. In that case, you're correct. Facts are not in debate.

**If you do not "believe" in evolution you should do some research on anti-biotic resistence and let me know how to explain what happens. I won't hold my breath.**

Perhaps if you did some research, you'd see that we've shown how antibiotic resistance fails the test as evidence for evolution (see "Antibiotic Resistance of Bacteria: An Example of Evolution in Action?"[2] and "Is Natural Selection the Same Thing as Evolution?"[3]). Here's an example: how is *H. pylori* changing into defective *H. pylori* support for the general theory of evolution? First, the resistance is moving in the wrong direction for evolution (losses), and second, changing these bacteria into the same bacteria is not evolution!

I want to encourage you to reconsider your faith in the evolutionary worldview. That philosophy is a dead end logically, morally, scientifically, and obviously religiously. I encourage you to reconsider the claims of the Bible, particularly Christ, because that is what it is all about — we are all sinners and all have fallen short — even me. But by the grace of God, Jesus Christ, the infinite Son of God, took the infinite punishment from an infinite God, to make a way of salvation. Jesus is calling all people everywhere to repent. "The Lord is not slack concerning His promise, as some count slackness, but is longsuffering toward us, not willing that any should perish but that all should come to repentance" (2 Peter 3:9). It doesn't matter how many steps you've taken in the wrong direction, it is only one step back.

With kindness in Christ.

2. Dr. Georgia Purdom, "Antibiotic Resistance of Bacteria: An Example of Evolution in Action?" July 10, 2007, http://www.answersingenesis.org/articles/am/v2/n3/antibiotic-resistance-of-bacteria.

3. Ken Ham, gen. ed., *The New Answers Book 1*, "Is Natural Selection the Same Thing as Evolution?" by Dr. Georgia Purdom (Green Forest, AR: Master Books, 2006).

## Chapter 28

# ABSOLUTE DISGRACE TO THE PROGRESS OF MAN?

Letter, unedited:

> You're business is an aboslute disgrace and abomination to the progression of man. You should be absolutely ashamed of yourselves for wanting to teach kids such fallacies you have no evidence for as 'facts'. Though a complete picture of how the world was derived hasn't been totally identified, the evidence is so far stacked toward evolution that I pity how heavily you must have been brainwashed and how much you have to ignore and reject to maintain your selfish beliefs. I am truely embarrassed to be on the same planet as you backward idiots! I challenge you to spend a few months to IMPARTIALLY research opposing theories and the possiblilty your 'God' does not exist. If you dont think your faith can withstand this examination, then I guess ignorance is bliss!
>
> Who needs logic rationale and reason anyway. If you can believe a genocidal malevolant tyrant wants you to ignore science, then you better do it!

Response:

Thank you for contacting us. My comments are below and I really hope you consider these. Also note, they are said with sincerity and respect, though I am being direct in places.

**To whom it may concern, You're business**

It is actually a ministry and a nonprofit.

**is an aboslute disgrace**

First, I'm glad you believe in absolutes; and second, I'm glad you believe there are such moral things as respect, honor, and subsequently shame, from which disgrace stems. Most evolutionists would disagree about these things.[1] They say "there are no absolutes or shame or honor, etc." They argue that everything is material and all things happen — even your own thoughts — as mere chemical reactions that ultimately have no meaning, because there is nothing immaterial.

Of course, many evolutionists are being illogical when they claim there are no absolutes, as they just used an absolute! All this is to say that I'm glad you disagree with leading evolutionists about absolutes and morality. These are very Christian of you. However, by the email it seems the Bible (which is where morality comes from) is not a high priority, so *why* would you think there are absolutes and disgrace without the Bible being true?

**and abomination to the progression of man.**

But from an evolutionary perspective, why care about the progress of man? "Eat, pass on your genes, and die"; that is really the evolutionist's motto. Why would the evolutionist care about the next generation? Let the offspring fend for themselves before they die? Why care about anything? Really?

When you care about people or society, that is Christian attribute (people are made in the image of God,[2] Genesis 1:26–27, 9:5–6), and I'm glad you do, but you must borrow from the Bible to make sense of it.

**You should be absolutely ashamed of yourselves for wanting to teach kids such fallacies you have no evidence for as 'facts'.**

We are not ashamed since we are teaching the truth, but evolutionists should be ashamed that they teach kids lies about God, morality, truth, science, and justice . . . and even kill them in "abortion factories" like "weeding the garden" (recall that it is the evolutionists that teach that children are just animals that are disposable).

But let me ask . . . what fallacies? And furthermore, in an evolutionary worldview where everything is material, why would truth and logic even exist? These things are NOT material, they are abstract. It is a Christian worldview based on the Bible from which we can have a basis for knowledge, logic, reasoning, morality, and so on. The non-Christian must borrow from the Bible just to try to argue against it.

---

1. Evolution is an atheistic worldview and one of the popular forms of secular humanism. Sadly, some Christians try to mix this religion with biblical Christianity. This is no different from what many Israelites did when mixing their religion with Baal worship, and God was not happy with them. Is God happy with mixing evolution and Christianity?

2. See also: http://www.answersingenesis.org/articles/2010/06/08/satan-the-fall-good-evil-image-of-god.

**Though a complete picture of how the world was derived hasn't been totally identified,**

Then why believe it is "absolute" enough to argue against other worldviews as the absolute standard?

**the evidence is so far stacked toward evolution**

Such as? We have the same evidence as the evolutionists and God disagrees with the evolutionists who make such claims. He says all of it is stacked His way: "The earth is the LORD's, and all its fullness, the world and those who dwell therein" (Psalm 24:1). So what is the *best* evidence that evolution is true (even though evolutionists say there is no such thing as truth)?

**that I pity**

Why "pity" if people are just chemicals? Chemicals don't "pity." Again, pity is a Christian thing, and I'm glad you have pity, even though it is misguided, because it refutes the position that evolutionists are arguing for (that pity and other immaterial things do not exist) and verifies that you are indeed *made in the image of God.*

**how heavily you must have been brainwashed and how much you have to ignore and reject**

I was brainwashed by public education that taught me that I was just a chemical and a "waste of space" in a "billions of years" universe where nothing matters and when you're dead . . . you're dead. But then I actually studied the subject. And I found out who was doing the brainwashing.

I thank the Lord God for saving me from the secular humanist religion (evolution and millions of years are aspects of this religion) that I was taught in school and university. It sounds like this religion was forced on you without question, too. I want to encourage you to question it.[3]

**to maintain your selfish beliefs.**

How is being loving and caring to others selfish? How is teaching people the truth selfish? How is taking a stand to save lives of children selfish? How is loving and being obedient to the God who died to save us from sin and death selfish? How?

---

3. Please don't get me wrong — there are many great Christian teachers in the secular system and they need your prayers, but the system is now set up to oppose Christianity and promote the religion of secular humanism.

But in an evolutionary worldview where it is a "free-for-all" evolutionary world . . . why not be selfish?

### I am truely embarrassed

Again, consistent evolutionists have no basis for truth, so why maintain this belief? If you want to be consistent, then either give up on truth and logic or give up on an evolutionary worldview.

But what I don't get is . . . why not be embarrassed about fellow evolutionists like Hitler or Stalin who killed many kids and adults or that maniac evolutionist Anders Behring Breivik who killed all those little kids in Norway . . . and yet email us saying we who preach righteousness should be the ones embarrassed?

### to be on the same planet as you backward idiots!

How are we backward and how are we ignorant? Such a claim is merely a question begging epithet fallacy.

### I challenge you to spend a few months to IMPARTIALLY research opposing theories and

Like this "impartial" email? The fact is, no one is impartial. There is no such thing as impartial research. This email and others we have received like it are evidence that those who criticize the biblical position clearly haven't "lifted a finger" to honestly research what the Bible teaches about creation, truth, knowledge, science, and so on.

Furthermore, I *have* searched hosts of religious beliefs, including the six differing views of evolution (Epicurean, Lamarckian, traditional Darwinism, neo-Darwinism, punctuated equilibrium, and hopeful monster).[4] Since you've professed a belief in evolution, out of curiosity, which of these do you believe right now and why are the others wrong?

As a matter of note, what Lamarck and Darwin did in trying to find a mechanism for evolution was really just a rehash of trying to make some Greek mythology work. The Epicurean Greeks proposed the myth of evolution; it was one popular form of Greek mythology — even Paul refuted it thousands of years ago in Acts 17.

But with aspects added by Lamarck and Darwin, they simply made variations in this mythology. Rightly, it is still Greek mythology, but their

---

4. For a concise review of some of these positions see: *The New Answers Book 3*, Ken Ham, gen. ed. (Green Forest AR: Master Books, 2010), p. 271–282.

new aspects can also be dubbed French mythology (Lamarck was from France) or English mythology (Darwin was from England). Sadly, WWII in Europe was instigated by Adolf Hitler, who bought into English mythology of evolution. . . .[5]

**the possiblilty your 'God' does not exist. If you dont think your faith can withstand this examination, then I guess ignorance is bliss!**

When it comes to the existence of God, I have searched the subject as well, be it the classical arguments that are still found wanting or the Transcendental Argument for the existence of God (TAG), which is foundational to the others.[6] How have you disproved the Transcendental Argument for the existence of the God of Christian theism?[7]

**Who needs logic rationale and reason anyway.**

Evolutionists don't consistently believe in such a thing since they are not material.

**If you can believe a genocidal malevolant tyrant**

Well, this is clearly not the God of the Bible as anyone could tell who has actually read the Bible. This is straw man fallacy that God-haters like Dr. Richard Dawkins have set up. Keep in mind that the last few genocidal, malevolent tyrants have been evolutionists, including Hitler and Stalin.

**wants you to ignore science, then you better do it!**

I love science and have a master's degree in it. It is sad when evolutionists can't tell the difference between evolution and science. It is a common equivocation fallacy on their part.

Mr. M., I would like to encourage you, though. You have expressed a belief in evolution (with its atheism, since evolution comes out of an atheistic worldview) and yet you are living your life borrowing from the Bible on the assumption that morality, logic, truth, and science exist.

---

5. Hitler was purely an evolutionist and gave up any thoughts of God. For more on this, see *Hitler's Second Book, The Unpublished Sequel of Mein Kampf*, dictated in 1928. It can be purchased offsite: http://www.amazon.com/Hitlers-Second-Book-Unpublished-Sequel/dp/1929631162.

6. See also *The New Answers Book 3*, Ken Ham, gen. ed. (Green Forest, AR: Master Books, 2010), p.263–270.

7. Being in the vein of Van Til in philosophy, I've tried to follow this debate. For a good summary of people's failed attempts to refute TAG, please see "The Transcendental Argument for God's Existence," Michael R. Butler, http://www.butler-harris.org/tag/.

I even suspect that you wear clothes — which come directly from a literal Genesis 3. Let's face it — frogs don't wake up in the morning and put their clothes on. The point is, you are living a life that is a contradiction — you follow the Bible in some areas (perhaps unknowingly) and yet you argue against its truthfulness.

> For the wrath of God is revealed from heaven against all ungodliness and unrighteousness of men, who suppress the truth in unrighteousness, because what may be known of God is manifest in them, for God has shown it to them. For since the creation of the world His invisible attributes are clearly seen, being understood by the things that are made, even His eternal power and Godhead, so that they are without excuse, because, although they knew God, they did not glorify Him as God, nor were thankful, but became futile in their thoughts, and their foolish hearts were darkened (Romans 1:18–21).

But it is time to stop and repent (Luke 13:3). It is time to change your life and start on the path of truth and righteousness. M., I would love to see you get saved. It seems you have a passion for standing up to things you feel are wrong, and that is a good Christian attribute. That is something I would hope you continue to do. But you need to understand what is right and wrong and have a basis for it — the Bible. I want to encourage you to begin the journey. For a good overview of who God is and what the Bible is all about, with selected Scriptures in the Bible, read *Begin,* compiled by myself and Ken Ham (Master Books, Green Forest, AR, 2011).

At the very least, it would help teach you who God is and what the Bible teaches on a number of subjects. With kindness in Christ.

SECTION 3:

~

# HOW TO RESPOND
# TO PEOPLE ON TOPICS
# ABOUT BIBLICAL
# AUTHORITY, THEOLOGY,
# AND COMPROMISED
# POSITIONS

Chapter 29

# $\mathcal{I}$S THE $\mathcal{Y}$OUNG EARTH $\mathcal{V}$IEWPOINT ABSURD?

Letter, unedited:

> I am furious with your explanation on the dinosaurs, suggesting that the dinosaurs lived alongside humans!!! THAT IS AB-SURD! I am 16 years old and trying to find a way to disprove evolution by logical means and this site does not give logical answers. I suggest an old-earth christian veiw be taken on every subject. This new earth explanation of the the world is just stupid . . . and I am apauled at the fact of a no proof pseudo-science. Ohh and by the way . . . You need all my information such as my name and e-mail as a sign of good faith! HA! I will be suprised if I even recieve feedback!
>
> C., Texas, U.S.

Response: [Editor's note: We receive emails from people of all ages, but rarely respond publicly to someone in primary or high school. However, we selected this email to show that kids are having the millions-of-years message drilled into their heads at such a young age that by the time they are 16, many believe it without questioning it, and likewise attack those who do believe what the Bible teaches about the age of the earth.]

Thank you for contacting Answers in Genesis. My comments are said with kindness and respect.

> **I am furious with your explanation on the dinosaurs, suggesting that the dinosaurs lived alongside humans!!!**

Actually, that concept came from God, not us. God made it clear in Genesis 1:24–31 that man and land animals (such as dinosaurs) were made on the same day. Moses penned this about 3,500 years ago, so the belief that land animals — such as dinosaurs — walked with man is not a new idea.

**THAT IS ABSURD!**

This is an attack on the Word of God, not us. On what basis do you think you know better than God? He was there to witness history. *Were you there?*

### I am 16 years old and trying to find a way to disprove evolution by logical means

There are many logical ways to do it that don't require one to appeal to evolutionary long ages (don't answer a fool according to his folly — Proverbs 26:4–5). Speaking of logic, are you trying to say that God is right and the evolutionists are wrong? If so, why compromise what God says for what the evolutionists say?

If you believe in the God of the Bible, then why not believe Him when He speaks in all areas? And, if you believe Genesis is true about man being specially created (as opposed to evolving), then why not believe Genesis is true when it says that God made land animals on the same day He made man?

Sadly, what you are doing is replacing the foundation of God's Word with an evolutionary premise, because long ages *aren't* biblical.

The concept of millions of years was read into the geologic layers back with non-Christians Charles Lyell and James Hutton, and is based on uniformitarian assumptions. If the geologic layers *did* represent billions of years of earth history, it would mean there was death before Adam was created and sinned. Hence death, in and of itself, would be "very good" and "perfect" according to Genesis 1:31 and Deuteronomy 32:4. One of Adam and Eve's punishments for their sin was death (Genesis 3:19; Romans 5:12). But this would be illogical if death already existed and God considered it "very good."

Additionally, indications of the Curse in the fossil record, which would have formed prior to Adam's sin, would also contradict other passages of Scripture. Take, for example, Genesis 1:30:

> "Also, to every beast of the earth, to every bird of the air, and
> to everything that creeps on the earth, in which there is life, I have
> given every green herb for food"; and it was so.

Animals were originally vegetarian. Yet with the millions-of-years scenario, the *Repenomamus robustus* that had the remains of a small dinosaur (a psittacosaur) in its gastrointestinal tract died 130 million years ago — which would make the Bible wrong about original vegetarianism.[1]

---

1. Ryan McClay, "Dino Dinner Hard to Swallow?" Answers in Genesis website, January 21, 2005, http://www.answersingenesis.org/articles/2005/01/21/dino-dinner-swallow.

Then to Adam He said, "Because you have heeded the voice of your wife, and have eaten from the tree of which I commanded you, saying, 'You shall not eat of it': Cursed is the ground for your sake; in toil you shall eat of it all the days of your life. Both thorns and thistles it shall bring forth for you, and you shall eat the herb of the field" (Genesis 3:17–18).

Thorns didn't exist until after sin. Yet, according to uniformitarian interpretations of the geologic record, thorns have been around for over 350 million years, since they have been found in the Devonian layers of the fossil record.[2] God would be wrong again if thorns were supposed to come after Adam's sin and yet actually came 350 million years *before* Adam.

The list could go on. Of course, neither of the above are problematic if the vast majority of the fossil record was laid down during the Flood of Noah's day, *after* Adam sinned. As you can see, we are not disputing the fact of geologic layers laden with evidence of death and the Curse, but the interpretation of when and how these layers were formed.

**and this site does not give logical answers.**

Such as? How are these illogical?

1. All land animals were made on day 6.

2. Dinosaurs were land animals.

∴ Dinosaurs were made on day 6.

1. Dinosaurs were made on day 6.

2. Man was made on day 6.

∴ Dinosaurs and man were made on the same day.

**I suggest an old-earth christian veiw be taken on every subject.**

It is not a matter of what *you* suggest but a matter of what God *said*. He is the authority — not scientists, not theologians, not me, not you. Believing in a young earth of about 6,000 years is based on trusting what is written in God's Word.

Of course, the Bible doesn't come out and say that the earth is 6,000 years old, and it's a good thing it doesn't — otherwise, it would only be right

2. https://answersingenesis.org/days-of-creation/is-the-young-earth-viewpoint-absurd/#fn-List_1_1.

for one year! But we wouldn't expect an all-knowing God to make that kind of mistake.

Instead, God gave us something better. He basically gave us a "birth certificate." For example, using my personal birth certificate, I can calculate how old I am at any time. It is the same with the earth. Genesis 1 makes it clear that the earth was created on day 1. From there, we can calculate the age of the earth.

Let's do a rough calculation to show how this works. The age of the earth can be estimated by taking the first five days of creation (before Adam was created on day 6) and then following the genealogies from Adam to Abraham. If you add up the dates from Adam to Abraham, you get about 2,000 years using the Masoretic Text. Most scholars — religious or otherwise — agree that Abraham would have lived about 2000 B.C. (4,000 years ago).

So a simple calculation is as follows: 5 days + ~2,000 years + ~4,000 years = ~6,000 years.

(Of course, the first five days are virtually negligible in the context of 6,000 years.) Quite a few people have done this calculation, and almost all calculate approximately 6,000 years for the age of the earth, or a creation date around 4000 B.C., when using the Hebrew Masoretic Text.[3]

| Who? | Age calculated | Reference and date |
|---|---|---|
| Archbishop James Ussher | 4004 B.C. | *The Annals of the World*, A.D. 1658 |
| Dr. Floyd Nolen Jones | 4004 B.C. | *The Chronology of the Old Testament*, A.D. 1993 |

**This new earth explanation of the the world is just stupid. . .and I am apauled at the fact of a no proof pseudo-science.**

This is not a good argument to help your case. You need to show why long ages are biblically necessary for proper doctrine or that young-earth interpretations are incorrect — and that would not be by saying "most teachers and professors think the earth is old." Investigate for yourself and see the assumptions that are involved in their assessment of old age. There is no reason to fall for the recent aberration of old-earth belief (e.g., no one believed the age of the earth was 4.5 billion years until 1956!). And there is

3. Ken Ham, gen. ed., *The New Answers Book 2*, "How Old Is the Earth?" by Bodie Hodge (Green Forest, AR: Master Books, 2008).

every reason to see that a recent creation does matter and can be logically defended.

**Ohh and by the way. . .You need all my information such as my name and e-mail as a sign of good faith! HA!**

Yes, as a sign of good faith, and we thank you for filling them out. We obviously need your email address — otherwise, we would have no way of replying to you! We do not add your information to any sort of subscriber lists unless you ask.

**I will be suprised if I even recieve feedback!**

Surprise! ☺

I hope this challenges you to get into God's Word and trust what it says. Sincerely in Christ.

*Chapter 30*

# THE BIBLE AND EVOLUTION COMPATIBLE?

Letter, unedited:

> I am just making a comment on multiple articles i have read on the topic of evolution on your site. I myself am a dedicated Christian; however, i also believe in evolution. This is due to my extreme interest in the whole debate which has raged about the topic for many many years, and being a zookeeper and animal trainer i felt i should personally educate myself as much as i could in the subject. The article which is based around proof of creation and presumptions, i think, is quite a shallow inlook to the situation. First of all, if this was the case the greater influence to evolutionary thinking, Charles Darwin would have never hypothesised natural selection, as he was a theological student and a dedicated christian at the time of his journey on the beagle. Also saying that because evolution theory has been constantly re written and the bible is not we should trust the bible, all it shows is that evolution is willing to move with the times and evidence.
>
> Thank you,
>
> C.C., Australia

Response:

Thank you for contacting Answers in Genesis. I want to encourage you to read Genesis and meditate on it because it simply doesn't mix with evolution. Years ago, I considered mixing them — more specifically, the evolutionary aspect of *millions of years* with the Bible. Regardless of how much I studied, it didn't work. So I know where you are coming from.

I am commenting below to help you get started, but I'm starting with a passage from Christ in Mark that is relevant to this discussion. My comments are intended with kindness and sincerity.

> I am just making a comment on multiple articles i have read on the topic of evolution on your site. I myself am a dedicated Christian; however, i also believe in evolution.

One of the problems I faced was Christ's comments in Mark. Jesus said:

> "But from the beginning of the creation, God 'made them male and female' " (Mark 10:6).

If you believe Christ is Lord and are dedicated to following the words of Jesus, then this becomes an enormous problem. According to the *general theory of evolution*, many billions of years ago the creation began, and man only evolved into the scene a few thousand years ago. Do you think that Jesus was in error and that human marriage between male and female (of which Jesus is speaking) has been around 13 or so billion years?

Jesus, the Creator, made it clear that the first marriage between man and woman (Adam and Eve) came at the beginning of creation. Tallying up the genealogies, Jesus was speaking about 4,000 years after this creation. So let's look at this in chart form:

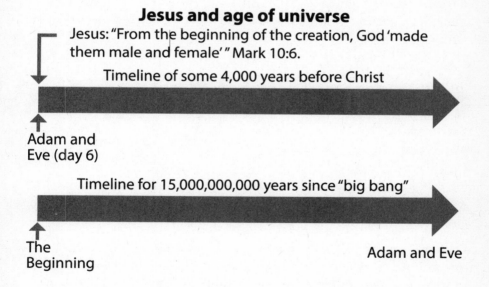

### Jesus and age of universe

Jesus: "From the beginning of the creation, God 'made them male and female'" Mark 10:6.

Timeline of some 4,000 years before Christ

Adam and Eve (day 6)

Timeline for 15,000,000,000 years since "big bang"

The Beginning

Adam and Eve

If the days in Genesis are regular solar days and Jesus was speaking about 4,000 years later, then, yes, the first marriage on day 6 was at the beginning of creation. If the earth is indeed billions of years old, then the first male and female came nowhere near the beginning of creation. This is a major theological problem. Either Christ is a liar in that view, or Christ told the truth and man-made evolution is a lie.

Those who religiously believe in evolutionary time over God's Word have tried to respond:

1. Some say biblical creationists have the same problem by appealing to Mark 10:6 as not being day 1 of creation.

2. Some insert words in the Bible to change the meaning (e.g., "beginning of the creation *of marriage*").

3. Some suggest that *beginning* is referring to an entire figurative "six-day" creation period or creation week, regardless of its length.

**Looking at point 1:** The argument incorrectly makes the assumption that the "beginning of creation" means the "first day of creation." The Bible doesn't say day 1 of creation; it says the beginning of the creation.

If one were to watch a movie, like *Expelled* by Ben Stein, and then tell a friend about the beginning of the movie, would that consist of the first word or frame of the movie only? Absolutely not; it would be a range of time surrounding the beginning of the movie and the events that get the movie going. Jesus' statement was reasonable and accurate, and any view of an old earth clearly falls flat.

The Bible points out that the term "beginning" has a bit of a range. For example, the devil was a sinner "from the beginning" (1 John 3:8), and yet this was after God's declaration that everything was very good at the end of day 6, as sin is not very good nor is the devil. The foundations of the earth were made on day 3 (God made the dry land) and that was "at the beginning" according to Hebrews 1:10.

Even if an "old earther" were to try to use point 1, he would be conceding that Jesus was wrong. Can Jesus err? No. If Jesus can err, then perhaps Jesus erred in passages concerning salvation. If this were the case, then the gospel and deity of Christ would be undermined.

**Looking at point 2:** Who is fallible, sinful mankind to try to add to Scripture to "correct" God? Sadly, when I hear someone add to Scripture in order to make it align with personal views, I think of Jehovah's Witnesses' treatment of John 1.[1]

Jehovah's Witnesses view Jesus as a created archangel, named Michael. So John 1 becomes a major problem for Jehovah's Witnesses because Jesus, the Word, is the Creator of all things. So they change the Scriptures to align with their viewpoint:

---

1. Bodie Hodge, "Is Jesus the Creator God?" Answers in Genesis website, December 12, 2007, http://www.answersingenesis.org/articles/aid/v2/n1/jesus-the-creator.

In the beginning was the Word, and the Word was with God, and the Word was God (John 1:1).

Jehovah's Witness change: In [the] beginning the Word was, and the Word was with God, and the Word was a god (John 1:1; NWT).

Notice how the change is that the Word was "a god" as opposed to "God." Sadly, this is done to change the Bible to conform to Jehovah's Witnesses' fallible theology. When people take Mark 10:6 and change it to conform to mankind's fallible theology, then what is the difference? Don't mistake what I'm saying here; "old earthers" are still saved as long as Jesus is their Savior, but their tack is the same as Jehovah's Witnesses'. Conforming ourselves to what Scripture says should be the goal of a Christian, not trying to change the meaning of Scripture.

**Looking at point 3:** If one goes on to conclude that "from the beginning of creation" (and likewise "from the beginning" in Matthew 19:4) means "all of the creative period, regardless of its length" then this implies 13–14 billion years of time in the "creative period," which is the beginning, middle, and end of the creation!

It is strange that one would think that 13 billion years or so have passed and that all of it is the beginning of creation — and now suddenly we are at the end after a few "measly" thousand years. Going back to our movie illustration, this would be akin to telling someone that the end was the last one second of a movie and that the other two hours of it were only the beginning.

First John 3:8 indicates that Satan was a sinner from the beginning and yet this was after creation week! So if point 3 is true, then 1 John 3:8 is wrong! It simply causes problems when one tries to add billions of years into creation week. Biblical creationists can say that the first six days are all part of the beginning of creation — and we can rightly argue this; an old earth creationist can't. I encourage you to trust Jesus over evolution stories.

> **This is due to my extreme interest in the whole debate which has raged about the topic for many many years, and being a zookeeper and animal trainer i felt i should personally educate myself as much as i could in the subject. The article which is based around proof of creation and presumptions, i think, is quite a shallow inlook to the situation.**

I'm not sure which article you are referring to, but the fact is that nothing makes sense without the Bible, and evolution has no basis in the Bible. And it should be the Bible that is the authority over any article.

**First of all, if this was the case the greater influence to evolutionary thinking, Charles Darwin would have never hypothesised natural selection, as he was a theological student**

Darwin didn't originally hypothesize natural selection; he merely gave it a name. Darwin was well aware of creationist Edward Blyth, who published several papers on the subject 20–25 years before. The idea was around before both of them, though.

You are correct: Darwin was not a scientist, but a theologian. I find it ironic that evolutionists often criticize creationists for saying anything outside of their field of study, and yet they do not question Darwin, who spoke about biology.

**and a dedicated christian at the time of his journey on the beagle.**

I seriously doubt Darwin ever gave his life to Christ. If he was saved, how could he walk away from Christ (Isaiah 43:10; John 10:28–30; 1 John 2:15–20; John 6:40:37–40)? Studying Scripture, and even a theology degree, won't get anyone into heaven. Jesus Christ is the only way (John 14:6).

Darwin described himself as an agnostic at best and even published that man, while evolving, invented the concept of God. Darwin wrote:

> What my own views may be is a question of no consequence to any one but myself. But, as you ask, I may state that my judgment often fluctuates. . . . In my most extreme fluctuations I have never been an Atheist in the sense of denying the existence of a God. I think that generally (and more and more as I grow older), but not always, that an Agnostic would be the more correct description of my state of mind.[2]

Fluctuation about whether there is a God or not has little to do with salvation, which is found in no other name under heaven than Christ (Acts 4:12).

**Also saying that because evolution theory**

2. Letter addressed to Mr. J. Fordyce, and published by him in his "Aspects of Scepticism" (1883) in Charles Darwin, *The Life and Letters of Charles Darwin, Including an Autobiographical Chapter*, Volume 1, Francis Darwin, ed. (London: John Murray, 1887).

"Theory"? Evolution is not a theory; it is a failed hypothesis at best, as its coherence leaves much to be desired.

> **has been constantly re written and the bible is not we should trust the bible, all it shows is that evolution is willing to move with the times and evidence.**

So are you saying that the Bible shouldn't be trusted? If evolution is true, then the Bible is false. Even evolutionists get this loud and clear:

> Christianity has fought, still fights, and will continue to fight science to the desperate end over evolution, because evolution destroys utterly and finally the very reason Jesus' earthly life was supposedly made necessary. Destroy Adam and Eve and the original sin, and in the rubble you will find the sorry remains of the Son of God. If Jesus was not the redeemer who died for our sins, and this is what evolution means, then Christianity is nothing.[3]

Since evolution is being rewritten every day, then it should be a red flag that there is something wrong with that belief system. Why add that belief system to the Bible? Would we want a Bible that changed or a God that did (Psalm 119:89; Hebrews 13:8)? The issue is simple: if you can't fully understand how God can create in six days as opposed to the atheistic belief in millions of years, then grant God the honor of being more learned than you are.

It is time to stop trusting in the "religion of the day," and get back to the authority of the Word of God.

With kindness in Christ.

---

3. G. Richard Bozarth, "The Meaning of Evolution," *American Atheist* (September 20, 1979): p. 30.

## Chapter 31

# TALKING SNAKES AND MYSTICAL TREES?

Letter, unedited:

> **Dear AiG,**
>
> **I've noticed a lot of evolutionists will try to mock creationists and make our beliefs seem ridiculous by saying things like "You creationists believe a woman was convinced by a talking snake to eat from a magical tree."**
>
> **How should creationists respond to remarks like that?**
>
> **Thanks and God bless,**
>
> **D.**

Response:

Thank you for contacting Answers in Genesis. Those making these sorts of comments are not likely even looking for a response, but are primarily poking fun without even knowing much about what they are ridiculing. In cases like this, sometimes it may be good to illuminate the humor of their own belief such as: "And evolutionists believe everyone in the world ultimately came from rock." Then point out that if they have trouble with talking animals then they mustn't believe parrots exist either!

In this case, explain that, like the talking donkey that Balaam rode, the talking serpent was a vessel enabled for another being to use or speak through — Satan, in the case of the serpent. And nowhere does the Bible call the Tree of the Knowledge of Good and Evil "magical." The curses and repercussions came from God as a punishment because of Adam and Eve's sin, not the tree. I suggest that they are confusing the Tree of Knowledge of Good and Evil with the Tree of Life, which one may mistake for having "magical" properties to make one live forever (Genesis 3:22). The Book of Revelation does mention that the leaves of the Tree will be used for healing (Revelation 22:2).

Humor aside, though, today we see people dying, which is exactly what God said would happen because of Adam and Eve's rebellion and sin. Today, we also see serpents slithering (snakes), which was what Genesis says. And yet, no one sees people coming from rocks, algae, or even lemurs! The Bible explains the world we live in, and it is the evolutionary position that simply begins with and ends with absurdity and irrationality.

When people do begin asking serious questions indicating they are truly looking for answers, I suggest you be prepared (1 Peter 3:15) to give good, solid answers. Study the Scriptures first, and then read up on common questions and answers in relation to challenges to the Bible, such as the New Answers Book series. Keep in mind an important Scripture as well:

> "If the world hates you, you know that it hated Me before it hated you" (John 15:18).

I pray this helps. God bless.

## Chapter 32

# DOES SCRIPTURE ALLOW FOR A GAP THEORY?

Letter, unedited:

> Wanted to make sure you knew that Genesis 1:2 says, "2 And the earth was without form, and void; and darkness was upon the face of the deep. And the Spirit of God moved upon the face of the waters."

> The first word for "was" is the word for "BECAME." (The second word for was is not in the text.) Just wanted to make you you knew this as it allows for all the prior life forms.

> Thanks.

> So, in Genesis 1:2 they would have been destroyed along with other life forms such as the cave man. When God created man in His own image that would have been Homo Sapiens with unique dna.

> S.C., U.S.

Response:

Thanks for contacting us. This common argument proposed by gap theorists in the past 200 years has major problems. Let's analyze it together in an iron-sharpening-iron fashion.

> Wanted to make sure you knew that Genesis 1:2 says, "2 And the earth was without form, and void; and darkness was upon the face of the deep. And the Spirit of God moved upon the face of the waters."

> The first word for "was" is the word for "BECAME." (The second word for was is not in the text.)

Actually, recognized grammarians, lexicographers, and linguists have almost uniformly rejected the translations "became" and "had become." It is a basic exegetical fallacy to claim that because *Strong's Concordance* lists "became" as one of the meanings of *haya*, it is legitimate to translate it this way *in the particular context of Genesis 1:2*. It is simply grammatically impossible when the verb *haya* is combined with a *waw* disjunctive — in the rest of the Old Testament, *waw* + a noun + *haya* (*qal* perfect, third person) is always translated "was" or "came," but *never* "became."

Additionally, the gap theory has many other problems, such as death for millions of years before sin, Satan in a sinful state, and sin being very good (Genesis 1:31).[1] There will be more on this in a moment.

**Just wanted to make you you knew this as it allows for all the prior life forms.**

Actually, it doesn't, because the Hebrew words that Moses (guided by the Holy Spirit) used in Genesis 1:2 make it very clear that there was no extended ("millions of years") gap of time that happened between the events described in these verses. Further, Moses also makes it very clear (e.g., Exodus 20:11) that *all things* were created in six actual days. Additionally, the idea that there were life forms that lived *and died* prior to the creation of Adam and the subsequent entrance of sin into the world undermines the gospel and denigrates the character of God.

You see, when He was finished creating, God looked at His completed creation and called it "very good" (Genesis 1:31). Accepting "millions of years" of prior life forms living and dying (and suffering from terrible diseases such as cancer or brain tumors) means that God labeled this process good. But can we honestly think death (and disease, pain, and suffering) is good? Paul calls it an *enemy* (1 Corinthians 15:26), and John tells us that it has no place in the new heavens and earth (Revelation 21:4). In fact, death was Adam's *punishment* for disobeying God (Genesis 2:17, Genesis 3:19, Romans 5:12). If Adam's punishment was *very good*, then why didn't he eat from the Tree of Knowledge of Good and Evil right away? And why would Jesus Christ come and die in our place to save us from death if death were a "very good" process that had been occurring for billions of years?[2]

**Thanks.**

**So, in Genesis 1:1 the dinasaurs would have existed**

---

1. Ken Ham, gen ed., *The New Answers Book 1*, "What about Gap and Ruin-reconstruction Theories?" by Ken Ham (Green Forest, AR: Master Books, 2006).

2. Bodie Hodge, *The Fall of Satan*, "Biblically, Could Death Have Existed before Sin?" (Green Forest, AR: Master Books, 2011).

That would mean dinosaurs *weren't* land animals. It seems pretty clear to me they were (with the exception of those sea and flying dinosaur-like creatures that were created on day 5); and God said He created land animals on day 6, not day 1. Even Job described one in Job 40, and numerous times dragons are mentioned in Scripture, the old name for dinosaurs prior to 1841.[3]

**and then by the time Genesis 1:2 they would have been destroyed along with other life forms such as the cave man.**

Elijah was a cave man! Some people today are cavemen. Caves make great shelters! Did you know that "cave men" like Neanderthals and *Homo erectus* have associated evidence with them of burying their dead, making and using elegant tools, religious ceremonies, and knowing how to manage fire (indicating they were human)? Accepting that cave men lived hundreds of thousands of years before Adam entered the scene means that Paul (and thus God, since Paul was being guided by the Holy Spirit to record the things that he did) was being deceitful in saying that Adam was the first man: "And so it is written, 'The *first man Adam* became a living being.' The last Adam became a life-giving spirit" (1 Corinthians 15:45). Furthermore, when it comes to men, even cave men, they are simply that. Caves are a great place to live when scattering from Babel to many places around the world. Cave men are not apes, as that would be cave-apes! And there is no such thing as a half human and half ape . . . just imaginary images.[4]

**When God created man in His own image that would have been Homo Sapiens with unique dna.**

All animals and plants have unique DNA. Being made in the image of God is what sets us apart from the plants and animals. I also recall Jesus' words in Mark 10:6 when He was asked about marriage and divorce. Jesus responded:

> "But from the beginning of creation, God 'made them male and female.' "

If the world really were billions of years old and man just showed up recently, then Jesus would be wrong — He should have said "*near the end* of creation." But since the world was only about 4,000 years old when Jesus

---

3. For more on this see *Dragons: Legends and Lore of Dinosaurs*, Bodie Hodge and Laura Welch (Green Forest, AR: Master Books, 2011).

4. For more see Ken Ham, gen. ed., *The New Answers Book 2*, "Did Humans Really Evolve from Ape-like Creatures?" by Dr. David Mention (Green Forest, AR: Master Books, 2008).

said this, and He had created man and woman on day 6 (only five days after "the beginning"), then Jesus was correct. Jesus believed in a young earth and not the "gap theory," so there is no reason for us to accept this unbiblical idea.[5]

I encourage you to read these.

Kind regards.

---

5. An entire book on the subject is *Unformed and Unfilled*, by Weston Fields (Collinsville, IL: Burgener Enterprises, 1976).

## Chapter 33

# Gap Theory – They All Have Problems!

Letter, unedited:

> I don't believe in the gap theory in that the original earth was destroyed. But why couldn't the planet earth and the heavens been created millions of years ago and remained null and void until God began 6000 years ago to create the atmosphere, land and life?

> B.C., U.S.

Response: [Special thanks to Troy Lacey, a colleague and friend who coauthored this with me.]

Thank you for contacting Answers in Genesis. The "modified gap theory" or "precreation chaos gap theory," which is the proposed "gap" between Genesis 1:2 and 1:3, is unscriptural, and ultimately unnecessary. In fact, several gap models have been proposed over the years for one reason — to add secular ideas of long ages to the Bible. Here are some of the various models:

1. Pre-time gap. This view adds long ages prior to God creating in Genesis 1:1. This falls short for a number of reasons. For example, how can one have millions of years of time prior to the creation of time?

2. Ruin-reconstruction gap. This is the most popular gap idea, which adds long ages between Genesis 1:1 and Genesis 1:2. It was popularized by Scottish pastor Thomas Chalmers in the early 1800s. This idea is promoted in the Scofield and Dake's study Bibles and is often associated with a Luciferian fall and flood.[1]

3. Modified gap/precreation chaos gap. This view adds long ages between Genesis 1:2 and 1:3, and is primarily addressed in this article.[2]

---

1. See refutation in *Unformed and Unfilled*, Weston Fields, and *The New Answers Book 1*, Ken Ham, gen ed., "What about Gap and Ruin-reconstruction Theories?" by Ken Ham (Green Forest, AR: Master Books, 2006).

2. One refutation of this view is in the *Proceedings of the Sixth International Conference on Creationism*, 2008, by John Zoschke, "A Critique of the Precreation Chaos Gap Theory," Andrew Snelling, ed.

4.  Soft gap. This also includes a gap between Genesis 1:2 and 1:3, but unlike previous views, it has no catastrophic events or destruction of a previous state. It merely proposes that God created the world this way and left it for long periods of time in an effort to get starlight here. In essence, this view has a young earth and old universe. The problem is that stars were created after the proposed gap (day 4), and it is unnecessary to make accommodations for long ages to solve the so-called starlight problem.[3]

5.  Late gap. This view has a gap between chapters 2 and 3 of Genesis. In other words, some believe that Adam and Eve lived in the Garden for long ages before sin. This view has problems, too. For example, Adam and Eve were told by God to be "fruitful and multiply" in Genesis 1:28, and waiting long ages to do so would have been disobedience. In addition, there is the problem of Adam only living 930 years (Genesis 5:5).

This modified gap theory is inconsistent with God creating everything in six days, as Scripture states. The plain meaning of the text is that everything was created sequentially: the earth, light, plants, sun, moon, stars, birds and fish, beasts, and man. The modified gap suggests that day 1 lasted for millions of years while the rest of the days were normal length.

> For in six days the LORD made the heavens and earth, the sea, and all that is in them, and rested the seventh day. Therefore the LORD blessed the Sabbath day, and hallowed it (Exodus 20:11).

Thus, the creation of the heavens and the earth (Genesis 1:1) and the sea and all that is in them (the rest of the creation) was completed in six days. Is there any room for an alternative interpretation that truly honors Scripture, based on this clear passage?

Since the sun, moon, and stars were not created until day 4, the modified gap theorist has to either accept billions of years with nothing in space but a lush earth, or rearrange the order of the Genesis 1 creation account without any hermeneutical basis.

Using Scripture as our starting point, we can show that the physical evidence is consistent with an earth being a few thousand years in age. There is significant evidence that can be discussed — the decay and rapid reversals of the earth's magnetic field, the amount of salt in the oceans,

---

3. See "Anisotropic Synchrony Convention," Dr. Jason Lisle, *Answers Research Journal*, September 22, 2010, http://www.answersingenesis.org/articles/arj/v3/n1/anisotropic-synchrony-convention.

the wind-up of spiral galaxies, helium in zircons, C-14 in diamonds, and much more.

The modified gap also calls into question the words of our Lord and Savior Jesus Christ. Consider that He said in Mark 10:5–8 that mankind was made from the beginning of creation, not billions of years later:

> And Jesus answered and said unto them, For the hardness of your heart he wrote you this precept. But from the beginning of the creation God made them male and female. For this cause shall a man leave his father and mother, and cleave to his wife; and [the two] shall be one flesh: so then they are no more [two], but one flesh (KJV).

The modified gap attempts to blend secular long ages with the Bible, but there is no need for a gap. The modified gap does not "bridge the gap" (pun intended) between biblical creation and long ages. Instead, it is an arbitrary attempt to compromise with secular interpretations of the age of the earth and universe.

It also opens up a major theological problem of *death before sin*.[4] This results in the idea of death being "very good" (Genesis 1:31) and undermines the reason for Christ's atonement to save us from sin and death. Death is the result of sin and did not occur millions of years before Adam. Please take some time to consider this with your Bible in hand.

With kindness and prayers that this helps. God bless.

---

4. *The Fall of Satan*, "Biblically, Could Death Have Existed before Sin?"

## Chapter 34

# ℘AIN AND SUFFERING: ℐS THIS ANSWER IN GENESIS?

Letter, unedited:

> I disagree with AiG that the answer to why there is pain and suffering is found in Genesis. If Genesis is true then it still doesnt explain why God allowed evil to continue and for all the horrors that were to follow and are happening today. To say that someone sinned in Adam and that's why we all have to suffer today makes no sense. The real question on people's mind is why does God allow all these things to happen, if He really loves us, why did He allow for all this to happen. There is an answer to why there is death and suffering but it's not in Genesis

H.M., Iceland

Response: [This response was coauthored with friend and co-laborer for Christ, Dr. Jason Lisle.]

> I disagree with AiG that the answer to why there is pain and suffering is found in Genesis. If Genesis is true then it still doesnt explain why God allowed evil to continue and for all the horrors that were to follow and are happening today.

The question of why pain and suffering *continues* today is a different question than why there is pain and suffering in the first place. The answer to why pain and suffering exists at all indeed goes back to Genesis.

Many people wonder why a good God would have created a world full of pain and suffering; but of course, He didn't. God created a "very good" world — a paradise for us to enjoy. But God gave Adam a command concerning the Tree of the Knowledge of Good and Evil: do not eat from it. And God told Adam what the consequences of disobeying that command would be. When Adam sinned, God gave Adam what he had earned (or at least a "taste" of it; the unbeliever does not receive the *full* payment of sin until death). Adam received the just reward for his actions.

By rebelling against God, Adam was in effect saying that he wanted to live by his own rules — separated from God. And God gave Adam a small taste of what he asked for. Pain and suffering exist because of what Adam did, so of course this all goes back to Genesis.

However, the question you raise is a legitimate question: basically, why does God allow the consequences of such evil actions to *continue*? We will deal with that below.

### To say that someone sinned in Adam and that's why we all have to suffer today makes no sense.

Actually, it does make sense. The consequences of sin are not confined to the sinner. They are often far-reaching and can affect many. In particular, many people have reaped the consequences of the wise or unwise actions of their parents. As one example, a pregnant woman who abuses alcohol or drugs can cause serious problems for her unborn child. So it is clear that children can certainly be harmed by the poor actions of their parents. Likewise, all humanity has suffered because of the sinful actions of our forefather Adam. In fact, since God gave Adam dominion over the world, all creation suffers (Romans 8:22) because of what Adam did.

We can all suffer because of the sinful actions of another. Perhaps this seems unfair? You might be tempted to think that it would have been better if God had created a universe where the *actions of another person affected only that person and no one else*. At first, this kind of spiritual "insulation" sounds great. But salvation would not be possible in such a universe — because Christ's actions on the Cross could have no effect on us. If we sinned even once, we would have no hope. Fortunately, God designed a universe where the actions of another person can be imputed to us; this means we can be redeemed *because of what Christ did in a similar way that Adam's sin affects us*. Christ doesn't have to die individually for each person but once for all. This is why Paul says:

> For the death that He died, He died to sin once for all; but the life that He lives, He lives to God. Likewise you also, reckon yourselves to be dead indeed to sin, but alive to God in Christ Jesus our Lord (Romans 6:10–11).

We are born with a sin nature because of what Adam did. But if we receive Christ as Savior, His righteousness is imputed to us (Romans 5:12–21). This is an amazing solution to sin, because it both satisfies God's justice (the penalty for sin is paid) and displays God's mercy (we can be reconciled with God).

Because of what Christ did, we who have received the free gift of eternal life have the hope that there will one day be a new heavens and a new earth without sin (Revelation 21:1–4, 27). This is the world one would expect a perfect God to have for eternity, not this temporary sin-cursed one.

Actions, such as man's sin, have consequences. When Adam sinned, the punishment was death (Genesis 2:17), and the punishment received was death (Genesis 3:19). And *we* were a part of Adam (Acts 17:26) so logically, it affected us as well.

He was the "federal head" of the human race. Expositor John Gill put it this way in his commentary on Romans 5:12:

> . . . besides, sin entered as death did, which was not by imitation but imputation, for all men are reckoned dead in Adam, being accounted sinners in him; add to this, that in the same way Christ's righteousness comes upon us, which is by imputation, Adam's sin enters into us, or becomes ours; upon which death follows. . . .

Gill continues further in the commentary on this verse:

> . . . all men were naturally and seminally in him; as he was the common parent of mankind, he had all human nature in him, and was also the covenant head, and representative of all his posterity; so that they were in him both naturally and federally, and so "sinned in him"; and fell with him by his first transgression into condemnation and death. The ancient Jews, and some of the modern ones, have said many things agreeably to the apostle's doctrine of original sin; they own the imputation of the guilt of Adam's sin to his posterity to condemnation and death.[1]

Consider Hebrews 7:9–10 where Levi (Abraham's great-grandson) was in the body of his ancestor Abraham when he paid tithes! Our life — all of us — was ultimately in Adam when he sinned. When Adam fell, we all fell with him.

We were a part of Adam (and Eve), and therefore, we sinned in Adam and his death sentence carries over to us. However, none of us can say that we have not disobeyed the Creator, as well. Regardless of the fact that we sinned in Adam, we still sin. You and I consciously sin as individuals, and therefore are genuinely blameworthy. So really, no one can blame God in any respect for the consequence of sin (the punishment of death and suffering) that we received. God made a righteous decision.

---

1. http://www.biblestudytools.com/commentaries/gills-exposition-of-the-bible/romans-5-12.html.

**The real question on people's mind is why does God allow all these things to happen, if He really loves us, why did He allow for all this to happen. There is an answer to why there is death and suffering but it's not in Genesis**

That we (in Adam) chose to rebel against our Creator is *our* fault — not God's. God gave Adam a command to follow, and Adam reaped the reward (death and suffering) of disobeying (James 1:14). Today, human beings (you and I) continue to sin and rebel against God, and we reap the consequences of our treason against the holy Creator. God's love for His children is expressed in His discipline of us (Hebrews 12:5–11). This is what we would expect in a sin-cursed world. But take heart, the curse will be removed (Revelation 22:3).

But what about those of us who have received Christ as Savior? We have been redeemed and have been made righteous in God's eyes by Christ's work on the Cross. Why must we continue to live in this world of sin? Consider Christ's parable here:

> Another parable He put forth to them, saying: "The kingdom of heaven is like a man who sowed good seed in his field; but while men slept, his enemy came and sowed tares among the wheat and went his way. But when the grain had sprouted and produced a crop, then the tares also appeared. So the servants of the owner came and said to him, 'Sir, did you not sow good seed in your field? How then does it have tares?' He said to them, 'An enemy has done this.' The servants said to him, 'Do you want us then to go and gather them up?' But he said, 'No, lest while you gather up the tares you also uproot the wheat with them. Let both grow together until the harvest, and at the time of harvest I will say to the reapers, 'First gather together the tares and bind them in bundles to burn them, but gather the wheat into my barn' " (Matthew 13:24–30).

Hypothetically, if God would take us away the instant we received Christ as Savior, we would never have the opportunity to share Christ with others. Actually, we would probably never have heard about Christ anyway, since the person(s) who helped lead us to Christ would have been taken away the moment they were saved (and so on).

What about those who will never return to a right, saving relationship with God? Why doesn't God simply remove them? God can even use the "tares" of this world to draw His children closer to Him. Many of us at Answers in Genesis have *benefited* from hearing those who preach out *against* the Bible. (Yes, you read that correctly.) It forces us to go back and study and learn to defend the faith and accordingly grow in our faith. This also enables us to better share the gospel so that people may be saved. Also, many non-Christians have produced children or grandchildren that will later become Christians. So uprooting the non-Christians would uproot many who would become Christians ("children of God," Romans 8:18).

God is permitting the seed, which is the Word of God, to grow in many people, who would otherwise not hear. We can't really see the entire "big picture"; we don't know how all the intricacies of the actions of every person affect every other person. But God orchestrates these actions to bring people to Him (Acts 17:26–27). God even uses evil actions to bring about good. Not that God approves of evil actions in any respect, but to clarify, God is so great that He can still make good come from it. And one particular example of this is found in Genesis (50:20).

Perhaps the supreme example of God using evil to bring about good is the Cross. The horrific death of the innocent Christ was used by God to bring about the salvation of all those who would trust in Him (Acts 2:23–24). Aren't you glad that God allowed/used such an evil action?

In this world, God can use evil to bring about good, and He leaves the wheat with the tares so that many might be saved. Therefore, God permits the consequences of sin, which is death and suffering until the time of the harvest. Paul continues on this: "I consider that the sufferings of this present time are not worthy to be compared with the glory which shall be revealed in us" (Romans 8:18). "The creation waits in eager expectation for the sons of God to be revealed. For the creation was subjected to frustration, not by its own choice, but by the will of the one who subjected it, in hope that the creation itself will be liberated from its bondage to decay and brought into the glorious freedom of the children of God" (Romans 8:19–21; NIV).

By your email, you appear to be eager (as are we) for the death and suffering in the world to end. However, Paul makes it clear that present suffering is not worth comparing with the glory that will be revealed in us.

Knowing that people are still coming to Christ is why we need to be patient in affliction (Romans 12:12). God knows better than we do the reasons for His patience, and this is just a small glimpse as to why. It is refreshing that God was kind enough to reveal in part why the present sufferings are still being permitted. We pray this helps clarify.

God bless.

## Chapter 35

# WHY DO YOU TAKE THE BIBLE LITERALLY?

Letter, unedited:

> **Dear AiG, Don't you take the Bible literally in every instance? How do you deal with metaphors in the Bible?**
>
> **B., U.S.**

Response: [I've used this same response to a number of people asking similar questions.]

Thank you for contacting Answers in Genesis. I think you've misunderstood how we interpret the Bible. You incorrectly state that we take the Bible *literally*, which we don't, although we understand that the events recorded in Genesis are *literal* history. Let me explain in more detail to avoid confusion.

The Bible gives us principles of interpretation in 2 Corinthians 4:2 and Proverbs 8:8–9:

> But we have renounced the hidden things of shame, not walking in craftiness nor handling the word of God deceitfully, but by manifestation of the truth commending ourselves to every man's conscience in the sight of God (2 Corinthians 4:2).

> All the words of my mouth are with righteousness; nothing crooked or perverse is in them. They are all plain to him who understands, and right to those who find knowledge (Proverbs 8:8–9).

In other words, we are to read and understand the Bible in a *plain* or *straightforward* manner. This is usually what people mean when they say "literal interpretation of the Bible" (this phrase is common among those not well-versed in hermeneutics). I try to use the term "plainly" so I don't confuse people.

Reading the Bible "plainly" means understanding that literal history is literal history, metaphors are metaphors, poetry is poetry, etc. The Bible is written in many different literary styles and should be read accordingly. This is why we understand that Genesis records actual historical events. It was written as historical narrative.

Reading the Bible plainly/straightforwardly (taking into account literary style, context, authorship, etc.) is the basis for what is called the *historical-grammatical* method of interpretation, which has been used by theologians since the church fathers. This method helps to eliminate improper interpretations of the Bible.

For example, I once had someone who is not a Christian say to me, "The Bible clearly says 'there is no God' in Psalm 14:1." When you look up the verse and read it in context, it says:

> The fool has said in his heart, "There is no God." They are corrupt, they have done abominable works, there is none who does good (Psalm 14:1).

So the context helps determine the proper interpretation — that a *fool* was saying this.

I also once had someone tell me, "To interpret the days in Genesis, you need to read 2 Peter 3:8, which indicates the days are each a thousand years." Second Peter 3:8–9, in context, says:

> But, beloved, do not forget this one thing, that with the Lord one day is as a thousand years, and a thousand years as one day. The Lord is not slack concerning His promise, as some count slackness, but is longsuffering toward us, not willing that any should perish but that all should come to repentance.

This passage employs a literary device called a *simile*. Here, God compares a day to a thousand years in order to make the point that time doesn't bind Him, in this case regarding His patience. God is not limited to the time He created — that would be illogical.

Also, this verse gives no reference to the days in Genesis, so it is not warranted to apply this to the days in Genesis 1. When read plainly, these verses indicate that God is patient when keeping His promises.

At any rate, I pray this helps to clarify why we advocate reading and understanding the Bible in a plain or straightforward manner, and why Genesis should be understood as actual history.

Kind regards in Christ.

*Chapter 36*

# ONE BIBLE, MANY INTERPRETATIONS?

Letter, unedited:

> I thought the Scopes Trail was over, evolution is the deal here folks. I am so proud to be a Jew, a Jew who understands that the bible has many interpretations and shouldnt be read in a fanatical one sided view. Your Museum is an affront to education and crosses the same line as Christianity in the separation of church and state.
>
> M.P., U.S.

Response:

It is nice to hear from you. Please see my sincere comments below.

**I thought the Scopes Trail was over, evolution is the deal here folks.**

Actually, the Butler Act, which forbade the teaching of *human* evolution, was upheld at the Scopes Trial, and John Scopes was fined for teaching human evolution (although this was later overturned on a technicality). The main setback to Christianity came when William Jennings Bryan, who accepted long-age ideas despite the clear teaching of Scripture to the contrary, was unable to provide sound answers to questions that merely require a straightforward reading of the Word: Who was Cain's wife?[1] Were the days in Genesis 1 normal length days?[2]

Today, the situation has reversed, and laws in certain places forbid the teaching of creationism and the questioning of evolutionism. Even evolutionary scientists who thrive on questioning ideas and hypotheses are restrained because they cannot critique aspects of evolution.

This also brings up other important points: one should not judge God and His Word based on the actions of fallible and sinful Christians; and compromising Genesis leads to unbelief in subsequent generations.

**I am so proud to be a Jew,**

---

1. For a thorough answer see *The New Answers Book 1*, Ken Ham, gen. ed., "Cain's Wife — Who Was She?" by Ken Ham (Green Forest, AR: Master Books, 2006).

2. For a thorough answer see *The New Answers Book 1*, "Could God Really Have Created Everything in Six Days?"

The Jews were entrusted with the oracles of God; they are descendants of Abraham, Isaac, and Jacob; and they were the people group to whom Jesus Christ first brought His message of reconciliation with God (Luke 3; John 1), but keep in mind that pride is a dangerous thing (James 4:6). But thanks be to God who, through the work of Christ, has made Jews and Gentiles one:

> There is neither Jew nor Greek, there is neither slave nor free, there is neither male nor female; for you are all one in Christ Jesus. And if you are Christ's, then you are Abraham's seed, and heirs according to the promise (Galatians 3:28–29).

Sadly, due to an evolutionary mindset, Nazis tried to exterminate the Jews throughout Europe. Darwin heavily influenced these Nazis, and Hitler in particular, when he wrote that the "civilized Caucasians" should exterminate the other "races." It is too bad they didn't listen to God's Word about all people being of the same race — the human race!

**a Jew who understands that the bible has many interpretations and shouldnt be read in a fanatical one sided view.**

Using this philosophy of multiple interpretations, how do you know a Jew is a Jew? Perhaps "Jew" is better understood as "Gentile" so as not to have a "one-sided" or "fanatical" view. But instead of this all-is-relative approach to understanding Scripture (which is a humanistic belief), God's Word dictates that we stick with the plain reading of the Bible, understanding it as the original authors intended it and as the original audiences would have understood it (2 Corinthians 4:2; Proverbs 8:8–9).

For example, we need to accept historical narrative passages as actual history and poetical passages as poetry. We must use Scripture to interpret Scripture, taking into account the language and culture of the original audience.

Further, we need to consider that the God who established the rules of logic could not possibly contradict Himself in His Word, so the "many interpretations" idea doesn't work. God does not allow for interpretation A to be equal to interpretation not-A at the same time in the same instance. In today's culture, many people appeal to relative truth, but truth is not truth if it's relative — it's merely fallible opinion. The God of the Bible is the absolute truth, and His Word is a reflection of His truth, and His purpose was to communicate this truth to us through it.

**Your Museum is an affront to education**

Actually, the Creation Museum is an educational institution, although the main message isn't new. For thousands of years, people taught biblical truths such as creation in six days, a global Flood, and an earth thousands (not billions) of years old. In fact, educational institutions such as Harvard, Oxford, Yale, and Princeton once taught these truths. Are you suggesting that these institutions were an affront to education for so long?

**and crosses the same line as Christianity in the separation of church and state.**

So you were opposed to King David, King Hezekiah, and others who mixed Judaism with state affairs? It is interesting to note that the oft-used "separation of church and state" clause isn't found anywhere in the U.S. Constitution; it comes from a Supreme Court ruling regarding the First Amendment of the Constitution, which prohibits *government and government-funded places* from endorsing religion. In fact, the Constitution protects the right to freedom of religious expression elsewhere.

But keep in mind that the Supreme Court also stated that African Americans were not protected by the Constitution and could not be U.S. citizens in the Dred Scott decision . . . so the Supreme Court isn't perfect like God's Word is. It can make mistakes.

Keep in mind that the Creation Museum isn't a state-run organization as many natural history museums are. It is a privately owned museum with the ability to speak freely about religious issues. If you truly want to keep religion separate from state institutions, then consider challenging the religion of humanism that is promoted in state schools and museums that are state funded.

With kindness in Christ.

## Chapter 37

# ℐS THE ℬIBLE INCOMPLETE?

Letter, unedited:

> I've read all the articles on your web-site regarding the Apocry-phal Gospels, but I need some more insight. The Catholics be-lieve our Bible is incomplete. I understand that 1 Maccabee 9:27 says there were no prophets, but so does Psalm 74:9. If God's Word expands further than my Bible I need to know.
>
> B.B., U.S.

Response:

Thank you for contacting Answers in Genesis. As you surely know, the Roman Catholics have the same New Testament as Protestants. The issue is solely over the Old Testament books. Even then, the list given by the Roman church is different than that given by Orthodox churches, whose division with Rome occurred far earlier than later Protestant reformers.

When 1 Maccabees 9:27 says "prophets ceased to exist among them" at that time, that eliminates the book itself — as well as the second book, also by Maccabees — as Scripture. One may too quickly assume the same thing must be the case with Psalm 74; however, the styles of both are immensely different.

First and Second Maccabees are written as *literal history*, discussing events between Malachi and Christ, whereas Psalm 74 is a poetic piece writ-ten by Asaph. This psalm is also not necessarily referring to the time at hand, but a time when Israel will be cast off (verse 1) and a time when the temple sanctuary will be destroyed (verses 3–8). So it may not be wise to interpret this psalm as literal history of the day, but instead keep it as it was intended: a verse discussing a future event and the destruction of the Temple. (As a side note, it was more likely the destruction of the second Temple, not Sol-omon's, as prophets existed in the days of Nebuchadnezzar when the first temple was destroyed — e.g., Daniel.)

When the second temple was destroyed, the *Apostles* spoke for God; no longer were there any prophets "in the sense" of the Old Testament to call that nation back to God. Also, the nation of Israel was "cast off," fulfilling

Psalm 74:1 with the new covenant in Christ, that is, there is no longer any difference between Jew and Gentile (Romans 10:12; Galatians 3:28). Of course, this leads to a much deeper discussion about the biblical relationship between Israel and the Church, which is beyond the scope of this response.

The issue of the canon of the Old Testament ultimately comes down to Christ, though. Jesus came from heaven to earth and did not challenge the canon of the Jews, but affirmed it. The canon of the Jews is identical to the Protestant canon, and many, even the Roman church, agree with this canon, such as Jerome until 1546 with the Council of Trent, where apocryphal writings were elevated to a full canon status by the Roman church. Of course, Protestants and Jews never affirmed such a thing for the Apocrypha — though they are seen as valuable for historical issues much like the church fathers.[1] I pray this helps and God bless.

---

1. For more on the canon, please see "A Look at the Canon," Bodie Hodge, Answers in Genesis website, January 23, 2008.

## Chapter 38

# ℐMPOSSIBLY OLD... THE PATRIARCHS?

Letter, unedited:

> Regarding the ancient patriarchs living for several centuries I don't believe that would be possible. Apart from the fact that the nose and ears continue to grow, so a 900 man would look like an elephant, there is senility. It happens to 1 in 5 over 80's, and I should imagine if people could live for even 200 years, it would be close to 100%. The main problem however is potential. 200 years ago, most were dead by age 40. They had the same potential as us, but living conditions meant they died early. For the patriarchs, they would not have had medical care or medicines. They would not have had sanitary conditions. They would have had a very poor diet (hard things like seeds would quickly have ruined their teeth so after the first century, they would have lived on soups). They would have worked very hard. Like people in Jesus's time, even with a possibility of living over 900 years, most would have been dead in their thirties. Living so long was just not possible.
>
> M.H., France

Response:

Thank you for contacting Answers in Genesis regarding the article on the age of the patriarchs. Please see my comments below and note that they are said with sincerity.

> Regarding the ancient patriarchs living for several centuries I don't believe that would be possible.

God disagrees in the Bible as witnessed by the genealogies. So the issue is trust — you or God? God was there; He eyewitnessed it and knows everything and cannot lie!

Although it is difficult for us to imagine someone living as long as the patriarchs lived, given current experience and conditions, this really isn't an issue of whether or not someone believes it. Imagine if someone came up and said, "I don't believe that it would be possible for water to exist at over 100 degrees Celsius." Would such an argument be valid? No, this is dependent upon other variables, such as pressure.

> **Apart from the fact that the nose and ears continue to grow, so a 900 man would look like an elephant, there is senility. It happens to 1 in 5 over 80's, and I should imagine if people could live for even 200 years, it would be close to 100%.**

But how do we know at what rate the ears and nose grew for those who lived to the age of around 900 years, 5,000 years ago? The point is that it would not be wise to assume that their rates of growth and renewal were the same as today. Obviously something was different; otherwise they would have been dying in only about one-ninth of their life.

Consider if everyone today had the sad and tragic children's disease progeria. This disease causes the body to age and die by the time the person reaches age 12 or 13. The bones have osteoporosis; the skin appears severely aged; the hair grays; etc. If someone would say, "There is no way a person could have lived to 80 years old," based on the rates they were experiencing with progeria, does that mean it couldn't happen? Of course not.

> **The main problem however is potential. 200 years ago, most were dead by age 40. They had the same potential as us, but living conditions meant they died early.**

I agree. However, the potential for the patriarchs was much different, and this is the key.

> **For the patriarchs, they would not have had medical care or medicines.**

How could one know the patriarchs didn't know good medical practices? Genesis doesn't record this. They could have been much wiser to medicines and care than we may imagine. However, I don't believe this was the primary reason they could sustain such long lives.

> **They would not have had sanitary conditions.**

How could one know they didn't have sanitary conditions? Genesis doesn't record this. I'm sure someone living for 900 years could surely figure out how to properly dispose of unsanitary items and to clean things decently. Additionally, unsanitary conditions are a problem because of disease, which was not much of a problem back then and usually occurs in overpopulated areas, and that also would not have been such a problem in the world's early days.

> **They would have had a very poor diet (hard things like seeds would quickly have ruined their teeth so after the first century, they would have lived on soups). They would have worked very hard. Like people in Jesus's time, even with a possibility of living over 900 years, most would have been dead in their thirties. Living so long was just not possible.**

How could one know they had a poor diet? Genesis doesn't record this. In fact, their diets/food may well have been superior — especially before the Flood.

Do you realize that these last three assumptions are actually founded in a religious evolutionary perspective? The assumption is that people were not smart enough to have invented good medical care and not advanced enough to wash their hands, brush their teeth, or grow nutritious, sustaining food. In fact, the opposite was likely true. Mankind was smart right from the start — with Adam being programmed with language to know what was good, how to clean, how to tend plants, and so on. To accept these assumptions is to place our understanding above what is clearly presented in the Bible.

But even so, these things are still probably not the major factor that allowed them to live so long. Most creationists believe that it was genetic. In the same way that a single point mutation in the DNA can cause the massive age drop for those suffering from progeria, another mutation or series of mutations over time could easily account for the reduced ages. The loss of information as mutations continued to accumulate in the human genome after the Fall and Flood seems to be the best explanation for what the Bible teaches. Hence, we would have the loss of the great ages as given in Scripture.[1]

---

1. For more please see *The New Answers Book 2*, Ken Ham, gen. ed., "Did People Like Adam and Noah Really Live Over 900 Years of Age?" by Drs. Georgia Purdom and David Menton (Green Forest, AR: Master Books, 2008); see also the next chapter in this volume (Chapter 39).

## Chapter 39

# WHY DID PEOPLE'S AGE DROP AFTER THE FLOOD?

Letter unedited, other than adding a reference to the feedback in question:

**Dear AiG:**

In Feedback: A Life Sentence?[1] you stated that God was not giving men a lifespan, but rather he was giving men one hundred and twenty years to repent.

Now, I too am a Christian but I must ask one question: if God was not setting man's lifespan, then why is it that after the flood men started living for a shorter and shorter time? It would appear that men were gradually getting to be 120 years old. If this is not the result of God giving them a possible lifespan, then what is it the result of? Why did men gradually live younger?

And yet if it is indeed the result of God's judgment, then why do some people live past the age of 120? ICR did an article on a woman who claims to be 157 years old, and official documents would place her at at least 135 years old.

So, in a nutshell, why did men gradually get younger after the flood? I'd appreciate your response. Thanks.

J.W., U.S.

Response:

It is a pleasure to hear from you. I always enjoy the questions that make us get into the Word in more detail. It is actually exciting.

**In Feedback: A Life Sentence?** you stated that God was not giving men a lifespan, but rather he was giving men one hundred and twenty years to repent.

---

1. "Feedback: A Life Sentence," Answers in Genesis website, November 14, 2008; this is in reference to the Bible passage in Genesis 6:3 that says, "And the LORD said, 'My Spirit shall not strive with man forever, for he is indeed flesh; yet his days shall be one hundred and twenty years.'"

**Now, I too am a Christian but I must ask one question: if God was not setting man's lifespan, then why is it that after the flood men started living for a shorter and shorter time? It would appear that men were gradually getting to be 120 years old. If this is not the result of God giving them a possible lifespan, then what is it the result of? Why did men gradually live younger?**

Remember that just because men began to live shorter lives does not prove that God set a limit on man's life span. The fact is that they were still well over 120 years until the time of Moses, about 1,000 years later. So God would have been wrong had this declaration been about the 120-year life spans. The 120 years is the countdown to the Flood. In fact, this begins the timeline of the Flood.[2]

| Years until the Flood | Event | Bible Reference |
| --- | --- | --- |
| 120 | Countdown to the Flood began | Genesis 6:3 |
| 100 | Noah had Japheth, the first of his sons, when he was 500 years old | Genesis 5:32; 10:21 |
| 98 | Noah had Shem, who was 100 two years after the Flood | Genesis 11:10 |
| ? Perhaps 95 or 96, the same time between Japheth and Shem. | Ham was the youngest one born to Noah and was aboard the ark, so he was born prior to the Flood | Genesis 9:24; Genesis 7:13 |
| ? Perhaps 20–40 years for all of the sons to be raised and find a wife | Each son was old enough to be married before construction on the ark began | Genesis 6:18 |
| ~ 55–75 years (estimate) | Noah was told to build the ark for himself, his wife, his sons, and his sons' wives | Genesis 6:18 |
| Ark Completed | | |
| ? | Gather food and put it aboard the ark | Genesis 6:21 |
| 7 days | Load the ark | Genesis 7:1–4 |
| 0 | Noah was 600 when the floodwaters came on the earth | Genesis 7:6 |

2. A discussion on this countdown and events associated with it can be found at: "How Long Did it Take for Noah to Build the Ark?" Bodie Hodge, Answers in Genesis website, June 1, 2010, http://www.answersingenesis.org/articles/2010/06/01/long-to-build-the-ark.

We would end up with a tentative range of about 55 to 75 years for a reasonable *maximum* time to build the ark, regardless of the 120-year countdown to the Flood.

> **And yet if it is indeed the result of God's judgment, then why do some people live past the age of 120? ICR did an article on a woman who claims to be 157 years old, and official documents would place her at at least 135 years old.**

Since this is not in reference to living over 120 years, then this is acceptable. In fact, this is a good article to read by our friends at ICR (The Institute for Creation Research).[3]

> **So, in a nutshell, why did men gradually get younger after the flood? I'd appreciate your response. Thanks.**

*This* is really the crux of the issue here. The ages *did* drop off over the next millennium or so. Several people have proposed ideas as to why this happened.

### Diet

Some thought it had to do with diet. People were first permitted to eat meat after the Flood (Genesis 9:3), so some scholars thought the original vegetarian diet (Genesis 1:29) would have helped people live to such great ages. Some have further pointed toward Daniel and his request of a vegetarian diet (Daniel 1:8–16).

However, vegetarian diets have never allowed people to live to such ages as 900 years, even today. In fact, there's little evidence that vegetarians attain a life span much different than those who retain meat in the diet.

### Increased Oxygen

Some have proposed that increased oxygen levels prior to the Flood (which surely changed significantly after the Flood) would allow the body to better heal and eliminate disease. And although there are some benefits to a temporary increase in oxygen in some cases (e.g., hyperbaric medicine), in other cases it is detrimental to your health (e.g., birth defects such as blindness in children due to supplemental oxygen, oxygen toxicity, swelling of lenses in the eye causing blurred vision, etc.).

Increased oxygen levels can cause a host of other problems because oxygen is extremely reactive, causing oxidation where your body doesn't

---

3. "Is Indonesian Woman Really 157 Years Old?" Brian Thomas, ICR website, June 17, 2010, http://www.icr.org/article/5496/.

want it. People often eat foods that are high in antioxidants to reduce these extra "free radicals" of oxygen. Regardless, the simple fact is that such experiments have not permitted people to live to ages remotely close to 900 years.

## Environmental Changes

The world changed significantly due to the Flood. Vegetation, as well as land and sea life, were drastically reduced and made to virtually "start all over again." But did this cause aging to significantly drop off?

Noah, who was already 600 years old, stepped off the ark into this new world as well. If the environment was the cause of the reduced age, why did Noah live 350 more years? Noah was the third longest-lived person recorded in the Bible (after Methuselah and Jared)! If the environmental effects were the cause, then this does not make sense — unless these environmental effects were more gradual. This is not to say environmental changes had no impact, but those effects were not the *primary* cause of life spans dropping about nine times below what they were.

## Genetics

In fact, genetics were likely the primary culprit. Dr. David Menton and Dr. Georgia Purdom look specifically at genetics and resulting functions of anatomical features with regard to aging in the chapter "Did People Like Adam and Noah Really Live Over 900 Years of Age?" from the *The New Answers Book 2*.[4] We need to keep in mind that there were two major genetic bottlenecks:

1. at the Flood
2. at the Tower of Babel

## Flood Bottleneck

Genetic bottlenecks cause a significant loss of access to other people's versions of genes (called alleles) that are *essentially lost*. The obvious loss of pre-Flood people reduced the alleles in the gene pool in humanity to only eight people, but really only six. Scripture reveals that Noah and his wife had no more *sons* after the Flood (Genesis 10). So, this leaves Shem, Ham, and Japheth and their wives, and, of course, these three men each inherited their genes from the same two parents.

So early generations after the Flood, like early generations after the Garden of Eden, saw marriages between people who are close relatives. Of

---

4. Ken Ham, gen. ed., *The New Answers Book 2*, "Did People Like Adam and Noah Really Live Over 900 Years of Age?" by Drs. Georgia Purdom and David Menton (Green Forest, AR: Master Books, 2008).

course, such close intermarriage was not forbidden until the time of Moses (Leviticus 18). Regardless, this bottleneck saw the loss of a great many alleles from the gene pool of those who died in the Flood.

## Tower Bottleneck

If you look at the ages of people born after the Flood, the ages do a sudden drop but are stabilized at about 445 years or so:

1. Arphaxad     438     Genesis 11:12–13
2. Shelah     433     Genesis 11:14–15
3. Eber     464     Genesis 11:16–17

So the ages seem to drop significantly, where Shem, who was born prior to the Flood, lived to 600. After the Tower, ages suddenly drop from about 450 to about 235 or so for three generations:

1. Peleg     239     Genesis 11:18–19
2. Reu     239     Genesis 11:20–21
3. Serug     230     Genesis 11:22–23

Even two generations after this, Terah lived to only 205. But age limits trickle down from there.

## Genetic Bottleneck Conclusion

So the Flood and the Tower bottlenecks did something significant to cause ages to drop. In both cases, there is a loss or splitting up of the gene pool. Consider also how mutations can affect age with an extreme example like progeria.[5]

With these bottlenecks, a host of alleles would have been filtered out and lost. For example, immune systems may not be as good, resulting in more infectious disease.

## Shem: An Intriguing Clue

Another interesting clue comes from Shem. The bottleneck at the Flood would not have affected Noah, as his genetics were not bound by that event. And he lived 350 years after the Flood and died at 950 years.

Ham and Japheth's ages are not recorded in Scripture. But Shem was 600 years when he died. Either of the above bottlenecks, the Flood or the Tower, would not have affected Shem's longevity.

---

5. Bodie Hodge, "One Tiny Flaw, and 50 Years Lost!" *Creation* magazine, December 1, 2004, http://www.answersingenesis.org/articles/cm/v27/n1/flaw.

And yet, his age was significantly reduced from his father's. The Bible does not record the cause of death, so it is possible that something caused a premature death. However, it seems likely that he died of old age. And this is a clue that there may have been a genetic problem that passed through Noah to Shem (and perhaps Ham and Japheth, too) to trigger a drop in ages. After all, all of the descendants of Noah's three sons live shorter lives now.

Lamech, Noah's father, only lived to 777. In the reality of his day, he was a young pup! Methuselah, Lamech's father, lived nearly 200 years longer than Lamech! So, it is possible that there was a genetic mistake hidden within Lamech that occurred between Methuselah and his son, Lamech.

If this defective gene had been passed to Noah from Lamech, and yet masked by a good gene from Noah's mother, it may not have affected him, and, hence, he still lived to a ripe old age of 950 years. But Noah could still pass this defect along to his sons, such as Shem, who lived to 600 years. But why couldn't this have been masked by a good gene from Noah's mother . . . unless she, too, had this defective gene?

After the Flood in Genesis 9 (prior to the assembly at Babel while Noah and his descendants were still living in tents west of Shinar, Genesis 11:2), righteous Noah became rather drunk — so drunk, in fact, that he lay naked in his tent and failed to recognize that his son Ham had gazed into the tent and observed him and then proceeded to spread the word in a derogatory sense about his father (Genesis 9:21–22).

So it was Shem and Japheth's responsibility to walk in backward, not looking at their father's nakedness, and lay a covering over him (Genesis 9:23). Why was it *their* responsibility to cover Noah? Where was Noah's wife? According to Archbishop Ussher, the events at Babel occurred about 106 years after the Flood (according to the Bible about three to four generations had been born, so this makes sense).[6] Thus, this event occurred before Babel, but with enough time for Canaan (Ham's youngest) to be born and be cursed by Noah when he awoke. Noah cursed the youngest son of Ham whose behaviors may have been similar to Ham's. Noah knew better than to curse Ham, whom God had blessed (Genesis 9:1).

If this were the case, then Noah and Mrs. Noah could have had defective genes that were passed to their sons, and this could explain why Shem only lived to 600 years, why Noah's wife is missing in Genesis 9, and why ages began dropping. Further, this explains one aspect of how this could

---

6. James Ussher, *The Annals of the World*, translated by Larry and Marion Pierce (Green Forest, AR: Master Books, 2003), p. 22.

have coupled in subsequent generations to drop the ages even further. But, of course, this is biblical speculation.[7]

**Common Denominator of All People Today**

All people today go back to Noah and his wife (Mrs. Noah). So, the genetics of reduced age has to come through them. Consider the name of Noah and the prophecy associated with it:

> And he called his name Noah, saying, "This one will comfort us concerning our work and the toil of our hands, because of the ground which the LORD has cursed" (Genesis 5:29).

Noah's name literally means "rest." This verse is obviously looking back to Genesis 3:17–19, where the ground was cursed due to sin and man would now sweat and have painful toil when working the ground. How can we have rest or comfort in this? It is by either finding better ways of doing the work . . . or not doing it as long. Commentators have long stated many ideas on this, such as Noah comforting us in being a type of Christ with the ark. Others have pointed out that this relates to the post-Flood statement by God that He would no longer curse the ground for man's sake, among other comments.

Some have said that this was the advent of farming; however, Adam worked the ground (Genesis 3:23) and so did Cain (Genesis 4:2–3). So, this may not be the best interpretation. Consider this verse:

> Then I heard a voice from heaven saying to me, "Write: 'Blessed are the dead who die in the Lord from now on.' " "Yes," says the Spirit, "that they may rest from their labors, and their works follow them" (Revelation 14:13).

This verse gives support to the idea that rest from work and labor means that you have died. Let's face it: the people after Noah did not work for 900 years, but far less than that by the sheer fact that they did not live that long.

Could Genesis 5:29 mean that through Noah people would not live as long and therefore have rest concerning their work and toil? It is possible. I'm sure an entire book could be written on the subject, but I hope this response helps you think about the ages in more detail.

With kindness in Christ.

---

7. Furthermore, like many biblical patriarchs who searched for a wife, they returned to their own lineage (think of Isaac and Rebekah) to find a *godly* wife. It is possible that Noah married someone of his own lineage, perhaps even a sister, like Abraham did, or a close cousin? If so, this would help explain why Noah's wife may have also had the same defective gene that Lamech possessed. Hence, there could be a coupling action to reduce ages or, at the very least, begin a bottleneck immediately prior to the Flood that affects Shem, Ham, and Japheth.

## Chapter 40

# YOUNG IS THE NEW OLD!

## Preface

Dear readers,

In this response, I depart from the usual manner of answering emails in a straightforward fashion because I felt this one would make a good point by, instead, endeavoring (in a lighthearted manner) to show the fallacy of reinterpreting a letter when it isn't warranted by the context. Language and communication are possible because of meaning and context, and the plain meaning should be taken unless context warrants otherwise.

In today's culture, though, this concept of trusting what is plainly written in the Bible is often ignored and the plain meaning is reinterpreted. In trying to justify a different position from the plain meaning in Genesis, the author of this letter, like others before him, tries to reinterpret words and meaning, and neglects context in the Bible.

In this satirical response, I will be doing to this letter what the author [and many others] do to the Bible — that is, neglect the plain meaning and reinterpret it to fit "different ideas than what the author meant to say." This is not meant to mock but to illustrate the dangers of ignoring the plain meaning of the text. And it is addressed to you, not back to the author the same way, sadly, that people reinterpret the Bible to other people. Essentially, I am taking his argument to its fullest extension of absurdity by apply to his letter what he is doing to God's Word.

Letter, unedited:

> **Do young-earth creationists believe that the animals on Noah's ark evolved into all of the species we see today? I agree with Dr. Hugh Ross that although the flood killed all mankind except Noah and his family, it was not necessarily global and that the flood was about 20,000 years ago. I am an old-earth creationist and believe the earth is 4.6 billion years old. I believe in a literal interpretation of Genesis also. I believe that while there is micro-evolution, there is not any macro-evolution. The Hebrew word yom translated as "day" can also literally mean "an indefinite**

period of time" as in Gen. 2:4. Also, boqer for "morning" can also literally mean "beginning", and 'ereb for "evening" can also literally mean "completion". I think the geneologies list only the most important names. Old-earth creationism is not the same thing as believing in darwinism. Old-earth creationism is also a literal interpretation of the Genesis creation account.

J.K., U.S.

Response:

**Do young-earth creationists believe that the animals on Noah's ark evolved into all of the species we see today?**

When the author speaks of "young-earth creationists," this often refers to creationists who hold to an extremely old earth and universe of about 6,000 years in age! So, young-earth creationists can easily be called "old-earth creationists." So, if one says "old earth," then that is really no different from "young earth," which views the earth as pretty old. So, the two (old earth and young earth) can be used almost interchangeably. This concept is vital throughout the exposition of this email.

*Evolved* can be interpreted to mean "change," and so, this author's question is asking if the animals on Noah's ark have undergone any changes since Noah's ark. Of course they did: they died. But even their descendants have undergone some minor changes. Some deer today, in one generation, are taller or shorter than their parents, but the deer is still a deer — and this is not evolution in the sense of molecule-to-man evolution (which is the common meaning of the word "evolution").

**I agree with Dr. Hugh Ross that although the flood killed all mankind except Noah and his family, it was not necessarily global and that the flood was about 20,000 years ago.**

Since the author placed the word "necessarily" in the sentence above, then it also means they may not necessarily believe it was a local Flood either, and therefore it can still refer to a global Flood. This was a significant placement for the word "necessarily," and it shouldn't be neglected.

Also, 20,000 is a round number signifying that it isn't exact, and therefore, it can and should simply be representing a number whether longer or shorter than 20,000. Furthermore, even the English word *year(s)* has a semantic range that can mean a literal year or simply a period of time (e.g., "In the year of my grandfather"). Therefore, this can easily be interpreted to support the Flood occurring about 4,300 years ago and being global in extent.

[FYI, Dr. Hugh Ross believes in wildly interpreting the Bible by inserting geological and astronomical evolution into the Bible to reinterpret it.]

### I am an old-earth creationist

Building on what was stated previously that an old-earth creationist is really the same as a young-earth creationist, since about 6,000 years *is* old, therefore, the interpretation of the conclusion is that the author is openly stating a belief in an old earth of about 6,000 years old.

### and believe the earth is 4.6 billion years old.

We know from science that the age of the earth is not more than 20,000 years old (e.g., earth's magnetic field is decaying too rapidly), so this can't be speaking of actual "years." Besides, from previous examples in this email, we found that numbers are not an exact figure — especially if rounded — and therefore merely represent a range that can include a number either higher or lower, so 4,600,000,000 is obviously a round number and, in comparison to infinity, is really no different from 6,000.

Again, years can merely represent a period of time. Since the number (*4.6 billion*) merely represents a range that is really no different than 6,000 and the noun (*years*) is merely signifying a period of time, this can be interpreted as 4.6 billion periods of time, so this can easily be subdivided into about 6,000 years of true time.

### I believe in a literal interpretation of Genesis also. I believe that while there is micro-evolution, there is not any macro-evolution.

In the same way that the author proposes, a literal interpretation of this letter is being done. A literal interpretation of Genesis has the sun on day 4 — well after the earth — and therefore doesn't support models like the big bang, which has it vice versa. This confirms that the author believes the days in Genesis were really approximately 24 hours in length. [FYI: Micro-evolution is a term representing small changes in living things (for example, a difference in hair color or height from a previous generation), while macroevolution refers to the aforementioned molecules turning into man.]

### The Hebrew word *yom* translated as "day" can also literally mean "an indefinite period of time" as in Gen. 2:4.

Likewise, the Hebrew word for day (*yom*) also means day (~24-hour period).

**Also, *boqer* for "morning" can also literally mean "beginning",**

Likewise, the Hebrew word for morning (*boqer*) also means "morning."

**and *'ereb* for "evening" can also literally mean "completion".**

Likewise, the Hebrew word for evening (*ereb*) also means "evening." And since context determines meaning in each of these, it is clearly a real evening, morning, and day of about 24 hours, which has an evening and a morning, just like the author really means.

**I think the geneologies list only the most important names.**

And this is a great point because Jesus is of utmost importance, and being God, there is no reason to think that Jesus' ancestors were not important, for without even *one* of them, Jesus would not have been born. So, Jesus' entire genealogy is important — after all, His genealogy (not mine) made it in the Bible.

Many names in Jesus' genealogy are people whom we have no clue as to who they were, and yet they are recorded, along with Abraham and David and other well-known historical people. Thus, it further indicates that all of Jesus' earthly ancestors were important. If God left some out, why would He not leave out the ones that we know nothing about except their names? Therefore, Jesus's genealogy in Luke 3, from Him back to Adam, does list the most important names — which are *all* of them — supporting the time frames that yield about 4,000 years from Christ to Adam (giving an approximately 6,000-year-old earth).

**Old-earth creationism is not the same thing as believing in darwinism.**

This is a very astute observation. Believing the age of the earth to be about 6,000 years (which is old, remember) and having Jesus Christ, the Word, as the Creator and Redeemer is not even remotely close to Darwinism.

**Old-earth creationism is also a literal interpretation of the Genesis creation account.**

Old-earth creationists believing that the earth is about 6,000 years old (as shown above) makes sense because there were six literal days, plus about 2,000 years until Abraham and about 2,000 years until Christ and about

2,000 years until today. This makes it about 6,000 literal years old and keeps with the literal curse in Genesis 3 and literal global Flood, literal genealogies and literal days of the creation week of about 24 hours in duration.

In conclusion, it is great to read such an inspiring email of one who clearly believes in an old earth of about 6,000 years old and approximately 24-hour creation days — when interpreted "correctly."

## Postscript

Although the above satire was done to show the dangers of reinterpreting what doesn't need reinterpretation, the reality is that, sadly, the clear teaching of God's Word is misinterpreted to mean something it clearly doesn't, based on preconceived ideas such as the big bang and millions of years. Please be in prayer that people will learn to trust what the Bible says in context and learn to view it as authoritative.

With kindest regards in Christ.

*Chapter 41*

# WHEN DID ADAM AND EVE SIN?

Letter, unedited:

> I am wondering if there is any Biblical indication of the specific length of time between the creation of man/woman (Gen. 1:29–30) and the fall of mankind (Gen. 3:6)?
>
> I found the 1991 article from James Stambaugh, which talked about the diet change that occurred, but nothing else specifically addressing this question.
>
> Thank you and God bless your ministry.
>
> R.H., U.S.

Response:

Thank you for contacting Answers in Genesis. Many people assume that there was a long period of time between the creation and the Fall: as if it is difficult to believe that man (or Satan) could possibly have fallen right away, but a careful look at Scripture reveals a different story. Although the Bible doesn't reveal the exact timeline, we can deduce an approximate time from the text.

In Genesis 1:28, God commanded Adam and Eve to be fruitful and multiply. Had they waited very long, they would have been sinning against God by not being fruitful, or their perfect bodies were no better than those of a current healthy couple who commonly conceive within a year. So, it couldn't have been for long.

In Genesis 3, Adam and Eve sinned (following Satan's temptation) and were kicked out of the Garden of Eden. This was prior to conceiving Cain. Genesis 5:3 indicates that Adam had Seth at age 130, and that Seth was a replacement for Abel after he was killed. Adam had at least three children before Seth: Cain (Genesis 4:1), Cain's wife (Genesis 4:17), and Abel (Genesis 4:2). He likely had many more during this time as well. So the maximum time before the Fall would have to be much less than 130 years.

If we jump back to creation week, Adam and Eve couldn't have sinned on day 6 (the day Adam and Eve were created), since God declared that everything was "very good" — otherwise sin would be very good. It was likely not on day 7, since God sanctified that day. Therefore, it had to be soon after this.

Archbishop Ussher suggests that Adam sinned on the tenth day of the first month in Ussher's chronology, which is the Day of Atonement.[1] The Day of Atonement is presumably representative of the first sacrifice, which God made by killing animals (from which He made coats of skins in Genesis 3:21) to cover Adam and Eve's sin.

One lady pointed out to me that if Adam and Eve had perfect bodies, which is expected in a perfect world (Deuteronomy 32:4), then there would have been no problem conceiving on the first try. And although we have no idea of the exact cycles and functions for those who were designed to live forever, if their reproductive abilities were anything like ours, then in about two weeks Eve would have been ready to conceive (ovulate). And yet they sinned prior to conceiving Cain (Genesis 4:1). So logically it would have to be prior to two weeks after the creation of Adam and Eve.

Although we can't be certain of this exact date that Ussher gives, for the reasons stated above, we know it had to be soon after day 7.

I pray this helps, God bless.

1. Ussher, *The Annals of the World*.

## Chapter 42

# WHO SINNED FIRST: ADAM OR SATAN?

Letter, unedited:

> While reading a chapter out of one of your resources (I believe it was The Great Dinosaur Mystery Solved!) about the Fall, I found myself with a rather perplexing question. It is one I may have heard before, but cannot find an answer to by searching on your site. If you do have a page on it, please send it to me. If not, I would ask that you answer this theological inquiry.
>
> The question is over sin, and when did it start. AiG, as well as the Bible (as far as I can tell), clearly states that sin started with Adam and Eve sinning. It also defines sin as a rebellion, or turning away from God or His Will.
>
> So, then, by the above definition, would sin not have started when Satan rebelled against God, which clearly happened before Adam and Eve took the fruit? Not only that, but Satan also sinned when he lied to Eve in the Garden, saying "ye shall not surely die," when they would. There are two clear examples of sin before the Fall, so why did "all of Creation groan" only after Adam?
>
> S., U.S.

Response:

When Answers in Genesis or others speak of Adam being the first sinner, they're referring to Paul's words in Romans 5:12:

> Therefore, just as through one man sin entered into the world, and death through sin, and thus death spread to all men, because all sinned.

It means that sin *entered* the world through Adam — that is, Adam is the one credited with sin's entrance and hence the subsequent entrance of death and suffering and the need for a Savior and a last Adam (1 Corinthians 15:45). When we look back at Genesis 3, we see it is true that Satan had rebelled and also that the woman (later named Eve) sinned prior to Adam.

## The Sin of the Woman (Eve)

There were several things that Eve did wrong prior to eating the fruit. The first was her misspeaking while responding to the serpent. When the serpent (who was speaking the words of Satan) asked in Genesis 3:1: "Has God indeed said, 'You shall not eat of every tree of the garden'?" her response was less than perfect:

> And the woman said to the serpent, "We may eat the fruit of the trees of the garden; but of the fruit of the tree which is in the midst of the garden, God has said, 'You shall not eat it, nor shall you touch it, lest you die' " (Genesis 3:2–3).

Compare her words to what God had commanded in Genesis 2:16–17:

> And the LORD God commanded the man, saying, "Of every tree of the garden you may freely eat; but of the tree of the knowledge of good and evil you shall not eat, for in the day that you eat of it you shall surely die."

The woman made four mistakes in her response:

1. She added the command not to *touch* the fruit ("Nor shall you touch it"). This may even be in contradiction with the command to tend the Garden (Genesis 2:15), which may have necessitated touching the tree and the fruit from time to time. This also makes the command from God to seem exceptionally harsh.

2. She amended that God allowed them to *freely* eat. This makes God out to be less gracious.

3. She amended that God allowed them to freely eat from *every* tree. Again, this makes God out to be less gracious.

4. She amended the meaning of "die." The Hebrew in Genesis 2:17 is "die-die" (*muwth-muwth*), which is often translated as "surely die" or literally as "dying you shall die," which indicates the beginning of dying, an ingressive sense. In other words, if they ate the fruit, then Adam and Eve would *begin to die* and would return to dust (which is what happened when they ate in Genesis 3:19). If they were meant to die right then, Genesis 2:17 should have used *muwth* only once as is used in the Hebrew meaning "dead," "died," or "die" in an absolute sense and not *beginning to* die or *surely* die as die-die is commonly used. What Eve said was "die" (*muwth*) once instead

of the way God said it in Genesis 2:17 as "die-die" (*muwth-muwth*). So she changed God's Word to appear harsher again by saying they would die almost immediately.

And although it is not wrong to call God "God," Eve did adopt the serpent's use of merely "God." Up to this point in history, when the Lord God had interacted with man beginning in Genesis 2:4, the Lord God was typically addressed as "Lord God" (*Jehovah Elohim*). Yet she adopted the serpent's use of "God" and not "Lord God." So essentially, this was a type of mistake, too.

Often we are led to believe that Satan merely deceived Eve with the statement "You will not surely die" in Genesis 3:4. But we neglect the cleverness/cunningness that God indicates that the serpent had in Genesis 3:1. Note also that the exchange seems to suggest that Eve may have been willingly led: that is, she had already changed what God had said. We sometimes miss this in our English translations.

If you take a closer look, the serpent argued against Eve with an extremely clever ploy. He went back and argued against her incorrect words using the correct phraseology that God used in Genesis 2:17 ("die-die" — *muwth-muwth*). This, in a deceptive way, used the proper sense of die that God stated in Genesis 2:17 against Eve's mistaken view. Imagine the conversation in simplified terms like this:

> **God says**: Don't eat or you will begin to die.
> **Eve says**: We can't eat or we will die *immediately*.
> **Serpent says**: You will not begin to die.

This was very clever of Satan, who was influencing the serpent. This is not an isolated incident, either. When Satan tried tempting Jesus (Matthew 4), Jesus said, "It is written," and quoted Scripture (Matthew 4:4). The second time Satan tried quoting Scripture (i.e., what God said) he did it deceptively by trying to take poetry as literal history when quoting a psalm (Matthew 4:5–6). Satan is not afraid to use Scripture in a false way. Of course, Jesus was not deceived, but corrected Satan's twisted use of Scripture (Matthew 4:7) by quoting the Word of God in the correct context. But because of Eve's mistaken view of God's Word, it was easier for her to be deceived by Satan's misuse of Scripture.

From there, she started down the slope into sin by being enticed by the fruit (James 1:14–15). This culminated with eating the forbidden fruit and giving some to her husband and encouraging him to eat. Eve sinned against God by eating the fruit from the Tree of the Knowledge of Good and Evil prior to Adam. However, upon a closer look at the text, we see that their eyes were not opened until after Adam ate — likely only moments later (Genesis 3:7). Since Adam was created first (Eve coming from him, but both being created in God's image) and had been given the command directly, it required his sin to bring about the Fall of mankind (one of the two who had dominion had still not fallen so the dominion had not yet fallen, but when Adam ate . . .). When Adam ate and sinned, they knew something was wrong and felt ashamed (Genesis 3:7). Sin and death had entered into the creation, the dominion God had given them (Genesis 1:26–27).

## The Sin of Satan

Like Eve, Satan had sinned prior to this. His sin was pride in his beauty (Ezekiel 28:15–17) while in a perfect heaven (Isaiah 14:12), and he was cast out when imperfection was found in him (Isaiah 14:12; Revelation 12:9; Ezekiel 28:15). Then we found him in the Garden of Eden (Ezekiel 28:13; Genesis 3).

Unlike Adam, Satan was not created in the image of God and was never given dominion over the world (Genesis 1:28). So his sin did not affect the creation, but merely his own person. This is likely why Satan went immediately for those who were given dominion. Being an enemy of God (and, thus, those who bear His image), he apparently wanted to do the most damage, so it was likely that his deception happened quickly.

## The Responsibility of Adam

Adam failed at his responsibilities in two ways. He should have stopped his wife from eating, since he was there to observe exactly what she said and was about to eat (Genesis 3:6). Instead of listening to (and not correcting) the words of his wife (Genesis 3:17), he ate while not being deceived (1 Timothy 2:14).

Adam also arguably failed to keep/guard the garden as he was commanded in Genesis 2:15. God, knowing Satan would fall, gave this command to Adam, but Adam did not complete the task. But God even knew that Adam would fall short and had a plan specially prepared.

I've had some people ask me: "Why do we have to die for something Adam did?" The answer is simple — we are without excuse since we sin, too (Romans 3:23, 5:12). But then some have asked, "Why did we have to inherit sin nature from Adam, which is why we sin?" We read in Hebrews:

> Even Levi, who receives tithes, paid tithes through Abraham, so to speak, for he was still in the loins of his father when Melchizedek met him (Hebrews 7:9–10).

If we follow this logic, then all of us were ultimately in Adam when he sinned. So although we often blame Adam, the life we have was in Adam when he sinned, and the sin nature we received was because we were in Adam when he sinned. We share in the blame and the sin as well as the punishment.

But look back further. The life that we (including Eve) all have has come through Adam and ultimately came from God (Genesis 2:17). God owns us and gives us our very being (Hebrews 1:3), and it is He whom we should follow instead of our own sinful inclinations. Since this first sin, we have had the need for a Savior, Jesus Christ, the Son of God who would step into history to become a man and take the punishment for humanity's sin. Such a loving feat shows that God truly loves mankind and wants to see us return to Him. God — being the Author of life, the Sustainer of life, and Redeemer of life — is truly the One to whom we owe all things.

In Christ.

*Chapter 43*

# THE MESSAGE, NOT THE LITERAL MEANING, IS WHAT MATTERS?

Letter, unedited:

Dear Members of the AnswersInGenesis organization,

I must admit, I am severely disappointed in some of the materials and positions posted on your website. So much of modern medicine and pharmaceutical development comes from evolutionary theory and genetic analysis. Science particularly evolutionary theory and biomedical engineering offer incredible benefits to the world at large.

Why cant the members of this site accept the idea that science and religion can mesh? I reconcile faith and science by taking the Bible as a timeless allegory where the message, not the literal meaning, is what matters. For example, the story of the garden of Eden and the Fall can be taken to mean that, while God created a world where humans have the ability and means to live their lives according to (from our perspective) the New Covenant, people made mistakes and sinned a flaw that is universal in humanity becomes the meaning of the Fall.

I felt the need to write and voice my opinions after reading your incredibly poor outlook on Darwin Sunday. These pastors and churches recognize that the relationship between you and God is more important than the idea that a book must be taken literally. Almost everyone today reads the King James Version of the Bible: this book was translated in the Middle Ages, but where do we hear that King James is a prophet? While we can say that it is a faithful translation, it is not the literal word of God.

In any case, there doesnt need to be a conflict between science and religion if one accepts the allegorical meaning of the Bible. I feel that the way you refuse to present this to your readers does a disservice to both them and the global community as a whole.

Thank you,

N.W., U.S.

Response:

**Dear Members of the AnswersInGenesis organization,**

**I must admit, I am severely disappointed**

I want to encourage you to be patient from the start. Do not be upset or disappointed (in this response, either) but sincerely seek to understand — it is meant to help, not to harm.

**in some of the materials and positions posted on your website. So much of modern medicine and pharmaceutical development comes from evolutionary theory**

Such as? Dr. Tommy Mitchell on staff at Answers in Genesis disagrees here:

> As a practicing physician, I have had to examine these claims about the importance of evolutionary thought in my daily interaction with patients. I have also sought the input of many colleagues as to whether or not any evolutionary input is needed for them to adequately serve society in their capacity as physicians. Regardless of any individual's particular religious persuasion (many of my colleagues are avowed atheists or theistic evolutionists who mock me for my young-earth creationist stance), not one example could be put forth of the need for evolution (or belief in its tenets) in order to practice modern medicine.

**and genetic analysis.**

Thus, we agree that modern medicine has been helped by genetic analysis, which has been able to help uncover causes of genetic defects and diseases. For example, genetic analysis has helped us realize that HGPS (Hutchinson-Gilford progeria syndrome) or simply "progeria" is caused by a single point mutation, where a thymine has replaced a cytosine. This simple substitution causes children to age rapidly and die by the time they are about 13 years old. By knowing this, we now have a potential opportunity to help correct the problem.[1]

**Science particularly evolutionary theory**

You are mistaking molecules-to-man evolution as a *subset* of science (even though science is repeatable and observable and molecules-to-man evolution isn't). In fact, it is a *subset* of the teachings of the religion of humanism. You

---

1. Bodie Hodge, "One Tiny Flaw, and 50 Years Lost!" *Creation* magazine, December 1, 2004, http://www.answersingenesis.org/articles/cm/v27/n1/flaw.

may not realize that evolution is a subset of a religion in the same way creation is a subset of Christianity (though both creation and evolution have been borrowed and incorporated into other religions).

It is also true that evolutionary ideas were around prior to the Humanist Manifestos (one being that form of Greek mythology, Epicureanism), but the creation view was also around prior to the completion of the Bible. In both cases, these are foundational to the rest of the belief. The Humanist Manifesto I in 1933 says in its first two tenets:[2]

> FIRST: Religious humanists regard the universe as self-existing and not created.

> SECOND: Humanism believes that man is a part of nature and that he has emerged as a result of a continuous process.

These are exactly what goo-to-you evolution teaches. The Humanist Manifesto II in 1973 is also clear about its adherence to the belief in evolution:[3]

> . . . alter the course of human evolution. . . .

> Rather, science affirms that the human species is an emergence from natural evolutionary forces.

Even the latest manifesto, the Humanist Manifesto III, in 2003 affirms its allegiance to evolutionary dogma:[4]

> Humans are an integral part of nature, the result of unguided evolutionary change. Humanists recognize nature as self-existing.

All three manifestos are clear that evolution is a vital part of the humanist belief system, and may well be the foundation for humanism. In the same way, Genesis 1–11 is directly or indirectly foundational to the rest of the doctrines in the Bible.

Both religions, Christianity and humanism, have roots in events that describe the beginnings of all things, but only one real history actually exists. Christianity has an eyewitness to the origin of the universe, earth, and man — and that is God, who has given us an error-free written record of the key things we need to know about those events.

---

2. American Humanist Association, "Humanist Manifesto I," http://www.americanhumanist.org/Who_We_Are/About_Humanism/Humanist_Manifesto_I.

3. American Humanist Association, "Humanist Manifesto II," http://www.americanhumanist.org/Who_We_Are/About_Humanism/Humanist_Manifesto_II.

4. American Humanist Association, "Humanist Manifesto III," http://www.americanhumanist.org/Who_We_Are/About_Humanism/Humanist_Manifesto_I.

When it comes to past events, you have two choices in which to place your faith: imperfect men who weren't there or a perfect God who was and has spoken — and keep in mind that Jesus Christ is the only name that can save you in the end (Acts 4:12).

**and biomedical engineering offer incredible benefits to the world at large.**

Biomedical engineering indeed offers incredible potential benefits.

**Why cant the members of this site accept the idea that science and religion can mesh?**

We do. Remember, we all have the same science.

**I reconcile faith and science by taking the Bible as a timeless allegory where the message, not the literal meaning, is what matters.**

So you think an all-knowing God couldn't get it right in Genesis? That He couldn't communicate the historical facts correctly and in a way that readers, who are made in His image, could understand? What about the other Bible writers (who were inspired by God) who believed Genesis was literal history — do you think they were wrong, too? What about Jesus, who is God? He took it as literal history. This becomes a major theological problem if you continue to hold to this view.

Don't be so quick to question the Bible's veracity. Perhaps you should consider questioning imperfect man's ideas about the past. Why not take the secular belief system and interpret its story about the origin of things as a timeless allegory? That is what Paul did to the evolutionary Epicureans as well as the Stoics in Acts 17; he took their story as a springboard (altar to the "unknown god") to teach creation as stated in the Bible for evangelism to lead to Christ!

Since you've tried to reinterpret the Scriptures to mean something that they *don't* say, then why not try this with evolutionary teachings? When a secular belief says

1. "life came from non-life," then why don't you reinterpret it as God created plants, animals, and man on days 3, 5, and 6.
2. "the earth is millions of years old," then reinterpret it as really being about 6,000 years old.
3. "man evolved from an ape-like ancestor," then reinterpret it to really mean Adam and Eve.

**For example, the story**

By calling it a "story," you have already discounted it as history. When Luke 3:23–38 records the genealogies from Christ to Adam, at what point do the men in this list stop being real people and begin to be allegories? On what Scriptures can this claim be made?

> **of the garden of Eden and the Fall can be taken to mean that, while God created a world where humans have the ability and means to live their lives according to (from our perspective) the New Covenant, people made mistakes and sinned a flaw that is universal in humanity becomes the meaning of the Fall.**

Why can't it mean what it says? Besides, why do you think the events that introduce sin are an allegory and yet believe that sin itself isn't an allegory? That doesn't make sense. On what basis do you decide which part is allegory and which part is not? By doing so, you are inadvertently elevating yourself to the position of determining truth OVER God. One needs to be careful of such things.

**I felt the need to write and voice my opinions after reading your incredibly poor outlook on Darwin Sunday.**

Opinions are not what matters — it is God's Word. Everyone has opinions, including me, but each of us is fallible and imperfect, whereas God is not. He is perfect, so we need to swallow our pride and trust God and His Word over our opinions. Sadly, if these churches who honor Darwin actually read what Darwin wrote they should be appalled, as Darwin was a sexist,[5] racist[6]

---

5. ". . . a higher eminence, in whatever he takes up, than can women — whether requiring deep thought, reason, or imagination, or merely the use of the senses and hands. If two lists were made of the most eminent men and women in poetry, painting, sculpture, music (inclusive of both composition and performance), history, science, and philosophy, with half-a-dozen names under each subject, the two lists would not bear comparison. We may also infer, from the law of the deviation from averages, so well illustrated by Mr. Galton, in his work on 'Hereditary Genius' that . . . the average of mental power in man must be above that of women." Charles Darwin, 1896. *The Descent of Man and Selection in Relation to Sex* (New York: D. Appleton and Company, 1896), p. 564.

6. "Remember what risk the nations of Europe ran, not so many centuries ago of being overwhelmed by the Turks, and how ridiculous such an idea now is! The more civilised so-called Caucasian races have beaten the Turkish hollow in the struggle for existence. Looking to the world at no very distant date, what an endless number of the lower races will have been eliminated by the higher civilized races throughout the world." Francis Darwin, ed., *The Life and Letters of Charles Darwin*, Charles Darwin to William Graham, July 3, 1881 (London: John Murray, 1887).

non-Christian[7] who believed man invented the idea of God[8] and wanted to exterminate everyone who was not a Caucasian![9]

**These pastors and churches recognize that the relationship between you and God is more important than the idea that a book must be taken literally.**

We agree that the relationship between God and man is of utmost importance. But taking the stance that you don't have to believe what God plainly says in Genesis could be a hindrance to a relationship with Him. For example, if your spouse asked to spend more time with you and you didn't believe that meant "*to spend more time with her*," and took it to mean something else, does this help make your relationship stronger? It should be obvious that it would cause a barrier in the relationship.

It is the same with God. Recall the many instances where the Israelites didn't listen to what God plainly said. Did the Israelites grow closer to God or further away? They went further away. It is better to trust what God says, and that will help you grow closer to God.

The Apostle John wrote, "If we receive the testimony of men, the testimony of God is greater" (1 John 5:9; NASB). And Jesus said, "Do not think that I will accuse you before the Father; the one who accuses you is Moses, in whom you have set your hope. For if you believed Moses, you would believe Me, for he wrote about Me. But if you do not believe his writings, how will you believe My words?" (John 5:45-49; NASB) We cannot *consistently* say we believe Jesus if we don't believe Moses in Genesis.

7. "What my own views may be is a question of no consequence to any one but myself. But, as you ask, I may state that my judgment often fluctuates. . . . In my most extreme fluctuations I have never been an Atheist in the sense of denying the existence of a God. I think that generally (and more and more as I grow older), but not always, that an Agnostic would be the more correct description of my state of mind." Darwin, ed., *The Life and Letters of Charles Darwin*, Charles Darwin to J. Fordyce, 1883.

8. "The same high mental faculties which first led man to believe in unseen spiritual agencies, then in fetishism, polytheism, and ultimately in monotheism, would infallibly lead him, as long as his reasoning powers remained poorly developed, to various strange superstitions and customs." Also: "The idea of a universal and beneficent Creator does not seem to arise in the mind of man, until he has been elevated by long-continued culture." Charles Darwin, *The Descent of Man*, chapter 3 and chapter 21 respectively, 1871.

9. "At some future period, not very distant as measured by centuries, the civilized races of man will almost certainly exterminate and replace the savage races throughout the world. At the same time the anthropomorphous apes . . . will no doubt be exterminated. The break between man and his nearest allies will then be wider, for it will intervene between man in a more civilized state, as we may hope, even than the Caucasian, and some ape as low as a baboon, instead of as now between the negro or Australian [Aborigine] and the gorilla." Charles Darwin, *The Descent of Man* (New York: A.L. Burt, 1874, 2nd ed.), p. 178.

When we trust Genesis as actual history, we have a basis for understanding sin and death in the world. Based on this history, we have a reason to accept Jesus Christ to save us from sin and death. If we remove this foundation in Genesis, then there is no reason to accept Jesus as our Savior from sin and death.

**Almost everyone today reads the King James Version of the Bible:**

Actually, only about 20 percent of the Bibles sold today are KJV, so I doubt this statistic. The KJV is an excellent and time-honored translation, though many find it more difficult to understand than modern translations.

**this book was translated in the Middle Ages,**

Well, it was actually later — originally translated in 1611 and then there were several revisions since then, including 1629, 1762, and 1769. Perhaps the most popular is the 1769 version.

**but where do we hear that King James is a prophet?**

Prophet? No informed Christian says this. He was an English king to whom the translation project was dedicated. That's why his name is on the translation. King James had nothing to do with the actual work of translation — the godly translators did the work.

**While we can say that it is a faithful translation, it is not the literal word of God.**

I agree that any translation needs to be checked against the Greek, Hebrew, and Aramaic texts. Our statement of faith says:

> The 66 books of the Bible are the written Word of God. The Bible is divinely inspired and inerrant throughout. Its assertions are factually true in all the original autographs. It is the supreme authority in everything it teaches.

The original autographs are what were inerrant and it is up to the translators to make an accurate translation into English. (I agree the KJV is a faithful, though not inerrant, translation into English.)

**In any case, there doesnt need to be a conflict between science and religion if one accepts the allegorical meaning of the Bible. I feel that the way you refuse to present this to your readers does a disservice to both them and the global community as a whole.**

There doesn't need to be any conflict between science and the Bible, if you take the Bible as the original authors intended it and as the original audiences would have understood it, and if you don't equate science with the *religion of humanism* but actually view it as a good repeatable and observable work in science fields.

God's Word is sufficient to give you a big picture of history so you can properly explain the world. The only reason someone would reject the Bible's plain reading is due to man-made beliefs that conflict with the Bible. I want to encourage you to trust the Bible *first*, and man's ideas *second*. If man's ideas ever conflict with God's, then you should reevaluate man's fallible ideas, because God doesn't get it wrong.

Please understand that our goal isn't to win or lose an argument but to get people to think, to help people understand their need for a Savior and to disciple them as Jesus commanded in Matthew 28. I'm sure you've heard the "good news" of Jesus Christ before, but I'm not sure if you understand what this means. Please read the good news (see appendix 4).

I want to encourage you to consider this.

Kind regards in Christ.

*Chapter 44*

# HOSTILE GAP THEORY CALL!

A fellow called up our customer service at Answers in Genesis and told the receptionist that he had "one question about dinosaurs." When the receptionist rang me for some advice, I thought that we could send him a complimentary copy of a booklet on dinosaurs that would answer a number of related questions on the topic. So the receptionist asked for his address so we could send him a complimentary booklet on dinosaurs. He refused and said he really wanted to talk to someone. That threw up a red flag to me.

So I said to send his call down, but I told her I thought this was a "setup." I answered with my name and he didn't respond with his, but he said he "had one question about dinosaurs." But he asked several about dinosaurs and I could tell this gent knew a bit about the Bible and Answers in Genesis and the biblical answers we provide as well as the debate, even though he tried not to let on that he knew much — yet he knew each answer as I was saying it.

But quickly he turned the conversation to gap theory by trying to take geological evolution, which is millions of years, and astronomical evolution like aspects of big bang and place them between Genesis 1:1 and 1:2). He raised his voice and began cutting me off quite often. Apparently, he had talked to another person at Answers in Genesis before, which meant he was obviously familiar with our ministry and knew exactly what we believed. So what he was asking was indeed a setup. He was calling because he was mad and wanted to take it out on us.

As he began to push around old-earth ideas such as gap theory as the truth, I responded about the Hebrew *waw* disjunctive to refute the alleged millions of years split between Genesis 1:1 and 1:2. I discussed death before sin, which is a major theological problem. I also pointed out that if Satan fell between Genesis 1:1 and 1:2, then Satan, in his sinful state, would be very good and sin would be very good. He really didn't want to talk much about this but kept trying to change the subject.

I then brought up Mark 10:6 and said that gap theorists have no choice but to say Jesus was in error on this point (Jesus said human male and female came at the *beginning of creation*, which is the basis for marriage). He said he didn't want to talk about that either. So he was avoiding the major theological problems in his professed gap theory worldview.

I could tell he was angry at this point and didn't want to learn but had the mindset to attack. He tried cutting me off on all sorts of stuff at this point. So I had no choice but to step up to the challenge-riposte method by which he was attacking — I was going to be direct in response.

What he really wanted to push was that the sun (and *somewhat* the moon) and stars were allegedly created on day 1. Of course, gap theory people must have this for their alleged previous creation. Further, he tried to use the laws of thermodynamics to say matter could neither be created nor destroyed, effectively saying God couldn't create them on day 4. I pointed out that this law works *within* the universe and that God, who created the universe, had every right to create or destroy and is not bound by His created laws. He was trying to appeal to this law for uniformitarian sake and make God bound by such a law! I pointed out that the God of the Bible is not bound to His creation, but beyond it.

I asked if he really thought God cannot create. He really struggled to answer this and I asked again, but to no avail. It was almost like he was appealing to an infinite and eternal creation and God was bound to this universe — which is not the God of the Bible! His argument was that God somehow did manage to create (or more properly move into place) all the heavenly host (stars, sun, etc.) on day 1 and God is merely stating on day 4 that they are to give light on the earth. So I asked — what did God make on day 4?

He struggled with this one, too. I pointed out that in his theology, God essentially rested on day 4 and that is inconsistent with the Bible. Finally, he said that God made the moon on day 4, but then I said that contradicts his worldview where he said these things were made on day 1 as part of the heavens. His lousy counter was that God basically had it in his back pocket and flung it, and gravitational forces grabbed it to go around the earth. So I reiterated that the theology he was presenting really had God resting on day 4 and not making anything.

He wanted to discuss the light, so I pointed out that the light source on day 1 was simply unknown to us since God doesn't inform us what it is. He said then that is a contradiction in our worldview, and I ask how so? He really couldn't prove his claim. I pointed out that whatever that light source was doesn't matter, as the sun took over those responsibilities on day 4. He was adamant that the light was the sun — but I pointed out that light can come from sources other than the sun. I told him I have a flashlight and it gives off light. He really didn't have much to counter with!

Then we got to the crux of his issue and why he was mad. He said that it was due to people like us that kids are walking away from the faith because we say that God made the sun on day 4 and plants can't survive without the sun. I came back and said plants can easily survive without the sun for a day (12 hours — it happens all the time as the earth rotates), so why is that a problem? He said kids are walking away from the faith because we say the sun was made on day 4 and people see through this logic — even his own kids have walked away from the faith! I asked on what basis do non-Christians have to say logic even exists in their worldview — they must borrow from the Bible to even make a case. I received no answer when I pointed this out.

Then I corrected him and said that the reason kids are walking away from the faith is due to Christian leaders (and parents) who say you can trust millions of years or evolution, and not trust Genesis as it is written (hypocrisy). Essentially, Christian leaders are saying the Bible is not true and kids believe the Bible is not trustworthy because of *them*. Kids can read Genesis and they do not get big bang, evolution, millions of years, and the like out of it. I pointed out that there was a book with stats addressing why kids walked away from Christianity called *Already Gone* that gives reasons from the kids themselves who have walked away![1] I said I would send him a copy. But he apparently didn't want one. He gave me no name and no address.

He continued to want to argue about moving things around in Genesis 1 and attacking biblical creation without much support. I asked a number of times where these things were in the Bible and his response fell short over and over. He was pushing strange views in an unchristian-like manner but obviously not wanting to trust Genesis the way it is written. He refused to listen and continued to just be "nasty." I even asked several times: "Why not just trust what Genesis says?" and repeatedly he refused to answer.

After all of his aggressiveness and attacks, I decided to call him on something. I said, "Didn't you tell the receptionist that you had '*one* question on dinosaurs,' and when I answered didn't you also tell me you had '*one* question on dinosaurs'?" He agreed. I asked, "Did you lie to us?" He seemed flustered as he knew I had caught him in this lie. He knew that he had called up for another reason.

He changed the subject to talk about something else. I asked again, "Did you lie to us?" Again, he wanted to change the subject and continued attacking. I realized at this point we were getting nowhere. Though interestingly, he did not deny that he was intentionally lying to us.

---

1. Ken Ham and Britt Beemer, *Already Gone* (Green Forest, AR: Master Books, 2009).

So, to make a long story short, after a very heated discussion about these and other things in Genesis 1, I had to tell him the conversation was over. I wished him the best and he acted as though he had done nothing wrong.

It is sad to hear he did not want to trust the Bible and that he wanted to blame everyone else for the problem of his children walking away from the faith. His was not the first call I've received from someone whose children had walked away from the faith and who wanted to blame us. All the while, *they* were telling their children not to believe the Bible as written but to accept many of the secular claims (like millions of years, big bang, and evolution), and then they wonder why their kids stop trusting the rest of the Bible.

So often this is the case. It is the children in the next generation that suffer by walking away when their parents or Christian leaders compromise the faith. And yet, they want to blame others instead of repenting and getting back to the Word of God. It makes you wonder what kind of example parents could set for their children if they repented and got back to the authority of the Word of God and openly told their children that they had been wrong. I'd suggest that many of the children would have a new respect for God and His Word, as well as a newfound respect for their parents who had been compromised.

But be praying for this man. We don't know his name, but God does. Even though he had premeditated to call and lie to us just to attack us in an effort to blame us, God knows what his underlying issue is. Be praying that he will learn to trust God over secular ideas and repent.

And this is a reminder to all of us. It is time to recognize the real culprit — sin! It is time to get back to the authority of the Word of God. And it is time to do it for the sake of this next generation.

## Chapter 45

# THEOLOGY OF GOD WITH MIRACLES AND THE LAWS OF SCIENCE

Letter (via a friend), unedited:

> As a believer I would like to believe that Genesis is a literal account of Creation. I feel that theistic evolution particularly by our Churches leads to credibility issues. However the account of creation seems very simplistic and yet very profound at another level. Are we to assume that when God 'made' things he did so in a non scientific way (ie totally supernatural) and if so does that make all scientific explanation redundant?

Response:

It is nice to hear from you. You are absolutely right in that buying into theistic evolution really does have credibility issues. The Bible and evolution are simply incompatible by orders of events, theological problems, and so on.[1]

## Creation is simple yet profound!

Also, you are right about Genesis 1 being both simplistic and yet profound. And this makes sense, as God didn't write the Bible or specifically the account of creation just for the highly educated, but so that even children can understand such a theme. Kids can read Genesis 1 and get it; and yet professors can read it over and over and get something new each time.

Consider for a moment Genesis 1:1: *In the beginning God created the heavens and the earth*. A child can grasp this simple statement. But consider it from another angle. God refutes all other worldviews with this statement: polytheism, atheism, agnosticism, unitarianism (using the majestic plural *Elohim* for God with singular verbs, of course other Scriptures confirm

---

1. Dr. Terry Mortenson, "Evolution vs. Creation: The Order of Events Matters!" Answers in Genesis website, April 4, 2006, http://www.answersingenesis.org/articles/2006/04/04/order-of-events-matters; Bodie Hodge, "Biblically, Could Death Have Existed Before Sin?" Answers in Genesis website, March 2, 2010, http://www.answersingenesis.org/articles/2010/03/02/satan-the-fall-good-evil-could-death-exist-before-sin.

this), etc. Such a profound statement is a great opening for the triune God of the Bible.[2]

But further, God created time, which proceeds as triune (past, present, and future); God created space (heavens and earth), which is triune, having length, width, and height. There was water on the first day, a triune molecule, that even has a triple point where it is solid, liquid, and gas at the exact same time! Light was also on the first day, which is also triune in nature, having an electrical component, magnetic component, and velocity.

But note the complexity and yet simplicity. God was not unwise in the least when writing Genesis 1 about what He did during creation week.

### Creation is unique!

But creation week *is* unique in that creation is not something that we typically observe or quantify through our everyday scientific methodology (observe and repeat). It was an event in the past. One law that now operates *within the creation* as upheld by God is that we can neither create nor destroy matter and energy.

Science laws, by their very nature, work *within the creation* and could not rightly be in place until creation occurred. Upon creation, God was upholding things in a particular fashion and has even promised that it would basically be like that until the end (Genesis 8:22; Hebrews 1:3). That is the basis for being able to do science in the first place, and why many founders of scientific disciplines were Bible-believing Christians like Newton, Faraday, Boyle, and Pasteur. The secular world must borrow from the Bible in order to make sense of this uniformity. (If the universe blew up from nothing, why would we have these beautifully ordered sets of laws that the universe obeys?)

Some get hung up on the issue of God being allegedly bound to His creation (e.g., saying things like: "God can't do miracles, as that violates the laws He made"). First, how do we know that God violates God's laws, since we don't understand all the laws in the universe yet anyway!

Second, the Creator is not bound to His creation. He is not held to the laws by which He upholds the creation. In other words, God is not subservient to such laws, but they are subservient to Him. God can create and destroy if He wishes, and has done so when creating food for 5,000, for example. So creation week *could* have been entirely supernatural and

2. Bodie Hodge, "God Is Triune," Answers in Genesis website, February 20, 2008, http://www.answersingenesis.org/articles/2008/02/20/god-is-triune.

creative powers of God in no way violate scientific principles that the rest of creation is normatively bound to.

However, God likely used a combination of the two from many examples in Genesis. For example, water is held together by forces that God upheld and put in place on day 1, when water was formed (the earth was originally formless and pure water according to Genesis 1:2). But God then applied formative actions (e.g., separating and gathering waters) whether making things from material He created (generally *asah* in Hebrew) or creating *ex-nihilo* (generally *bara* in Hebrew) throughout the rest of the creation week, though there is some overlap in these Hebrew terms.[3]

The point is that God is not bound as part of His creation and hence not bound to mere scientific principles that are just our man-made descriptions of the creation and how it works today. But creation week was indeed unique, and upon creation's completion, God generally upheld the universe in a consistent fashion as He alluded to, until the end, that is, with the exception of His rare intervenings (Genesis 2:1, 8:22, etc.). But God is by no means obligated to remain subject to those physical laws that apply to the physical world.

I pray this helps clarify. And with this, all scientific explanation should not be rendered redundant, but placed, like all things, under the interpretive lenses of God Word, not a finality based on man's fallible and imperfect ideas. God bless.

---

3. Dr. Terry Mortenson, "Did God Create (*bara*) or Make (*asah*) in Genesis 1? Answers in Genesis website, August, 15, 2007, http://www.answersingenesis.org/articles/aid/v2/n1/did-god-create-or-make.

*Chapter 46*

# ᏆOLERANCE, OR THE GOSPEL?

Letter, unedited:

**Dear Answers,**

**I have a friend who was raised as a Christian, but is being exposed to different religions. One of her new friends is a Hindu. She is confused between tolerance and having an open mind about other religions.. She said, "It seems wrong that they would be thrown into the pit of hell for doing the same thing that we're doing... I just can't grasp that.." What do I need to tell her? What kind of Godly advice can I give her? I know God says that he is the only way to Heaven... but she has a good piont... Are there any verses I can give her?**

**M.C., U.S.**

Response:

Thank you for contacting Answers in Genesis. My hope is that you will receive some insight so that you can respond to your friend. Remember that it is not you versus her, but an issue of biblical authority: God's Word versus other religions.

**I have a friend who was raised as a Christian, but is being exposed to different religions. One of her new friends is a Hindu. She is confused between tolerance and having an open mind about other religions..**

Tolerance is very similar to *having an open mind to other religions*. Christ, however, was not open to false religions, but stood solidly on the truth (John 14:6). In today's culture, most students have been taught the religion of secular humanism. This is important in this discussion because your friend is raising herself up to be the judge of religions to then "pick and choose." Take note of the humanistic view in her sentence:

**She said, "It seems wrong that they would be thrown into the pit of hell for doing the same thing that we're doing... I just can't grasp that.."**

Your friend is setting herself up to be the higher standard by judging God and His Word as being subpar right from the start. Who is she (or any human) to judge the Creator God? This attitude is a humanistic belief, that is, putting oneself as the ultimate authority, even over God. So, even if she were to say something like "I pick Hinduism," the religion and "gods" of Hinduism really are not going to be her highest authority — she is. The act of comparing and choosing is sitting in judgment of the religion of Hinduism and the associated "gods."

By her statement, she is already claiming to be able to also sit in judgment over God and His Word. And so she reveals that she is really a humanist, although she may not realize it. Christians need to be aware that children today are being taught humanism — and they are often imbibing it whether they realize it or not.

Also, take note of another misconception in her statement. She assumes that Hinduism is "doing the same thing we're doing." If by "we" she means Christians, then there are two problems.

First, she views Christianity as a religion of works. When she states "doing," she implies that one can avoid damnation by doing works. This is false. Salvation is a free gift by faith in Christ through grace alone:

> For by grace you have been saved through faith, and that not
> of yourselves; it is the gift of God (Ephesians 2:8).

Second, the goals of Hinduism are not really close to the goals of Christianity. In other words, even the works for both worldviews are entirely different.

**What do I need to tell her? What kind of Godly advice can I give her?**

The first thing to do is pray for her. Pray that the Holy Spirit will open her eyes. Then I suggest inviting her to study the Bible with you to show what the Bible really does say about being the one true God's only fully inspired revelation to mankind. Continually point her back to God's Word — the only source of truth — as humans are all fallible.

**I know God says that he is the only way to Heaven... but she has a good piont... Are there any verses I can give her?**

A final note with regards to Hinduism — God's Word reveals that He is the only God and that there are no other "gods" besides Him (Exodus 20:2–6). There are many other passages that reveal that, in light of the Bible, Hinduism is a false religion. So there is no reason — in the eyes of God — to raise up Hinduism or any other religion to be equal to God and His Word or to lower His Word so that fallible sinful human beings sit in judgment over Him.

In Hinduism, there is a belief in "Moksha" or "Mukti," which is supposed to be the liberation of the soul from the endless cycles of Karma, or the binding life-cycles (also called "samsara"). They often strive to get closer to liberation via several means (primarily devotion to a "god," good works, or understanding). But the good news of Jesus Christ is that a *completed* work of salvation has come to mankind once for all. When Hinduism began after the Tower of Babel, it began as a corruption of truth and has deviated ever since. Even the old Vedas (wisdom books for Hinduism) list Pra-Japati — a variation of Noah's son Japheth. And by then, corruption had already set in, elevating this real person to the level of a "god" as the sun and lord of creation!

> Knowing that Christ, having been raised from the dead, dies no more. Death no longer has dominion over Him. For the death that He died, He died to sin once for all; but the life that He lives, He lives to God (Romans 6:9–10).

Those who have been taught Hinduism may be receptive to repentance and the gospel. Such would be ultimate completion to return to the true God. Please be praying that many in Hinduism and other false religions would consider the true and living God and be saved through Jesus Christ. Also, keep in mind that Hindus are not the enemy, but the false philosophy that has deceived our relatives (Ephesians 6:12).

Really, though, you need to get her into the Scriptures: "So then faith comes by hearing, and hearing by the word of God" (Romans 10:17).

With kindness for the gospel.

Bodie Hodge, a sinner saved by grace. . . .

# CONCLUSION

As you could probably tell, many common claims were brought up over and over again (which made it difficult to know where to place letters in the three sections of the book). And you may have noticed that I had to use recurring themes in some instances, too. But remember that such things are often new to unbelievers or people who have not stood on the authority of God's Word. So please be patient with people when replying.

Remember, too, even if a letter is rather hostile, try to be kind and forgiving while still being bold for the Word of God. They are not the enemy, but it is these false philosophies that they have been taught that are the enemy. People are made in the image of God and have value and . . . they are also your relatives. It brings about a whole new perspective when we look at people this way.

The goal is to teach and preach the Word of God, but remember, you are not the one to persuade them (1 Corinthians 12:3). One apologist once said the job of the Christian is not to change the mind of the unbeliever, as that is the Holy Spirit's job, but our job is to help silence their false arguments.

There is a difference between proof and persuasion. The Bible is the proof and is what we use in our responses, but the persuasion is that of God — the Holy Sprit. And may God receive the glory in salvation, not us, though we, too, are overjoyed when non-Christians get saved! This is why it is good to answer questions, then *present* the gospel of Jesus Christ as a twofold apologetic. It is good to present the gospel whenever we can, but remember that the gospel often needs a foundation, and Genesis and biblical authority are that foundation.

Always be in prayer when replying to people — and for those reading this, please be in prayer for me as I answer. There are many more responses that will likely never be seen. Many others can be found at our website: www.answersingenesis.org. But let's not make a long conclusion out of this. I hope you enjoyed the book and its conversational style. But in all things give God the glory and praise that is due Him.

# ℒOGICAL FALLACIES

**Non-exhaustive abbreviated fallacies of reason (not necessarily in the common Latin titles)**

## 1. Linguistic (language)

a.  Emotive language fallacy (words lacking defined language — usually to upset someone)

b.  Ambiguity fallacy (vague general words)

c.  Equivocation fallacy (using more than one sense of the word, tone, paraphrasing, multiple interpretations of a word, or incorrect assumption about a word)

d.  Misinterpretation of a statement fallacy (not just a word — violations of context)

e.  Figure of speech fallacy (misusing idioms)

f.  Composition fallacy (using a statement to judge the whole, using some small thing to illustrate the whole thing) — *part-to-whole*

g.  Fallacy of division (dividing things that are not divisible or using the whole to judge one statement [opposite of Composition]) — *whole-to-part*

h.  Vicious abstraction fallacy (changing the argument to something else to try to prove the other point)

i.  Either-or fallacy (making someone choose between two things when there are other possible options)

## 2. Irrelevant evidence

a.  Irrelevance fallacy (introducing and disproving the wrong point) — *red herring*

b.  Ignorance fallacy (assuming something is true because one is ignorant about the subject)

c.   Pity fallacy (pity or looking for sympathy)

d.   Respect fallacy (assuming arbitrarily that something is true because of the prestige or respect of the person who is saying it)

e.   Disrespect fallacy (condemning an argument because of where/how/who began it) — *genetic fallacy*

f.   By force fallacy (making everyone think it is the truth by force and power)

g.   Attack the person fallacy (attacking the person not the point) — *ad hominem*

h.   Prejudice/masses fallacy (appeal to masses, prejudice of groups) — *appeal to the people*

## 3. Material Fallacies

a.   Fallacy of accident (apply a general rule because of an obscure event)

b.   Converse fallacy of accident (come up with science rules and laws based on accidents)

c.   False cause fallacy (because something randomly happened by accident doesn't mean it always will or just because something happened before something else doesn't mean it *caused* the other) — *post hoc*

d.   Failed step fallacy (conclusions do not follow the logic)

e.   Compound questions fallacy (combine several questions to try to trick the opponent) — *loaded question*

f.   Begging the question fallacy (using itself to prove itself) — *circular reasoning*

g.   Agreeable fallacy (agree because you do it yourself) — *tu quoque*

h.   Misplaced authority fallacy (asking an expert to give an opinion about something he is not an expert in) — *faulty appeal to authority*

i.   Genetic error fallacy (determining if it is true by who is saying it *now*)

j.   False analogy fallacy (using a similar argument to argue the point regardless of different circumstances) — *weak analogy*

k.  Insufficient evidence fallacy (inadequate evidence and then jumping to a conclusion) — *lack of evidence*

l.  Contrary to fact conditional error fallacy (alters historical facts and draws conclusions from them)

m.  Contrary to premise fallacy (self-contradicting right from the start)

n.  Reification fallacy (giving distinctive human qualities to beliefs or ideas or other abstract concepts); variant is a personification fallacy (giving distinctive human qualities to animals, plants, and objects)

o.  Hasty generalizations (generalizing about a class or group based on a small sample)

## 4. Propaganda Types

a.  Appeal to fear (trying to get people to do something or else there may be consequences that you don't want to happen)

b.  Appeal to pity (trying to get you to do something out of pity)

c.  Bandwagon (pressuring because many others are doing it)

d.  Exigency (giving time limits to influence you)

e.  Repetition (repeating something so many times that people begin to believe it regardless of the facts)

f.  Transfer (trying to transfer a thought of one thing/person to another thing/person)

g.  Snob appeal (trying to get people to think they are better than everyone else)

h.  Appeal to tradition (trying to influence due to tradition or age)

i.  Appeal to technology (trying to influence via the latest thing)

# HOW TO RESPOND TO A "REPEAT OFFENDER"

**(Bodie Hodge and John Upchurch using challenge-riposte)**[1]

Letter (unedited):

> I have read through all of your links you sent me . . . and I must say that I am deeply disturbed but what I read. I understand what you said about people having presuppositions. There is a very big problem that you are not seeing. You, and all creationists, presuppose something that invokes paranormal behaviors. You accept these ideas as being truth because you presuppose that the bible is the true word of god. You are not giving your observations an unbiased look. Clearly you start with the answer and look for things to prove your answer to be true. That is why you are not scientific-based. You are completely faith-based. Thats fine and dandy, but you are stepping into the realm of science when you make wild claims that go against what roughly 98% of the scientific population has decided to be true.
>
> The presupposition that "evolutionists" start with is the theory that life changes over time. This does not invoke anything paranormal and it surely does not provoke anything that cannot be tested or falsified. Your website is cluttered with logical fallacies like false analogies, false dichotemies, and arguements from final consequences. Your presuppositions cloud your judgment in a very negative way because you are working backwards. You cannot start with answers and then find the questions. It is, in fact, the exact opposite. You start with a hypothesis and test it to see if it works or if it fits. If it does, you test it again. If it works again, you make some predictions that should be true if your hypothesis is true. If that works, you write down your steps and have someone

---

1. This response is coauthored with friend and former colleague from Answers in Genesis, John Upchurch.

else try it for themselves. This is the scientific method. I assume you know what this is, but you do not use it at all.

Finally, your presupposition is that the bible is the true word of god. That it is factual truth. That it has been kept perfect through generations. And that everything is meant to be as literal as it is written. You start with this presupposition, as you have said. This makes everything you have written on AIG sompletely tainted and biased. This means that you have never given the bible a critical once over. Or if you did, you already started with the presupposition that it is the true word of god. You have just shown the most blatant form of circular logic possible. This essentially discredits what you say about almost anything.

Help me out, where am I wrong?? If you dont think you are biased, explain. I see nothing but circular logic and multiple logical fallicies.

## Our response using challenge-riposte

Since you really haven't taken past Answers in Genesis correspondence to heart and genuinely learned, we will take this to the challenge-riposte style. Though direct, the hope is that you will take this to heart and be challenged by it.

> I have read through all of your links you sent me . . . and I must say that I am deeply disturbed but what I read.

Thank you for reading those links, but you also agreed to search the website for the relevant information, but by viewing your comments here, you obviously didn't. Why would you do that and continue to write in with the same misunderstandings?

> I understand what you said about people having presupposi- tions. There is a very big problem that you are not seeing.

Have you ever considered why "problems" are even an issue in your worldview, where all things are merely rearranged pond scum? Is this a "problem" only for us or do you not also have presuppositions?

> You, and all creationists, presuppose something that invokes paranormal behaviors.

"Paranormal behaviors"? Immaterial based behaviors? Perhaps you mean logical thoughts? Since logic is immaterial. I suppose that makes sense. In light of that, this sounds like a compliment, thanks. What you call "paranormal behaviors" (if we understand your use here correctly) are only "paranormal" to someone who believes that God either does not exist or does not interact with the universe.

**You accept these ideas as being truth because you presuppose that the bible is the true word of god.**

Keep in mind that in your naturalistic worldview, truth, which is not part of the physical realm, does not exist. Truth only exists if the Bible is true. If the Bible is not true, knowledge would not even be possible. The Bible, in fact, offers the only logical basis of all truth and knowledge.

**You are not giving your observations an unbiased look.**

You aren't either — and are therefore applying a double standard. No one is neutral. Jesus made this clear in Luke 11:23:

> He who is not with Me is against Me, and he who does not gather with Me scatters.

We openly affirm our allegiance to Christ, whereas you are actually borrowing from our presuppositions because your worldview simply has no basis for them. Many atheists and evolutionists honestly think that they are unbiased explorers who let the "evidence" lead where it may. But when we examine more closely, we find that there are some places they will not be led — no matter how loudly the creation declares a Creator. You, too, seem to have made up your mind about the truthfulness of the Bible, thinking you are unbiased. Perhaps you should take some time to examine why you refuse to accept the Bible for what it claims to be and why you assume that naturalism must be correct.

**Clearly you start with the answer and look for things to prove your answer to be true.**

Interesting — we make the same claim about evolutionists. Even though molecules-to-man evolution has never been repeated, observed, etc., it is still professed as alleged truth, all while efforts are made to find anything to help give some credence to the model. We work from the framework of the Bible to understand the world using scientific methodology. This allows us to build testable scientific models, firmly based on a trustworthy eyewitness description of events. Evolutionists approach any problem within the framework of billions of years, life from nonlife, and common ancestry. If something challenges this paradigm, the response is not to question the paradigm, but to create a new story in the evolution myth. The difference is that there will never be a written, eyewitness account to verify the claims.

**That is why you are not scientific-based.**

Of course, we are not "science based" — we are Bible-based, but the fact is that science comes out of a biblical worldview and can be done using the Bible as a basis (as evolutionists arbitrarily use naturalism as a basis). You have heard of Pasteur, Newton, and Faraday? Science is simply a means by which we discover information about the world.

**You are completely faith-based.**

All humans have beliefs rooted in faith. Even you have great faith . . . in humanism, as you have already appealed to its prime premise (i.e., man can determine truth apart from God). In other words, humanism claims that humans are the ultimate authority and judge — even over God. However, God says in Exodus 20:3, "You shall have no other gods before Me."

**Thats fine and dandy, but you are stepping into the realm of science**

Since God created the laws of nature, it has always been His realm. And since most fields of science have been developed by Bible believers, then this is a great confirmation of that. Naturalism and humanism (arbitrarily set forth as "pure science") have "hijacked" the field after the fact.

**when you make wild claims that go against what roughly 98% of the scientific population has decided to be true.**

And where did that number come from? Besides, popular vote is not a measure of truth. Imagine that all the evolutionary scientists decided to commit suicide because they realized that there is no purpose and meaning in their professed worldview. Based on your statement, that would mean our "wild claims" would suddenly become truth, since the only scientists left (the new majority) would be creationists. While this example is fanciful, it does show the problem with depending upon a majority to determine what is accurate.

**The presupposition that "evolutionists" start with is the theory that life changes over time.**

Then why do you have a problem with creationists? We agree that life changes over time.

### This does not invoke anything paranormal

Such as logic and truth? Speaking of "the whole truth," your statement does not reveal the true extent of what most believe evolution is. If it were simply the fact that life changes over time, there would be no argument. However, at issue is the belief that inanimate matter (think of dissolved rock pieces in a primordial stew) gave rise to the many complex life forms we see around us today (and all the extinct ones in the fossil record, too). I still find it funny that evolutionists criticize us for believing that all the people in the world came from two people (Adam and Eve), when they are really teaching that all the people in the world came from rocks! At least experiments reveal that people come from people, and not from rocks!

**and it surely does not provoke anything that cannot be tested or falsified.**

Based on what you just said, evolutionists cannot believe in a big bang. If evolution were simply understood to be change over time, then this can be tested in the present because we can study natural selection and speciation. But for it to mean that all species came from a common ancestor, then the claim is incorrect. Common ancestry can never be tested in a laboratory.

**Your website is cluttered with logical fallicies like false analogies, false dichotemies, and arguements from final consequences.**

Where? This is an unsubstantiated allegation, which you agreed not to do, when you agreed to the feedback rules of our website. While none of us here claim to be infallible, it would be helpful if you pointed out these errors.

### Your presuppositions cloud your judgment in a very negative way

As an evolutionist, what makes you think there is such a thing as good (positive) and evil (negative)? You are affirming the truth of the Bible, which teaches there is such a thing as a "negative." But I find it fascinating that you do not understand your own hypocrisy as your presuppositions are clouding your judgments in a very negative way.

**because you are working backwards.**

Again, you are trying to apply a double standard, as evolutionists are working backward all the time. In fact, their premise of naturalism is based on this principle. In essence, you are suggesting that the "forward" way of thinking is by coming at life with a *tabula rasa* (a blank slate) and being led by the "evidence."

Think of it this way: If you went to a traffic judge and said, "The foot pedal spoke to me and said that it needed to be pushed to the floor." The judge would consider mental capacities for listening to strange voices. And yet, many evolutionary scientists (and sadly some creationist ones, too) often appeal to evidence making claims. It is time for people to realize that evidence doesn't speak, let alone for "itself," but rather people interpret that evidence.

But I doubt that you yourself studied the universe and life with a blank slate anyway to come to the conclusion that evolution must be the best explanation. Instead, you learned the evolution story from teachers, books, TV shows, and other authority figures. This story that you learned has become the foundation for what you believe happened in the past. These presuppositions are darkening your eyes from seeing creation and the Word of God for what they are.

> **You cannot start with answers and then find the questions. It is, in fact, the exact opposite.**

It seems as though you are trying to force your religion of humanism on to me. Regardless, we don't necessarily start with answers, but even so, why would that be wrong in your worldview? Having the answer to a question before asking it does not invalidate the answer.

> **You start with a hypothesis and test it to see if it works or if it f**
> **its. If it does, you test it again. If it works again, you make some**
> **predictions that should be true if your hypothesis is true. If that**
> **works, you write down your steps and have someone else try it**
> **for themselves.**

Have you tested this very concept of the scientific method empirically? If not, how can you possibly know it is true? So this refutes your empiricist view. While we agree that the scientific method is very valuable (and, by the way, based upon belief in a universe of order because of an all-powerful, intelligent Creator), it does not and cannot apply to history that was not observed and cannot be repeated. So if you relied strictly on the scientific method, you would have to reject the naturalistic origin of life. It cannot be repeated by tests.

Even if life were generated in a lab, this does nothing to show that life could have come into existence without a Creator, since there is no evidence of life spawning from nonlife. And you must also reject the idea of a single-celled organism like an amoeba becoming a cow over millions of years. That has never been repeated by tests either. And you must also reject the big bang, as that was never repeated by tests. I could keep going. . . .

> **This is the scientific method. I assume you know what this is, but you do not use it at all.**

The funny thing is that you probably don't realize Francis Bacon, a young-earth creationist, came up with the scientific method because it is a logical outcome of a biblical worldview. And of course we use it, but not for truth claims, as it deals only with the physical world. But why would an evolutionist care? In an evolutionary worldview, everything came from nothing and is going to nothing, so who cares?

> **Finally, your presupposition is that the bible is the true word of god. That it is factual truth. That it has been kept perfect through generations.**

Since you have borrowed so many presuppositions (as evidenced from this email) from the Bible (such as logic, truth, and knowledge existing; morality; and science), why not accept the rest of it?

> **And that everything is meant to be as literal as it is written. You start with this presupposition, as you have said.**

False — we didn't say this — this is a vicious abstraction fallacy. Sections in the Bible that are literal history are to be taken as literal history, metaphors are metaphors, psalms are psalms, etc. This means we take the plain or straightforward reading of each passage *in context* (2 Corinthians 4:2; Proverbs 8:8–9).

> **This makes everything you have written on AIG sompletely tainted and biased.**

Biased, yes — in the same way that everything you have written in this email is biased. But if this statement were true, then that would mean that your email is tainted, too (notice how your comment is self-refuting). But tainted, no. In an evolutionary worldview, "tainted" would not be wrong anyway. It is only in a Christian worldview that tainting would be wrong.

**This means that you have never given the bible a critical once over.**

Recall the serpent speaking to Eve: "Did God really say. . . ?" Satan, while influencing the serpent, tried to get Eve to step back and judge God's Word on her own merits. And you — sadly — are doing the same thing — trying to get us to step back and view ourselves as gods to look down upon God and His Word and judge it, as you apparently have. You must assume that everyone at Answers in Genesis has always been a believer.

Even if that were true (it's not), your second assumption is that the only truly "critical" way to look at the Bible is to see it as not being what it claims to be. You assume that humans are capable of judging the merit of the claims in the Bible in an unbiased manner. That is, you (and those who believe as you) are not "tainted," but we at Answers in Genesis (and other Christians) are. However, the very premise of this claim reveals the bias that you have. You reject the Bible because you have a commitment to what naturalists tell you is "right." Have you ever critically examined their claims?

**Or if you did, you already started with the presupposition that it is the true word of god.**

If we didn't start with that presupposition, knowledge would not be possible. In fact, you are subtly borrowing from that biblical presupposition when you email us — thus proving the point.

**You have just shown the most blatant form of circular logic possible.**

False. In fact, it was you that assumed you were the authority and have tried to make a circular case that you are the authority. This is a vicious circular argument. I'm not starting with myself, but with God — what greater authority is there than the Creator of everything?

> For when God made a promise to Abraham, because He could swear by no one greater, He swore by Himself (Hebrews 6:13).

**This essentially discredits what you say about almost anything.**

This statement is false, as shown.

> **Help me out, where am I wrong??**

> **If you dont think you are biased, explain. I see nothing but circular logic and multiple logical fallicies.**

You seem to think that if you have shown we have biases that we are wrong. But that premise is flawed. We start with God; naturalists start with the belief that God cannot be involved. According to that sort of argument, no one could know anything because we are all biased.

Please suspend your presuppositions and bias momentarily and consider the biblical worldview. It is the only worldview that accounts for all aspects of reality. My goal is not to merely demolish the false worldview of humanism and evolution. It is ultimately about the gospel.

I encourage you to read the Bible, beginning in Genesis; then jump to John, then Romans, and then the last two chapters of Revelation as a good start. You can read these sections with connecting material and some basics in the book *Begin*.[2] This will provide a good overview of the Bible. Then you can go back and read it in its entirety. *The Ultimate Proof of Creation*[3] and the *New Answers Books*[4] are also good for providing answers. I pray this is helpful.

With kindness in Christ,
Bodie Hodge and John Upchurch

---

2. Ken Ham and Bodie Hodge, editors, *Begin* (Green Forest, AR: Master Books, 2011).
3. Dr. Jason Lisle, *The Ultimate Proof of Creation* (Green Forest, AR: Master Books, 2009).
4. The New Answers Book Series (Green Forest, AR: Master Books).

*Appendix 3*

# WHERE DO WE DRAW THE LINE?

Answers in Genesis (AiG) is a unique ministry for this age — a biblical authority ministry. Many people see us as just a creation and evolution ministry diving into scientific aspects of the creation. Many others view us as a worldview ministry, and yet others see us as an evangelical ministry stressing the gospel (which should be the focus of any ministry), and so on. Although these things may seem to make the Answers in Genesis ministry unusual, it is something else that makes us unique.

AiG is a *parachurch* ministry. It could also be called a non-denominational ministry, which means that AiG is not a church in and of itself, but is staffed by church members from various denominations (e.g., Baptist, Christian, Lutheran, Reform, etc.) to focus on specific issues and challenges of today's culture.

## Biblical authority

AiG is made up of Christians who unite to defend the authority of the Bible in today's secular culture. And that is what we are "on about" — the authority of the Bible, often in Genesis — a foundational book — but also other places (like the gospel message of the New Testament).

For example, the secular world has been teaching that the earth is billions of years old. The Bible, based on genealogies recorded throughout the Scriptures and the context of the Hebrew word *yom* (day) in Genesis 1, reveals that the earth is thousands of years old. So this question becomes a biblical authority issue. Is one going to trust a perfect God who created all things (Genesis 1:1), has always been there (Revelation 22:13), knows all things (Colossians 2:1–3), and cannot lie (Hebrews 6:18), or trust imperfect and fallible humankind who was not there and speculates on the past?

Also, take note that many of these issues ultimately overlap with worldview issues (biblical Christianity vs. secular humanism in this instance). Of course, this subject also gets into the character of Jesus Christ and His deity and, hence, the gospel. For a few other examples of biblical authority issues that Answers in Genesis gets into, see Table 1.

**Table 1: A sampling of biblical authority topics that Answers in Genesis actively deals with**

| Topic | A biblical authority issue? | Does AiG involve itself? |
|---|---|---|
| Millions of years | Yes. The Bible does not teach millions of years; this idea comes from a source outside the Bible. | Yes |
| Evolution | Yes. The Bible teaches man was specially created from dust, and the woman specially created from the man (Genesis 3), but in an evolutionary worldview, humanity came from an ape-like ancestor. | Yes |
| A local flood | Yes. Genesis 6–8 makes it clear that the Flood was global with the water over the highest mountain by over 15 cubits (Genesis 7:20). Those appealing to a local flood trust secular authorities who say that the rock layers are evidence of millions of years instead of mostly Noah's Flood sediment. | Yes |
| The Trinity | Yes. The Bible clearly teaches God is triune. So sources outside the Bible are going against the Bible (e.g., the Watchtower organization, Koran, etc.) | Yes |
| Racism | Yes. The Bible teaches there is one race that began with Adam and Eve, whereas the world had been teaching that there are perhaps four races (Caucasoid, Mongoloid, Negroid, and Australoid). | Yes |

This is, of course, only a small list of topics, but it should give the reader an idea of how and why we distinguish. Basically, Answers in Genesis is involved when any issue impacts the authority of Scripture — especially when human claims run counter to what God teaches.

## Are some controversial topics battles over biblical authority?

Being a subset of the Church as a whole is why this ministry is unique. Christians from various denominations can and should be able to come together to defend the authority of the Bible against sources that are claiming the Bible, and ultimately God, is false or wrong.

But there are many who do not fully understand (or may have simply missed) what we mean by biblical authority — even within the various denominations from which we all come. Some want us to dive into issues that are not biblical authority issues. And although these issues are important and may be worthy of careful thought and cordial debate, they are not a topic in which Answers in Genesis will get involved.

One of these is Calvinism vs. Arminianism. Although we encourage people to know what they believe and why, biblically, this is not a biblical *authority* debate. Both sides of this particular debate see the Bible as the authoritative Word of God and draw from its passages to make cases for their positions. Neither position is appealing to the Koran, autonomous human reason, or others for interpretation of these verses.

Another example would be eschatology. For the most part, each position in this debate readily views the Bible, including the Book of Revelation, as authoritative. So the debate is about Scripture interpreting Scripture regarding various passages. For this reason, Answers in Genesis does not comment on this debate or maintain a formal position. A few other examples can be seen in Table 2. This is a fairly short list, but it should give an idea of the debates AiG does not address and why. There may be instances where, even with these subjects, some try to insert an authority other than Scripture, and so it may *become* a biblical authority issue. For example, if someone said that "no one ever spoke in tongues," then this becomes a biblical authority topic and that particular point could be dealt with because Scripture reveals that speaking in tongues has indeed taken place (Acts 2:4).

### A fine line

The main reason we avoid some topics is due to our focus on biblical authority issues and our desire not to be distracted from what we have been called to do. It can be a difficult task to draw a fine line between the items we address and those we do not. In fact, it is often very difficult simply because all doctrines of Christianity ultimately interconnect.

There are times when we tread a fine line in an effort to word things in a way that each position would agree with. Of course, there are times when a fine line may get crossed in the eyes of some, especially when we work with outside authors that may be associated with one of these issues or who may not be aware of our avoidance of an issue. This is part of the reason why we have a statement of faith that reflects where we stand, and we try to remain within that limit.

**Table 2: Non-biblical authority topics for which Answers in Genesis has no formal position**

| Topic | A biblical authority issue? | Does AiG involve itself? |
|---|---|---|
| Calvinism vs. Arminianism | No. Both positions view the Bible as the authority. | No |
| Eschatology | No. Each position views the Bible as the authority.[1] | No |
| Modes of baptism | No. Each position views the Bible as the authority. | No |
| Speaking in tongues today | No. Both positions view the Bible as the authority. | No |
| Church government | No. Each position views the Bible as the authority. | No |
| Saturday vs. Sunday worship | No. Both positions view the Bible as the authority. | No |
| Covenant vs. Dispensational theology | No. Both positions view the Bible as the authority. | No |

## Conclusion

In reality, all doctrines are interconnected, which makes it difficult to remain silent in some areas and to be vocal in others. Some well-meaning Christians prefer us to focus on one area, and others prefer that we not be involved in some areas at all. We have to draw the line somewhere, and this is done so that we do not lose our focus on biblical authority — especially concerning origins, which is foundational to competing worldviews in today's culture. By carefully guarding the areas we choose to become

---

1. However, "Full" or "Hyper" Preterism (which teaches Christ has returned and we are living in a restored perfect world where the Curse has been removed and there is no more death and suffering) is rejected by Answers in Genesis due to the denial that Christ will have a future return and that the Curse has been removed; this would imply death, thorns, suffering, pain, etc., before sin and other theological problems. This is not to be confused with "Orthodox" or "Partial" Preterism in which Christ has not yet returned and the Curse has not yet been removed.

involved in, most denominations are readily open to working with and supporting Answers in Genesis so that we can have a common goal of promoting biblical authority.

We encourage Christians to know what their denomination believes and to respect issues of emphasis and importance for their church or the ministries that they're involved in. After all, those doing ministry at AiG are made up of Christians from various denominations.

# THE GOSPEL – GOING THROUGH THE MOTIONS

## The Genesis-Romans road to salvation

**Genesis 1:1** — [God made everything.]

> In the beginning God created the heavens and the earth.

**Genesis 1:31** — [God made everything perfectly — no death, no suffering.]

> Then God saw everything that He had made, and indeed it was very good. So the evening and the morning were the sixth day.

**Genesis 3:17–19** — [The punishment for sin is death, and because of sin the world is no longer perfect.]

**Romans 5:12** — [Because Adam, our mutual grandfather, sinned, we now sin, too.]

> Therefore, just as through one man sin entered the world, and death through sin, and thus death spread to all men, because all sinned.

**Romans 3:23** — [We need to realize that we are all sinners, including ourselves.]

> For all have sinned and fall short of the glory of God.

**Romans 6:23** — [The punishment for sin is a just punishment — death — but God came to rescue us and give the free gift of salvation by sending His Son Jesus.]

> For the wages of sin is death, but the gift of God is eternal life in Christ Jesus our Lord.

**Romans 10:9** — [To receive this free gift of salvation, you need to believe in Jesus as your risen Lord and Savior. Salvation is not by works, but by faith — see also John 3:15 and Acts 16:30–31.]

> . . . that if you confess with your mouth the Lord Jesus and believe in your heart that God has raised Him from the dead, you will be saved.

**Romans 5:1** — [Being saved, you are now justified and have peace with God.]

> Therefore, having been justified by faith, we have peace with God through our Lord Jesus Christ.

### Encouragement

Our hope is that you truly give your life to Christ. We want to see people saved from this sin-cursed, death-ridden, and broken world. It would be a shame to go through the motions all your life but never really receive God's free gift of salvation. The Bible says:

> "For what will it profit a man if he gains the whole world, and loses his own soul?" (Mark 8:36).

"Going through the motions" is not faith; it is works, so it cannot save you. You need Jesus Christ, the Son of God, who paid on the Cross the infinite punishment that you (and all the rest of us) deserve. Only God the Son, who is infinite, could take the infinite punishment from the infinite God the Father to make salvation possible. We, as mankind in Adam, messed up God's perfect world, and Christ, in His love, stepped in to save us (Romans 5:8). He is a truly loving God.

> But as many as received Him, to them He gave the right to become children of God, to those who believe in His name (John 1:12).

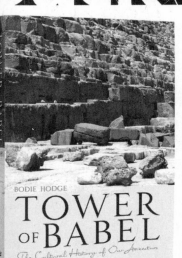

Fijians have a legend of Walavu-levu, a great deluge or flood, which was universal. Ndengei, their supreme god, who punished the people for wrongdoing, sent the great flood in response to the killing of his bird Turukawa by Ndengei's grandson. Ndengei called forth torrents of rain, wiping out cities and submerging mountains.

Hundreds of legends — possibly as many as 500 — seem to point to many of the details familiar to those who have read the Biblical account of Noah and the ark. Why are there so many similarities in these legends from all corners of the globe? Discover the legends, intriguing clues, common origins and exciting details presented with an interactive experience of flaps, mini-books, foldouts, a wheel chart, and more!

Available where fine books are sold or nlpg.com

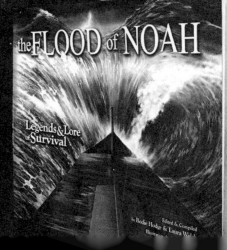

the FLOOD of NOAH

Legends & Lore of Survival

Edited & Compiled by Bodie Hodge & Laura Welch